A

DICTIONARY OF ACRONYMS AND ABBREVIATIONS

IN LIBRARY AND INFORMATION SCIENCE

SECOND EDITION

COMPILED BY

R. TAYYEB AND K. CHANDNA

CANADIAN LIBRARY ASSOCIATION

OTTAWA

Canadian Cataloguing in Publication Data

Tayyeb, R., 1936-
   A dictionary of acronyms and abbreviations
in library and information science

ISBN 0-88802-195-X

1. Library science--Acronyms. 2. Library
science--Abbreviations. 3. Information
science--Acronyms. 4. Information science--
Abbreviations. I. Chandna, K., 1935-
II. Canadian Library Association III. Title.

REF Z1006.T39 1985   020'.1'48   C85-090119-7
          69695

Published by the Canadian Library Association
151 Sparks Street, Ottawa, Ontario K1P 5E3
Copyright © 1985 The Canadian Library Association

ISBN 0-88802-195-X

Printed and bound in Canada

Since librarianship has entered the age of technology and has established a closer friendship with information science, its terminology and language have altered considerably.

The impact of automation, mushrooming of industrial, local, national and international library organizations, and expansion within its own boundaries have made library science a genuinely interdisciplinary field of endeavour.

For some time librarians have felt the need for an up-to-date list of definitions of abbreviations and acronyms used in library science, which have tended to proliferate during the past two decades.

Although there are several good dictionaries of abbreviations and acronyms, there are very few exclusively devoted to library and information science.

We have compiled this dictionary with a view to helping those seeking specific acronyms and abbreviations related to library and information science and frequently used by librarians, library science educators and information scientists. We have scanned major American and Canadian library science periodicals as well as personal and professional sources too numerous to mention.

The authors are aware that even this revised edition can not be considered definitive and that it will require further revision at fairly frequent intervals. However, it is our conviction that this list provides a good overview of the subject matter.

NOTES ON ARRANGEMENT OF TERMS

Terms are arranged in alphabetical order. Abbreviations having more than one explanation are noted as (1), (2), (3), etc. and are arranged alphabetically according to the definitions.

ABA (1)   American Booksellers' Association

ABA (2)   Antiquarian Booksellers Association (International)

Any reference to another abbreviation includes the appropriate number following the term referred to.

AAL   Association of Assistant Librarians (part of Library Association, U.K.; formerly LAA (1))

Minor parts of speech

Articles, punctuation marks or diacritics are ignored in

alphabetizing. Terms with hyphens, slashes or ampersand are filed letter by letter.

B/NA-MARC	BNA MARC
BNBC	British National Book Centre (now British Library Lending Division Gifts and Exchanges Section)
BNB MARC	British National Bibliography MARC
ISSN	International Standard Serial Number
ISTIM	Interchange of Scientific and Technical Information in Machine Language
IS & TP	Index to Scientific and Technological Proceedings

General Coverage

Acronyms and abbreviations for institutions of a general and popular nature are included if the institutions are actively involved in library services and programmes.

ACS (2)	American Chemical Society
API (2)	American Petroleum Institute
IBM	International Business Machines Corp. (U.S.)
ILO	International Labour Office (of U.N.)

Since a Canadian dictionary of acronyms and abbreviations ought to cover French-language terminology as well as English, an effort is made to include as many French Canadian abbreviations as possible.

For organizations which are known by more than one acronym or abbreviation, the equivalent abbreviations are cross-referred by means of a phrase (also known as ...)

ACUTE	Association of Canadian University Teachers of English (also known as APAUC (2))
ASD (2)	Association Suisse de Documentation (also known as SVD)

When available, the English translation of foreign language definition is noted in parentheses following the definition.

ABS (2)	Associazione di Bibliotecari Suizzeri (Association of Swiss Librarians; also known as VSB and ABS (1))

Sometimes, only the English translations of certain foreign-language acronyms have been supplied due to the non-availability of foreign-language explanations.

CEDAF   (Centre for African Studies and Documentation, Belgium)

An effort is made to include important Canadian educational institutions, and in most cases both the English and French abbreviations are recorded.

Abbreviations and acronyms related to computer science and technology have been greatly expanded in this edition, reflecting the increased used of these terms in the library literature.

ALU   Arithmatic Logic Unit (computer term)

ALGOL   Algorithmic Language (computer language)

Symbols and abbreviations for metric weights and measures and International System of Units (SI) are included as these have become increasingly relative to library and information science.

Geographic abbreviations to specify a jurisdiction have been taken from Anglo-American Cataloguing Rules (2nd ed.).

Finally, the authors will be grateful if readers would take time to suggest additions, deletions or corrections to any term used in this book.

R.T.
K.C.

Dedicated
to
our families
for their understanding and support

A	Ampere (SI) (electric current)
AAAA	American Association of Advertizing Agencies
AAAAAA	Association for the Alleviation of Asinine Abbreviations and Absurd Acronyms
AAAB	American Association of Architectural Bibliographers
AAAC	Archival Association of Atlantic Canada
AAACE (1)	American Association for Adult and Continuing Education
AAACE (2)	American Association of Agricultural College Editors (now ACE (1))
AAAE (1)	Alliance of Associations for the Advancement of Education (U.S.)
AAAE (2)	Association for African American Education
AAAH	American Association for the Advancement of the Humanities
AAAL	American Academy of Arts and Letters (now AAIL)
AAAS	American Association for the Advancement of Science
AAASS	American Association for the Advancement of Slavic Studies
AABB	Association des Archivistes et Bibliothécaires de Belgique (also known as VABB)
AABevK	Arbeitsgemeinschaft für das Archiv und Bibliothekswesen in der Evangelischen Kirche, Sektion Bibliothekswesen (Working Group for Archives and Libraries in the Lutheran Church Library Section, (W. Germany)
AABP	Association of Area Business Publications (U.S.)
AAC	Association of American Colleges
AACCCM	Anglo-American Cataloguing Committee for Cartographic Materials
AACHIR	Augusta Area Committee for Health Information Resources (U.S.)
AACI	American Association for Conservation Information
AACJC	American Association of Community and Junior Colleges

AACOBS	Australian Advisory Council on Bibliographic Sources/Services
AA Code	Anglo-American Cataloguing Code (1908)
AACR	Anglo-American Cataloging Rules (1967)
AACR II	Anglo-American Cataloguing Rules (2nd ed.)
AACR/BT	Anglo-American Cataloguing Rules - British Text (1967)
AACTE	American Association of Colleges for Teacher Education
AAEO	Association of Adult Education Organizations
AAF	American Advertizing Federation (formerly AFA)
AAHE	American Association for Higher Education (U.S.; formerly AHE)
AAHLA	Albany Area Health Library Affiliates (U.S.)
AAHSLD	Association of Academic Health Science Library Directors (U.S.)
AAIL	American Academy and Institute of Arts and Letters (formed through the merger of AAAL and the National Institute of Arts and Sciences)
AAIM	American Association of Industrial Management
AAL	Association of Assistant Librarians (part of Library Association, U.K.; formerly LAA (1))
AALC	Asian American Librarians Caucus (U.S.)
AALL	American Association of Law Libraries
AALO	Association of Academic Librarians of Ontario
AALS (1)	Association of American Library Schools (now ALISE)
AALS (2)	Association of American Law Schools
AALSED	Association of Assistant Librarians South East Division (Library Association, U.K.) (also known as SED)
AALT	Alberta Association of Library Technicians
AAMC	American Association of Medical Colleges

AAMRL	American Association of Medical Record Librarians
AAP (1)	Affirmative Action Program (U.S.)
AAP (2)	Association of American Publishers (formerly AEPI and ABCP (2))
AAPA	American Amateur Press Association
AAPIER	American Association for Public Information
AAPT	American Association of Physics Teachers
AAQ	Association des Archivistes du Québec
AARL	Advanced Automation Research Laboratory (Perdue University, U.S.)
AARLMP	Afro-American Resources and Library Manpower Project (Columbia University, U.S.)
AARP	American Association of Retired Persons
AAS (1)	American Antiquarian Society
AAS (2)	Asian and African Section (of ACRL)
AAS (3)	Association for Asian Studies (U.S.)
AASA	American Association of School Administrators
AASCU	American Association of State Colleges and Universities
AASDJ	American Association of Schools and Department of Journalism (Univ. of Minnesota)
AASL (1)	American Association of School Librarians (of ALA)
AASL (2)	American Association of State Libraries (also known as ASLA (2); now ASCLA)
AASL/EB	AASL Encyclopaedia Britannica (of AASL (1))
AASLH	American Association for State and Local History
AASL/NPSS	AASL Non-Public School Section (of AASL (1))
AASL/SS	AASL Supervisors Section (of AASL (1))
AAU (1)	Association of American Universities (also known as American Association of Universities)

AAU (2)	Association of Atlantic Universities (also known as AUA)
AAU/BNA Project	Association of Atlantic Universities/Blackwell North America (cataloguing support) Project (ceased 1979)
AAUC	Association d'Art des Universités du Canada (also known as UAAC)
AAULC	Association of Atlantic Universities Librarian's Council
AAUP (1)	American Association of University Professors
AAUP (2)	Association of American University Presses
AAUW	American Association of University Women
AAVRPHS	American Association for Vital Records and Public Health Statistics
AAVT	Association of Audio-Visual Technicians
ABA (1)	American Booksellers' Association
ABA (2)	Antiquarian Booksellers Association (International)
ABA (3)	Atlantic Booksellers Association
ABA (4)	Australian Boksellers Association
ABAA	Antiquarian Booksellers of America Association
ABACOS	A Bunch of Atari Computer Owners (U.S.)
ABACUS	Association of Bibliographic Agencies of Britain, Australia, Canada, and the United States (a group formed to discuss cooperation in cataloguing matters in March 1978)
ABADCAM	Association des Bibliothécaires, Archivistes, Documentalistes et Muséographes du Cameroun (Association of Librarians, Archivists, Documentalists, and Museum Curators of Cameroon)
ABAH	Asociación de Bibliotecarios y Archiveros de Honduras (Association of Librarians and Archivists of Honduras)
ABAK	Asociation di Biblioteka i Archivo di Korsow (Association of Libraries and Archives, Netherlands)
ABB	Asociación Boliviana de Bibliotecarios (Association of Bolivian Librarians)

ABC (1)	American Bibliographical Center
ABC (2)	American Book Center for War Devastated Libraries (now USBE)
ABC (3)	Asociación de Bibliotecarios de Córdoba (Argentina)
ABC (4)	Audit Bureau of Circulations (U.S.)
ABC (5)	Augmented Bibliographic Citation
ABC (6)	Automation of Bibliography through Computerization (American Bibliographical Center - Clio Press)
ABCA (1)	American Business Communication Association (formerly ABWA)
ABCA (2)	Association of British Columbia Archivists
ABC-Clio	American Bibliographical Center - Clio Press
ABCL	Association of British Columbia Librarians (dissolved 1975)
ABC Pol Sci	Advance Bibliography of Contents: Political Science (publication)
ABCU	Association of Burroughs Computer Users
ABD (1)	Administration des bases de Données (of UTLAS, Inc.)
ABD (2)	Area Business Databank (of Broward County Library in Florida and Dayton-Hudson Corp. Library in Minneapolis)
ABD (3)	Association des Bibliothécaires - Documentalistes de l'Institut d'Études Sociales de l'Etat (Association of Librarians and Documentalists of the State Institute of Social Studies, Belgium)
ABDF	Associação dos Bibliotecários do Distrito Federal (Brazil)
ABDP	Association of British Directory Publishers
ABE	Adult Basic Education (Provincial Institutional Program: Canada)
ABEBD	Associação Brasileira de Escolas de Biblioteconomia e Documentação (Brazilian Association of Library Science and Documentation Schools)
ABEF	Association des Bibliothèques Ecclésiastiques des France

ABELF	Association Belge des Editeurs de Langue Français (Belgian Association of Publishers of French Language Books)
ABES	Asociación de Bibliotecarios de El Salvador (Association of El Salvador Librarians)
ABF	Association des Bibliothécaires Français (France)
ABGILA	Annals, Bulletin and Granthlaya of the Indian Library Association (1949-53)
ABGRA	Asociación de Bibliotecarios Graduados de la República Argentina (Association of Graduate Librarians of the Republic of Argentina)
ABI (1)	Abstracted Business Information (Data Courier Inc., Louisville, Ky.)
ABI (2)	Adult Book Index
ABI (3)	Association des Bibliothèques Internationales (also known as AIL (1))
ABIESI	Asociacion de Bibliotecarios de Instituciones de Ensenanza Superior y e Investigacion (Mexico)
ABI/INFORM	Abstracted Business Information/Information Needs (Data Courier, Inc.)
ABIISE	Agrupación de Bibliotecas para la Integración de la Información Socio-Economica (Group of Special Libraries for the Integration of Socio-Economic Information, Peru)
ABIPAR	Asociación de Bibliotecarios del Paraguay (Association of Paraguay Librarians)
ABIPC	Abstract Bulletin of the Institute of Paper Chemistry (Appleton, Wis.)
ABIUC	Association des Bureau d'Information des Universités du Canada (also known as ACUIB)
ABL	Atlas Basic Language (computer language)
ABLE (1)	Academic Business Librarians Exchange (a network at UCLA)
ABLE (2)	Adult Basic and Literacy Education (Conference, Toronto, Aug. 1980)
ABLE (3)	Agricultural Biological Literature Exploitation (a systems study of NAL)

ABLEDATA	(an information system of the National Rehabilitation Information Center at the Catholic University of America, Washington, D.C.)
ABLISS	Association of British Library and Information Studies Schools (formerly SLC (1), then ABLS (1))
ABLS (1)	Association of British Library Schools (formerly SLC (1); now ABLISS)
ABLS (2)	Bachelor of Arts in Library Science (U.S.)
ABMG	Associação dos Bibliotecários de Minas Gerais (Brazil)
ABMI	Author Biographies Master Index (Gale Research)
ABN	Australian Bibliographic Network
ABO (1)	Association des Bibliotechniciens de l'Ontario (also known as OALT)
ABO (2)	Association des Bibliothèques d'Ottawa (also known as LAO)
ABP	American Business Press, Inc.
ABPA	Australian Book Publishers' Association
ABPC (1)	American Book Prices Current (periodical)
ABPC (2)	American Book Publishers Council (formerly AEPI; now AAP (2))
ABPR	American Book Publishing Record
ABQ	Association des Bibliothécaires du Québec (also known as QLA)
ABRACADABRA	Abbreviations and Related Acronyms Associated with Defense, Astronautics, Business and Radio-Electronics (publication)
ABRC	Association des Bibliothèques de Recherche du Canada (also known as CARL (2))
ABS (1)	Association des Bibliothécaires Suisses (Association of Swiss Librarians; also known as VSB and ABS (2))
ABS (2)	Associazione dei Bibliotecari Suizzeri (Association of Swiss Librarians; also known as VSB and ABS (1))
ABSC	Association des Bibliothèques de la Santé du Canada (also known as CHLA (1))

ABSS	Agriculture and Biological Sciences Section (of ACRL)
ABSTI	Advisory Board on Scientific and Technical Information (of NRC (1))
ABTD	American Book Trade Directory (publication)
ABTICS	Abstract and Book Title Index Card Service (U.K.)
ABTAPL	Association of British Theological and Philosphical Libraries (formerly SCOTAPLL)
ABU (1)	Agrupación Bibliotecologica del Uruguay (Library Science Association of Uruguay)
ABU (2)	Asociación de Bibliotecarios del Uruguay (Library Association of Uruguay)
ABUEN	Asociación de Bibliotecas Universitarias y Especializadas de Nicaragua
ABWA	American Business Writing Association (now ABCA (1))
ACA (1)	American Communications Association
ACA (2)	American Composers Alliance
ACA (3)	American Correctional Association
ACA (4)	Association of Canadian Archivists
ACAEN	Association Canadienne pour l'Avancement des Etudes Nederlandaises (also known as CAANS)
ACARU	Association Canadienne des Administrateurs de Recherche Universitaire (also known as CAURA)
ACATA	Association for Computer-Assisted Text Analysis (U.S.)
ACB (1)	Asociación Costarricense de Bibliotecarios (Costa Rican Library Association)
ACB (2)	L'Association Canadienne des Bibliothèques (now CLA)
ACBCU	Association Canadienne des Bibliothèques de Collège et d'Université (now CACUL)
ACBD	Association Canadienne des Bibliothèques de Droit (also known as CALL (1))
ACBLF	Association Canadienne des Bibliothécaires de Langue Française (now ASTED)
ACBM	Association Canadienne de Bibliothèques Musicales (also known as CAML)

ACC (1)   Accumulator (computer term)

ACC (2)   Amateur Computer Club (U.S.)

ACC (3)   Article Clearinghouse Catalog [number] (of UMI)

ACC (4)   Association des Cartothèques Canadiennes (also
             known as ACML)

ACCC   Association des Collèges Communautaires du Canada
             (Association of Canadian Community Colleges)

ACCE   Association Canadiennes des Chercheurs en Éducation
             (also known as CERA)

ACCESS (1)   Automated Catalog of Computer Equipment and
             Software Systems (U.S. Army)

ACCESS (2)   Automatic Computer-controlled Electronic Scanning
             System

ACCIS   (United Nation's Geneva-based program)

ACCL   Alberta Council of College Librarians

ACCOMP   Academic Computer Group (U.S.)

ACCORD   Acquisitions par CATSS/CATSS Ordering (of UTLAS Inc.)

ACCT (1)   AD Hoc Committee for Competitive Communications (U.S.)

ACCT (2)   Advisory Committee on Careers and Training (of LC)

ACCUC   Association Canadienne de Counseling Universitaire
             et Collégial (also known as CUCCA)

ACCWP   Acquisitions, Cataloguing and Circulation Working
             Party (Aslib Computer Applications Group, U.K.)

ACDDE   Association Canadienne des Doyens et Directeurs
             d'Éducation (also known as CADDE)

ACDEAULF   Association Canadienne des Dirigeants de l'Éducation
             des Adultes des Universités de Langue Française

ACDHE   Alabama Consortium for the Development of Higher
             Education

ACDL   Asynchronous Circuit Design Language (computer
             language)

ACDLS   Association Canadienne des Doyens des Facultés des
             Lettres et des Sciences

ACE (1)   Agricultural Communicators in Education (U.S.;
             previously AAACE (2))

ACE (2)   American Christians in Education

ACE (3)   American Council on Education

ACE (4)   Association Canadienne d'Éducation (also known
             as CEA (1))

ACEA (1)   Association Canadienne des Études Africaines (also
             known as CAAS (2))

ACEA (2)   Association Canadienne des Études Asiatiques (also
             known as CSAS)

ACEA (3)   Association Canadienne pour l'Éducation des Adultes
             (also known as CAAE)

ACEAS   Association Canadienne pour l'Étude de l'Adminis-
             tration Scolaire

ACEB   Association Canadienne des Écoles Bibliothécaires
             (also known as CALS)

ACEI   Association for Childhood Education International
             (Washington, D.C.)

ACEJ   American Council on Education for Journalism

ACELA   Association Canadienne des Études Latino-Américaines
             (also known as CALAS)

ACELF   Association Canadienne d'Éducation de Langue Française

ACELLC   Association Canadienne pour l'Étude de Langues et
             de la Littérature du Commonwealth (also known as
             CACLALS)

ACER   Australian Council for Educational Research

ACESS   Association Canadienne des Écoles de Service Social
             (also known as CASSW)

ACEUM   Association Canadienne des Écoles Universitaires
             de Musique (also known as CAUSM)

ACEUN   Association Canadienne des Écoles Universitaires
             de Nursing (also known as CAUSN)

ACEUR   Association Canadienne des Écoles Universitaires
             de Réadaption (also known as CAUSR)

ACF   Authorities Communication Format (of UTLAS Inc.)

ACFAS   Association Canadienne Française pour l'Avancement
             des Sciences

ACFB	Association Canadienne Fournisseurs Bibliothèque
ACFD	Association of Canadian Faculties of Dentistry (also known as AFDC)
ACFEE	Association Canadienne des facultés d'Études sur l'Environnement (also known as ACFES)
ACFEES	Association Canadienne des Facultés et Écoles des Études Supérieures
ACFES	Association of Canadian Faculties of Environmental Studies (also known as ACFEE)
ACFRSE	Association Canadienne des Femmes Responsables de Service aux Étudiants
ACH	Association for Computers and Humanities (U.S.)
ACHE	Alabama Center for Higher Education
ACI	Association Canadienne de l'Informatique (also known as CIPS)
ACIA	Asynchnonous Communications Interface Adapter (computer term)
ACIC	Aeronautical Chart and Information Center (U.S. Air Force)
ACIDA	Atlantic Coast Independent Distributors Association (U.S.)
ACL (1)	Association for Computational Linguistics (U.S.; formerly AMTCL)
ACL (2)	Audit Command Language (computer language)
ACLCP	Area College Library Cooperative Program of Central Pennsylvania
ACLNC	Association of Children's Librarians of Northern California
ACLO	Association of Cooperative Library Organizations (now part of ASCLA)
ACLS	American Council of Learned Societies
ACLU	American Civil Liberties Union
ACM	Association for Computing Machinery (U.S.) (see also several entries under SIG ... Special Interest Groups of ACM)

ACMC   Association of Canadian Medical Colleges (also
              known as AFMC)

ACML   Association of Canadian Map Libraries (also known
              as ACC (4))

ACMST   Association of Computers in Mathematics and Science
              Teaching

ACOMPLIS   A Computerised London Information Service (Greater
              London Council Research Library, U.K.)

ACONDA   Activities Committee on New Directions for ALA

ACORDD   Advisory Committee for the Research and Development
              Department (a Committee of ASLIB and the
              Confederation of British Industries)

ACORN   Associative Content Retrieval Network (A.D. Little,
              Inc., U.S.)

ACP (1)   Associated Collegiate Press (Univ. of Minnesota)

ACP (2)   Association of Canadian Publishers

ACPA (1)   American College Personnel Association

ACPA (2)   Association of Computer Programmers and Analysts (U.S.)

ACPAU   Association Canadienne du Personnel Administratif
              Universitaire

ACPD   Association Canadienne des Professeurs de Droit
              (also known as CALT)

ACPE   Association Canadienne des Professeurs d'Éducation
              (also known as CAPE)

ACPMSP   Association Canadienne des Professeurs de Médecine
              Sociale et Préventive (also known as CATSPM)

ACPU   Association Canadienne des Professeurs Université
              (also known as CAUT)

ACQ   Association des Collèges du Québec

ACR   Advisory Committee on Research (of Ohio State
              University Library)

ACRA   Associate Control, Research and Analysis, Inc. (U.S.)

ACRiLIS   Australian Centre for Research in Library and
              Information Science

ACRL	Association of College and Research Libraries (of ALA)
ACRL/AAS	ACRL Asian and African Section
ACRL/ABSS	ACRL Agriculture and Biological Sciences Section
ACRL/ANSS	ACRL Anthropology and Sociology Section
ACRL/ANTS	ACRL Anthropology Section
ACRL/ARTS	ACRL Art Section
ACRL/BIS	ACRL Bibliographic Instruction Section
ACRL/CJCLS	ACRL Community and Junior College Libraries Section
ACRL/CLS	ACRL College Libraries Section
ACRL/EBSS	ACRL Education and Behavioral Sciences Section
ACRL/JCLS	ACRL Junior College Libraries Section (now CJCLS)
ACRL/LPSS	ACRL Law and Political Science Section
ACRL/RBMS	ACRL Rare Books and Manuscripts Section
ACRL/SEES	ACRL Slavic and East European Section
ACRL/STS	ACRL Science and Technology Section
ACRL/ULS	ACRL University Libraries Section
ACRL/WESS	ACRL Western European Specialists Section
ACRPP	Association pour la Conservation et la Reproduction Photographique de la Presse (France)
ACRS	Association Canadienne de Recherche Sémiotique (also known as CSRA)
ACS (1)	Advanced Communications Service (a planned AT&T data transmission network)
ACS (2)	American Chemical Society
ACS (3)	American Culture Series (UMI)
ACS (4)	Australian Computer Society, Inc.
ACS (5)	Automated Circulation System
ACS/CLD	ACS Chemical Literature Division (of ACS (2))

ACS/DCD	ACS Division of Chemical Documentation (of ACS (2); now ACS/DCI)
ACS/DCI	ACS Division of Chemical Information (of ACS (2); formerly ACS/DCD)
ACS/DCL	ACS Division of Chemical Literature (of ACS (2))
ACSES	Automated Computer Science Education System (at the Univ. of Illinois at Urbana-Champaign)
ACSI	Association Canadienne des Sciences de l'Information (also known as CAIS (1))
ACSIL	Admiralty Centre for Scientific Information and Liaison (U.K.; later Naval Scientific and Technical Information Centre; now Defence Research Information Centre)
ACSTI	Advisory Committee for Scientific and Technical Information (U.K.)
ACSUS	Association for Canadian Studies in the United States
ACT (1)	Action for Children's Television (U.S.)
ACT (2)	Automatic Code translation
ACTIS	Auckland Commercial and Technical Information Service (N.Z.)
ACTP	Advanced Computer Techniques Project
ACTS	Acquisitions, Cataloging, Technical Systems (a fiche service of Richard Alde & Co.)
ACTSU	Association of Computer Time-Sharing Users (U.S.)
ACU (1)	Association of Commonwealth Universities
ACU (2)	Association of Computer Users (U.S.)
ACU (3)	Automatic Calling Unit
ACUG	Association of Computer User Groups (U.S.)
ACUIB	Association of Canadian University Information Bureau (also known as ABIUC)
ACUP	Association of Canadian University Presses (also known as APUC (2))
ACURIL	Association of Caribbean University, Research, and Institutional Libraries (formerly Association of Caribbean University and Research Libraries)

ACUTE	Association of Canadian University Teachers of English (also known as APAUC (2))
ACUTF	Association of Canadian University Teachers of French (also known as APFUC)
A/D	Analog to Digital (computer term)
ADA (1)	Automatic Data Acquisition
Ada (2)	(a programming language developed by U.S. Dept. of Defense)
ADABAS	Adaptable Data Base System (of WLN)
ADAM (1)	Advanced Data Management (Mitre Corp., U.S.)
ADAM (2)	Automatic Document Abstracting Method
ADAPSO	Association of Data Processing Service Organizations (U.S.)
ADBACI	Association pour le Développement de la Documentation, des Bibliothèques et Archives de la Côte d'Ivoire (Association for the Development of Documentation, Libraries and Archives of the Ivory Coast)
ADBPA	Association pour le Développement des Bibliothèques Publiques en Afrique (Association for the Development of Public Libraries in Africa)
ADBS	Association Française des Documentalistes et des Bibliothécaires Spécialisés (France; also known as AFDBS)
ADC (1)	Aid to Dependent Children (U.S.)
ADC (2)	Analog to Digital Converter (computer term)
ADCIS	Association for the Development of Computer-based Instructional Systems (Western Washington State College, Bellingham, Wash.)
ADCOM	Administrative Computing Center (Circulation Sytem of the Univ. of Virginia)
ADD (1)	Accessibility and Dissemination of Data
ADD (2)	American Doctoral Dissertations (Association of Research Libraries and University Microfilms, U.S.)
ADDS	Applied Digital Data Systems (U.S.)
ADE	Automatic Data Entry
ADEBD	Association des Diplômés de l'École de Bibliothécaires-Documentalistes (France)

ADES (1)   Association de la Documentation Economique et
            Sociale (France)

ADES (2)   Automatic Digital Encoding System (programming
            language)

ADI   American Documentation Institute (now ASIS)

ADIC   Aktueel Dokumentatie – en Informatie - Centrum
            (Current Information Centre, Amsterdam Public
            Library, Netherlands)

ADIS   Austrlasian Drug Information Services

ADL   Arther D. Little (Study) (a 1979 Study on the
            National Periodical Centre, U.S.)

ADLP   Association of Special Libraries of the Philippines

ADMIG   Australian Drug and Medical Information Group

ADMIRE (1) Adaptive Decision Maker in an Information Retrieval
            Environment (Stanford University, U.S.)

ADMIRE (2) Automatic Diagnostic Maintenance Information Retrieval

ADOK   Aufbau - Dokumentation (W.Germany)

ADONIS (1) Article Delivery Over Network Information Service (U.S.)

ADONIS (2) Automatic Digital On-line Instrumentation System
            (of Blackburn Electronics, U.S.)

ADONIS (3) (a computerized system that will use laser and
            optical discs to store and print journal articles
            for fast delivery to requestors, to begin operation
            from a center near London, Eng. 1984)

ADP (1)   Administrative Detail Program (of LC)

ADP (2)   Advanced Data Processing

ADP (3)   Automatic Data Processing

ADPE   Association of Data Processing Employees

ADPL   Association of Data Processing Librarians

ADPS (1)   Assistant Director for Public Services

ADPS (2)   Automatic Data Processing System

ADPSO   Association of Data Processing Service Organizations
            (U.S.)

ADRES	Army Data Retrieval Service (U.S. Army)
ADRIS	Association for the Development of Religious Information Systems (of Marquette University, Milwaukee, Wis.)
ADRS	Automatic Document Request Service (of BLLD)
ADSATIS	Australian Defence Science and Technology Information System
ADSDUC	Association des Dirigeants du Service de Développement des Universités Canadiennes (also known as CAUDO)
ADSTAR	Automatic Document Storage and Retrieval
ADSUP	Automatic Data Systems Uniform Practices (programming language)
ADU	Automatic Dialing Unit (computer term)
ADX	Automatic Data Exchange (computer term)
AEA	American Education Association
AEB	Asociación Ecuatoriana de Bibliotecarios (Ecuadorian Library Association)
AEBIG	Aslib Economics and Business Information Group (U.K.)
AEBQ	Association des Enseignants Bibliothécaires du Québec
AEC (1)	Association des Editeurs Canadiens
AEC (2)	Atomic Energy Commission (U.S.)
AECB	Association for the Export of Canadian Books
AECL	Atomic Energy of Canada Ltd.
AECT	Association for Educational Communications and Technology (U.S.; previously DAVI)
AED (1)	Atomkernenergie Dokumentation (Atomic Energy Documentation Centre, W. Germany; also known as ZAED)
AED (2)	Automated Engineering Design
AEDS	Association for Educational Data Systems (U.S.)

AEEP	Association of European Engineering Periodicals (initiated by UNESCO and World Federation of Engineering Organizations)
AEF	Aerospace Education Foundation (U.S.)
AEFUC	Association des Écoles Forestières Universitaires du Canada (also known as AUFSC)
AENSB	Association de l'École Nationale Supérieure des Bibliothécaires (Association of the National School of Librarianship, France)
AEOC	Association des Écoles d'Optometrie du Canada (also known as ASOC)
AEPI	American Educational Publishers Institute (formerly ABPC (2); now AAP (2))
AEPS	Alternative Education Programs Section (of PLA (6))
AEPUA	Association d'Éducation Permanente des Universités de l'Atlantique (also known as APACUE)
AEPUC	Association pour l'Éducation Permanente dans les Universités du Canada (also known as CAUCE)
AERA	American Educational Research Association
AERCC	Agricultural Economics Research Council of Canada (also known as CREAC)
AERE	Atomic Energy Research Establishment (U.K.)
AESC	American Engineering Standards Committee
AESL	Associated Engineering Services, Limited (Edmonton, Alta.)
AESOP	An Evolutionary System for On-line Processing
AEWIS	Army Electronic Warfare Information System (U.S.)
AFA	Advertising Federation of America (now AAF)
AFACO	Association Française des Amateurs Constructeurs l'Ordinateurs (French Association of Amateur Computer Builders, France)
AFB	American Foundation for the Blind
AFC (1)	American Folklore Center (of LC)
AFC (2)	Automated File Control

AFCAL	Association Française de Calcul (French Computing Association)
AFCET	Association Française pour la Cybernetique Economique et Technique
AFCRL	Air Force Cambridge Research Laboratories (U.S.)
AFDBS	Association Française des Documentalistes et des Bibliothécaires Spécialises (France; also known as ADBS)
AFDC	Association des Facultés Dentaires du Canada (also known as ACFD)
AFFS	American Federation of Film Societies
AFGL	Air Force Geophysics Laboratory (Library) (U.S.)
AFI	American Film Institute (Kennedy Center, Washington, D.C.)
AFIED	Armed Forces Information and Education Division (U.S.)
AFIPS	American Federation of Information Processing Societies
AFIRO	Association Française d'Informatique et de Recherche Opérationnelle (France)
AFIRSS	Automatic Fact Information Retrieval and Storage Systems
AFLA	Asian Federation of Library Association (Formerly FALA)
AFL/CIO	American Federation of Labor/Congress of Industrial Organizations
AFLI	Association for Library Information (U.S.)
AFLS	Armed Forces Librarians Section (of PLA (7))
AFMC	Association de Facultés de Médecine du Canada (also known as ACMC)
AFMVC	Association des Facultés de Médecine Vétérinaire du Canada (also known as AFVMC)
AFNIL	Agence Francophone pour la Numérotation Internationale du Livre (France)
AFNOR	Association Française de Normalisation (of ISO (2))
AFOSR	Air Force Office of Scientific Research (U.S.)

AFPC	Association des Facultés de Pharmacie du Canada (Association of Faculties of Pharmacy of Canada)
AFR	Automatic Field/Format Recognition (computer term)
AFSARI	Automation for Storage and Retrieval of Information
AFSCME	American Federation of State, County and Municipal Employees
AFTRA	American Federation of Television and Radio Artists
AFVMC	Association of Faculties of Veterinary Medicine in Canada (also known as AFMVC)
AGARJ	Associação dos Graduados em Arguivologíado Rio de Janeiro
AGB	Association of Governing Boards (of Universities and Colleges, U.S.)
AGE	Asian Information Center for Geotechnical Engineering (Thailand)
AGILE II	(a bibliographic utility of Auto-Graphics Inc.)
AGLC	Alberta Government Libraries' Council
AGLIB	Asociación de Bibliotecarios Graduados del Istmo de Panamá (Association of Graduate Librarians of the Isthmus of Panama)
AGLINET	Agricultural Libraries Information Network (of IAALD and FAO (UN))
AGM	Annual General Meeting
AGN	Archivos General de la Nación (National Archives, (Mexico)
AGO	Art Gallery of Ontario
AGREP	Agricultural Research Projects (Centre for Information and Documentation, European Communities)
AGRICOLA	Agricultural On-line Access Data Base (National Agricultural Library's Network)
AGRINTER	(an inter-American system of information for Latin American and Caribbean agricultural sciences)
AGRIS	Agricultural Information System (of FAO)

AGROINFORM Agricultural Information (Information Centre for the Ministry of Agriculture and Food, Hungary)

AGT Alberta Government Telephones

AHA American Historical Association

AHD Audio High Density Disc (computer term)

AHE Association for Higher Education (U.S.; now AAHE)

AHEC Area Health Education Center (S.C.)

AHEPA American Hellenic Education Progressive Association (order of, - Founded in 1929 in San Francisco)

AHIL Association of Hospital and Institution Libraries (of ALA)

AHL American History and Life (bibliographic data base)

AHLC Areawide Hospital Library Consortium (of Southwestern Illinois)

AHONDA Ad Hoc Committee on New Directions (for RTSD)

AHSIC Alaskan Health Sciences Information Center

A&I Abstracting and Indexing (also known as I&A)

AIA American Institute of Architects

AIAD Acronyms, Initialisms, and Abbreviations Dictionary (edited by Ellen T. Crowley)

AIB Associazione Italiana Biblioteche (Italy)

AIBDA Asociación Interamericana de Bibliotecarios y Documentalistas Agrícolas (Inter-American Association of Agricultural Librarians and Documentalists (Costa Rica)

AIBM Association Internationale des Bibliothèques Musicales (also knwon as IAML, IVM, IVMB)

AIC American Institute for Conservation (of Historic and Artistic Works)

AICA (1) Association Internationale pour le Calcul Analogique (International Association for Mathematics and Computer Simulation, Belgium)

AICA (2) Associazione Italiana per il Calco Automatico (Italian Association for Automatic Data Processing)

AICCE	Augmented Individualized Courses in Continuing Education (of ACS (2))
AICDT	International Advisory Committee on Documentation and Terminology (France)
AICRO	Association of Independent Contract Research Organisations (U.K.)
AID (1)	Agency for International Development (Washington, D.C.)
AID (2)	Air Information Division (of LC)
AID (3)	Association Internationale des Documentalistes et Techniciens de l'Information (International Association of Documentalists and Information Officers, France) (also known as IAD (2))
AID (4)	Automatic Information Distribution
AIDBA	Association Internationale pour le Développement de la Documentation des Bibliothèques et des Archives (for Africa) (also known as IADLA)
AIDC	Association of Information and Dissemination Centers (U.S. formerly ASIDC or ASIDIC)
AIDI	Associazione Italiana per la Documentazione e l'Informazione (Italian Association for Documentation and Information)
AIDS (1)	Aerospace Intelligence Data Systems (IBM Corp.)
AIDS (2)	Automated Information Directory Service (U.S.)
AIDS (3)	Automated Information Dissemination System
AIDUS (1)	Automated Information Directory Update System
AIDUS (2)	Automated Input and Document Update System
AIE	Associazione Italiana Editori (Italian Publishers Association)
AIESI	Association Internationale des Écoles des Sciences de l'Information
AIIM	Association for Information and Image Management (formerly NMA (2))
AIInfSc	Associate of the Institute of Information Scientists (U.K.)

AIISUP	Association Internationale d'Information Scolaire Universitaire et Professionelle (International Association for Education and Vocational Information)
AIL (1)	Association of International Libraries (also known as ABI (3))
AIL (2)	Australian Institute of Libraries (now LAA (3))
AILS	Automated, Integrated Library Systems
AIM (1)	Abridged Index Medicus (of NLM)
AIM (2)	American Institute of Management
AIM (3)	Associated Information Managers (U.S.)
AIM/ARM	Abstracts of Instructional and Research Materials in Vocational and Technical Education (Center for Vocational Education, Ohio State University)
AIMLO	Auto-Instructional Media for Library Orientation (Colorado State University)
AIMS (1)	Applied Information Management System (System Development Corp., U.S.)
AIMS (2)	Author Index Manufacturing System (of Chemical Abstracts Service)
AIMS (3)	Automated Instructional Materials Management System (System Development Corp., U.S.)
AIM/TWX	Abridged Index Medicus/Telex (of NLM)
AINAI	African Integrated Network of Administrative Information (Morocco)
AINTD	Association de l'Institut National des Techniques de la Documentation (Association of the National Institute of Documentation Technology, France) (also known as INTD)
AIOPI	Association of Information Officers in the Pharmaceutical Industry (U.K.)
AIPEQ	Association des Institutions de Niveaux Préscolaire et Élémentaire du Québec
AIR	American Institute for Research
AIRA	Alberta Information Retrieval Association

AIRHPER	Alberta Information Retrieval for Health, Physical Education and Recreation (Alberta University)
AIRS (1)	Alliance of Information and Referral System/ Services (U.S.)
AIRS (2)	Automatic Image Retrieval System
AIRS (3)	Automatic Information Retrieval System
AIT	Agency for Instructional Television (U.S.)
AIU	Association Internationale des Universités (also known as IAU)
AJBD	Arbeitsgemeinschaft für Juristisches Bibliotheks- und Dokumentationswesen (Association for Law Librarianship and Documentation, W. Germany)
AJL	Association of Jewish Libraries (U.S.)
AKB	Arbeitsgemeinschaft der Kunstbibliotheken (Working Group of Art Libraries, W. Germany)
AKLA	Alaska Library Association (also known as ALA (2))
AKThB	Arbeitsgemeinschaft Katholisch-Theologischer Bibliotheken (Study Group of Catholic Theological Libraries, W. Germany)
AKWIC	Author and Key Word in Context
AL (1)	American Libraries (periodical)
AL (2)	Assistant Librarian (periodical)
ALA (1)	Afghan Library Association (Afghanistan)
ALA (2)	Alaska Library Association (also known as AKLA)
ALA (3)	Alberta Library Association
ALA (4)	American Library Association
ALA (5)	Arizona Library Association
ALA (6)	Arkansas Library Association
ALA (7)	Associate of the (British) Library Association
ALA (8)	Authors League of America, Inc.
ALAA	Associate of the Library Association of Australia

ALAD   Academic Librarians Assisting the Disabled (of ALA)

ALADIN   Automation of Agricultural Information and
              Documentation (Netherlands)

ALAFR   ALA Filing Rules

ALAI   Association Litteraire et Artistique Internationale
              (France)

ALA/IRO   ALA/International Relations Office

ALA/ISAD   ALA/Information Science and Automation Division

ALANET   American Library Association Network (provides
              electronic mail and information services)

ALAO   Academic Library Association of Ohio

ALARM   Anaesthesia Literature Abstracting Retrieval
              Method (American Society of Anesthesiologists)

ALAS (1)   Army Library Automated System (U.S.)

ALAS (2)   Automatic Literature Alerting System

ALASA   African Library Association of South Africa

ALBIS   Australian Library-based Information System
              (National Library of Australia)

ALBOR   Asociacion Latinoamericana de Bibliotecarios

ALCL   Association of London Chief Librarians (U.K.;
              formerly AMCL)

ALCRLB   Association of Librarians in Charge of Regional
              Library Bureaux (U.K.)

ALD (1)   Aligned List of Descriptors (OECD)

ALD (2)   American Library Directory

ALDP   Academic Library Development Program (of UNCC, first
              initiated by CLR in 1975)

ALEBCI   Asociación Latinoamericana de Escuelas de
              Bibliotelogia y Ciências de la Information/
              Associação Latinoamericana de Escolas de Biblio-
              teconomia e Ciências da Informação (Latin American
              Association of Schools of Library and Information
              Sciences)

ALERT   American Library Early Response Team

ALERTS   Associated Library and Educational Research Team
              for Survival (U.S.)

ALESCO	American Library Educational Services Company
ALGOL	Algorithmic Language (computer language)
ALHRT	American Library History Round Table
ALI (1)	American Library Institute
ALI (2)	Associazione Librai Italiani (Italian Booksellers Association, Italy)
ALIS (1)	Association of Librarians in Schools (U.K.)
ALIS (2)	Automated Library Information System (developed by Dataphase Systems, Inc. Kansas City, Mo.; an inventory control system)
ALISE	Association of Library and Information Science Education (formerly AALS (1))
ALJ	Australian Library Journal
ALJH	Association of Libraries of Judaica and Hebraica in Europe
ALLCeD	Association of Library and Learning Center Directors (Oklahoma City)
ALLG	Australian Law Librarians Group
ALMA	Association of Literary Magazines of America
ALMIP	Academic Library Management Intern Program (U.S.)
ALMS (1)	Analytic Language Manipulation System
ALMS (2)	Automated Library Management System
ALOIT	Association of Library Officers-in-Training (Australia)
ALP (1)	Academic Library Program (of ARL)
ALP (2)	American Library in Paris
ALP (3)	Association of Little Presses (U.K.)
ALP (4)	Automated Language Processing
ALP (5)	Automated Library Program (U.S.)
ALPAC	Automatic Language Processing Advisory Committee (National Academy of Science, National Research Council, U.S.)

ALPC	Australian Library Promotion Council
ALPHA	Automated Literature Processing, Handling and Analysis (U.S. Army)
ALPL	Administrators of Large Public Libraries (of ALA)
ALPS (1)	Advanced Linear Programming System
ALPS (2)	Association of Laurentian University Part-time Students
ALPS (3)	Automated Library Processing Services (Systems Development Corp., U.S.)
ALQ	Associations des Libraries du Québec
ALRTS	Association for Library Resources and Technical Service (proposed name change of RTSD)
ALS (1)	Advanced Library Systems, Inc. (U.S.)
ALS (2)	American Library Society (defunct)
ALS (3)	Automated Library System
ALS (4)	Automated Library Systems Ltd. (U.K.)
ALSAs	Area Library Service Authorities (a network of several Indiana libraries)
ALSC	Association for Library Service to Children
ALSD	Annals of Library Science and Documentation (periodical)
ALSO	Area Library Service Organizations of Ohio
ALTA (1)	Alberta Library Trustees' Association
ALTA (2)	American Library Trustee Association
ALTA (3)	Australian Library Technicians Association
ALTRAN	(computer language developed for symbolic algebraic manipulation in FORTRAN)
ALTS	Automated Library Technical Services (Los Angeles Public Library)
ALU	Arithmatic Logic Unit (computer term)
AM	Amplitude Modulation (computer term)

AMA (1)	American Management Association
AMA (2)	American Medical Association
AMACUS	Automated Microfilm Aperture Card Updating System
AMBAC	Asociacion Mexicana de Bibliotecarios, A.C. (Mexico)
AMBAD	Association Malienne des Bibliothécaires, Archivistes et Documentalistes (Mali)
AMCL	Association of Metropolitan Chief Librarians (U.K.; now ALCL)
AMCOS	Aldermaston Mechanized Cataloging and Ordering System (Atomic Energy Authority, U.K.)
AME	Automatic Microfiche Editor
AMFIS	Automatic Microfilm Information System
AMFR	Activity Model Committee's Final Report (of ACRL)
AMIC	Aerospace Materials Information Center (U.S. Air Force)
AMIGOS	Access Method for Indexed Data Generalized for Operating System
AMIS	Agricultural Management Information System (Centre for Information and Documentation, European Communities)
AMLAC	Annual Medical Library Association Coference (U.S.)
AMLN	Arizona Medical Library Network (of Univ. of Arizona)
AMLS	Master of Arts in Library Science
AMMINET	Automated Mortgage Information Network (U.S.)
AMMLA	American Merchant Marine Library Association
AMNIPS	Adaptive Man/Machine Non-numeric Information Processing System (IBM Corp., U.S.)
AMOP	Association of Mail Order Publishers (U.K.)
AMP	Audiovisual Market Place
AMPA	American Medical Publishers' Association
AMPL	A Macro Programming Language

AMPLO	Administrators of Medium-size Public Libraries of Ontario
AMR	Automatic Message Routing (computer term)
AMRA	American Medical Record Association (Chicago)
AMRS	Australian Marc Record Service
AMS (1)	American Mathematical Society
AMS (2)	American Meteorological Society
AMTCL	Association for Machine Translation and Computational Linguistics (U.S.; now ACL (1))
AMTD	Automatic Magnetic Tape Dissemination Service (of Defence Documentation Center, U.S.)
AMTEC	Association for Media and Technology in Education in Canada (Association des Media et de la Technologie en Éducation au Canada)
AMWS	American Men and Women of Science (publication)
ANABA	Asociación Nacional de Bibliotecarios, Archiveros y Arqueólogos (National Association of Librarians, Archivists and Archaeologists, Spain)
ANABAD	Asociación Nacional de Bibliotecarios, Archiveros, Arqueólogos y Documentalistas (Spain)
ANACONDA	Ad Hoc Committee to Work with Activities Committee on New Directions for American Library Association Activities (U.S.)
ANAF	Automated Names Authority File (of LC)
ANAI	Associazione Nazionale Archivistica Italiana (National Association of Italian Archives)
ANB	Australian National Bibliography
ANBADS	Association Nationale des Bibliothécaires, Archivistes et Documentalistes Sénégalais (National Association of Librarians, Archivists and Documentalists of Senegal)
ANBEF	Association Nationale des Bibliothécaires d'Expression Française (National Association of French-Speaking Librarians, Belgium)
ANCCAC	Australian National Committee on Computation and Automatic Control

ANCIRS	Automated News Clipping, Indexing, and Retrieval System (Image Systems Ltd., U.K.)
ANCS	American National Standards Committee (of LC, operating under the procedures of ANSI)
ANDBP	Association Nationale pour le Développement des Bibliothèques Publiques (National Association for the Development of Public Libraries, France)
ANEDA	Association Nationale d'Études pour la Documentation Automatique (France)
ANIBIPA	Asociación de Bibliotecas Universitarias y Especializadas de Nicaragua
ANIRC	Annual National Information Retrieval Colloquium (U.S.)
ANL (1)	American National Standard Labels
ANL (2)	Australian National Library (also known as NLA (3))
ANOVA	(one way) Analysis of Variance Statistics
ANPA	American Newspaper Publishers Association
ANPB	Asociacion Nacional de Profesionales de Biblioteca (National Association of Professional Librarians, Cuba; now Colegio Nacional de Bibliotecarios Universitarios)
ANRIC	Annual National Information Retrieval Colloquim (U.S.)
ANRT	Association Nationale de la Recherche Technique (France)
ANS	American National Standards (of ANSI)
ANSCR	Alphanumeric System for Classification of Recordings
ANSI	American National Standards Institute (formerly ASA (1), USASI))
ANSI/SPARC	ANSI Standards Planning and Requirements Committee
ANSI/X3/ SPARC/SGDBMS	ANSI/SPARC Study Group on Data Base Management Systems
ANSI-Z39	(ANSI Committee on library work, documentation and related publishing practices)
ANSLICS	Aberdeen and North of Scotland Library and Information Cooperative Service

ANSS	Anthropology and Sociology Section (of ACRL)
ANSTEL	Australian National Scientific and Technological Library (of NLA (3))
ANSVIP	American National Standard Vocabulary for Information Processing
ANTS	Anthropology Section (ACRL)
ANYLTS	Association of New York Libraries for Technical Services (U.S.)
ANZLA	Associate of the New Zealand Library Association
AOIP	Assault on Illiteracy Program (U.S.)
AOIPS	Atmospheric and Oceanographic Information Processing System
AOLTI	Association of Ontario Library Technician Instructors
AOSP	Automatic Operating and Scheduling Program
AOTE	Associated Organizations of Teachers of English (U.S.)
AP	Access Point (records of LC)
APA (1)	Alberta Publishers' Association
APA (2)	Atlantic Publishers' Association
APACUE	Atlantic Provinces Association for Continuing University Education (also known as AEPUA)
APADI	Asosiasi Perpustakaan, Arsip dan Dokumentasi Indonesia (Indonesian Library, Archive and Documentation Association)
APAIS	Australian Public Affairs Information Service (of NLA (3))
APALA	Asian/Pacific American Librarians (U.S.)
APAM	Array Processor Access Method (computer term)
APAPUL	Association du Personnel Administratif et Professionnel de l'Université Laval
APAR	Automatic Programming and Recording
APAUC (1)	Association des Professeurs d'Allemand des Universités Canadiennes (also known as CAUTG)
APAUC (2)	Association des Professeurs d'Anglais des Universités Canadiennes (also known as ACUTE)

APB (1)	Arbeitsgemeinschaft Pädagogischer Bibliotheken und Medienzentren (Working group of Educational Libraries and Media Centres, W. Germany)
APB (2)	Associação Paulista de Bibliotecários (São Paulo Library Association, Brazil)
APBA	Atlantic Provinces Booksellers Association
APBB	Arbeitsgemeinschaft der Parlaments - und Behörden- bibliotheken (Working Group of Parliament and Government Libraries, W. Germany)
APBEG	Associação Profissional de Bibliotecários do Estado da Guanabara (Professional Association of Librarians in Guanabara)
APBSM	Association des Préposés aux Bibliothèques Scholaires de Montréal
APC	Alternative Press Centre (Toronto)
APDU	Association of Public Data Users (U.S.)
APEL	Associação Portuguesa dos Editores e Liveiros (Portuguese Association of Publishers and Booksellers)
APER	Association of Publishers Educational Representatives (U.K.)
a.p.f.	Access Point Files
APFS	American Prose Fiction Series (UMI)
APFUC	Association des Professeurs de Français des Univer- sités Canadiennes (also known as ACUTF)
APG	Application Program Generator (computer term)
APHA	American Printing History Association
API (1)	Alternative Press Index (Alternative Press Centre, Toronto)
API (2)	American Petroleum Institute
APICS (1)	Atlantic Provinces Inter-University Committee on the Sciences
APICS (2)	Air Pollution Information and Computation System (U.S.)
APIF (1)	Antioch Program for Interracial Education (Antioch College, U.S.)

APIF (2)   Automated Process Information File (of LC)

APILIT   (Index to API Abstracts of Refining literature;
              of API (2))

APIN   Automatyzacja Przetwarzania Informacji Naukowej
              (automation system for library and information
              processes, based on MARC format, Poland)

APLA (1)   Atlantic Provinces Library Association

APLA (2)   Authors' and Publishers' Lending Right Association
              Committee (U.S.)

APLIC (1)   Association of/for Population/Family Planning
              Libraries and Information Centers (U.S.)

APLIC (2)   Association of Parliamentary Librarians in Canada

APLO   Automation Planning and Liaison Office (of LC)

APLS   Alabama Public Library Services

APPLE   Associative Processor Programming Language

APPTR   Access Point Pointer (computer term)

APRIS   Alcoa Picturephone Remote Information System (U.S.)

APS   American Periodicals Series (UMI)

APSA   American Political Science Association

APSE   Abstracts of Photographic Science and Engineering
              Literature (Society of Photographic Scientists and
              Engineers, U.S.)

APSP   Array Processor Subroutine Package (computer term)

APT   Automatically Programmed Tools

APTIC   Air Pollution Technical Information Center (Franklin
              Institute Research Labs., Philadelphia, Penn.)

APUC (1)   Association de Placement Universitaire et Collégial
              (also known as UCPA)

APUC (2)   Association des Presses Universitaires Canadiennes
              (also known as ACUP)

AQL   Acceptable Quality Level (computer term)

AQPU   Association Québecoise des Presses Universitaires

ARAC	Arab Research and Administration Center (U.S.)
ARAL	Automatic Record Analysis Language
ARASCO	Arab Organization for Education Science and Culture (U.S.)
ARB	Associação Rio-Grandense de Bibliotecários (Brazil)
ARBA	American Reference Book Annual (publication)
ARBICA	Arab Regional Branch of the International Council on Archives
ARC	Action and Referral Center (Somerville Public Library, Mass.)
ARCHON	Archives On-line (Baltimore, Md.)
ARDIS	Army Research and Development Information System (U.S. Army)
AREA	Association of Records Executives and Administrators (U.S.; now part of ARMA)
ARGUS	Automatic Routine Generating and Updating System
ARIANE	Arrangement Réticule des Informations en vue de l'Approche des Notions par leur Environnement
ARIS	Association Referral Information Service (Ohio Education Association)
ARISE	Adult Referral and Information Service in Education (a database)
ARIST	Annual Review of Information Science and Technology (Encyclopaedia Britannica for ASIS)
ARKISYST	International Information System for Architecture and Urban Planning (Unesco)
ARL	Association of Research Libraries (U.S.)
ARLIS	Art Libraries Society (U.K.)
ARLIS/ANZ	ARLIS Australia New Zealand
ARLIS/NA	ARLIS North America
ARLO	Art Research Libraries of Ohio
ARL/OMS	Association of Research Libraries Office of Management Studies

ARLS	Algonquin Regional Library System
ARMA	Association of Records Managers and Administrators (U.S.)
ARMIS	Agricultural Research Management Information System (U.S.)
ARPA	Advanced Research Projects Agency (Department of Defense, U.S.)
ARPANET	Advanced Research Projects Agency Network (Department of Defense, U.S.)
ARPDP	Association of Rehabilitation Programs in Data Processing (U.S.)
ARRT	Art Reference Round Table (of ALA, ceased)
ARSC	Association for Recorded Sound Collections (N.M.)
ARSRCDS	Academia Republici Socialiste Romania Centrul de Documentare Stlintifica (Romania)
ART	Advanced Research and Technology
ARTEMIS	Automatic Retrieval of Text from Europe's Multi-national Information Service
ARTS	Art Section (of ACRL)
ARU	Audio Response Unit (computer term)
ARUCC	Association of Registrars of Universities and Colleges of Canada (Association des Registraires des Universités et Collèges du Canada)
ARUO	Association des Registraires d'Universités de l'Ontario (also known as OURA)
AS (1)	Acquisitions Section (of RTSD)
AS (2)	Adult Services
ASA (1)	American Standards Association (formerly USAI; now ANSI)
ASA (2)	American Statistical Association
ASA (3)	Australian Society of Archivists
ASAE (1)	American Society of Agricultural Engineers
ASAE (2)	American Society of Association Executives

ASALH	Association for the Study of Afro-American Life and History
ASB	Allgemeine Systematik für Büchereien (General Classification for Public Librararies, W. Germany)
ASBL	Association des Archivistes et des Bibliothécaires de Belgique (Belgium)
ASC (1)	Acquisitions and Serials Controls System (of UTLAS Inc.)
ASC (2)	Automatic Sequence Control
ASC (3)	Automatic Serials Control
ASCA (1)	American School Counselors Association
ASCA (2)	Automatic Subject Citation Alert (Institute for Scientific Information, U.S.)
ASCAP	American Society of Composers, Authors and Publishers
ASCD	Association for Supervision and Curriculum Development (U.S.)
ASCENT	Assembly System for Central Processor
ASCIDIC	Association of Scientific Information Dissemination Centres (U.S.)
ASCII	American Standard Code for Information Interchange (also called American National Standard Code for Information Interchange)
ASCLA	Association of Specialized and Cooperative Library Agencies (formed by the merger of ASLA (1) and HRLSD of ALA and ACLO)
ASCLA HCLS	ASCLA Health Care Libraries Section
ASCLA LSBPHS	ASCLA Library Service to the Blind and Physically Handicapped Section (previously HRLSD/LSBPH)
ASCLA LSDS	ASCLA Library Services to the Deaf Section
ASCLA LSIES	ASCLA Library Services to the Impaired Elderly Section
ASCLA LSPS	ASCLA Library Services to Prisoners Section
ASCLA MLCS	ASCLA Multitype Library Cooperation Section
ASCLA SLAS	ASCLA State Library Agency Section
ASCOBIC	African Standing Conference on Bibliographic Control

ASCOLBI	Asociación Colombiana de Bibliotecarios (Colombian Library Association)
ASCRT	Association for the Study of Canadian Radio and Television
ASD (1)	Adult Services Division (of ALA; merged with RSD to become RASD)
ASD (2)	Association Suisse de Documentation (also known as SVD)
ASDBAM	Association Sénégalaise pour le Développement de la Documentation, des Bibliothèques, des Archives et des Musées (Senegal Association for the Development of Documentation, Libraries, Archives and Museums)
ASDI	Automated Selective Dissemination of Information
ASDIRS	Army Study Documentation and Information Retrieval System (U.S.)
ASECS	American Society for Eighteenth Century Studies
ASECUC	Association des Services aux Étudiants des Collèges et Universités du Canada (also known as CACUSS)
ASEIB	Asociación de Egresados de la Escuela Interamericana de Bibliotecología (Association of Graduates of the Inter-American School of Librarianship, Colombia)
ASELT	Association Européenne pour l'Echange de la Littérature Technique dans le Domaine de la Sidérurgie (Luxembourg)
ASERL	Association of Southeastern Research Libraries (U.S.)
ASGL	Association of Saskatchewan Government Libraries
ASI (1)	American Society of Indexers
ASI (2)	American Statistics Index (Congressional Information Services)
ASI (3)	Analytic Subject Index (American Institute of Physics)
ASIDC	Association of Scientific Information Dissemination Centers (U.S.; now AIDC)
ASIDIC	Association of Scientific Information Dissemination Centers (U.S.; now AIDC)
ASII	American Science Information Institute
ASIN	Agricultural Sciences Information Network (National Agricultural Library, U.S.)

ASIRC	Aquatic Sciences Information Retrieval Center (U.S.)
ASIS	American Society for Information Science (formerly ADI) (see also entries under SIG/ for various Special Interest Groups of ASIS)
ASIS/Wes-Can	ASIS Western Canada Chapter
ASK (1)	Access to Sources of Knowledge (Service of NRC (2))
ASK (2)	Aerospace Shared Knowledge (an on-line total library system of Aerospace Corp., Charles C. Lauritsen Library, Los Angeles, Calif.)
ASL (1)	American Sign Language
ASL (2)	Association of State Libraries (U.S.; also known as AASL (2))
ASLA (1)	Association of State Library Agencies (of ALA; now ASCLA)
ASLA (2)	Australian School Library Association
ASLC	Association for Library Services to Children (of ALA; formerly CSD)
ASLIB	Association of Special Libraries and Information Bureaux (U.K.; now called Aslib)
ASLIP	Association of Special Libraries of the Philippines (also known as ASLP)
ASLP	Association of Special Libraries of the Philippines (also knwon as ASLIP)
ASLS	Academic and Special Libraries Section (of NLA (5))
ASLT	Advanced Solid Logic Technology
ASM	Association for Systems Management (U.S.)
ASMI	Agudat Ha-Sifriyot Hameyuhadot Imerkeze Ha-Meda Beyisrael (Israel Society of Special Libraries and Information Centres; also known as ISLIC)
ASN	Authority Sequence Number (of UTLAS Inc.)
ASNIBI	Asociacion Nicaraguense de Bibliotecarios (Nicaraguan Library Association)
ASO	Automated Systems Office (of LC)
ASOC	Association of Schools of Optometry of Canada (also known as AEOC)

ASODOBI	Asociación Dominicana de Bibliotecarios (Dominican Republic Library Association
ASP	Archival Security Program (of the Univ. of Illinois Library)
ASPA	American Society for Personnel Administration
ASPB	Arbeitsgemeinschaft der Spezialbibliotheken (Association of Special Libraries, W. Germany)
ASPER	Assembly System for the Peripheral Processors (of CDC (2))
ASPIRE	Access Service for Profitable Information Resource Exchanges (U.S.)
ASR	Automatic Send/Receive or Automatic Sending and Receiving (computer term)
ASSASSIN	Agricultural System for Storage and Subsequent Selection of Information (U.K.)
ASSPA	Association Suisse pour l'Automatique (Swiss Association for Automation; also known as SGA)
AST	Applied Science and Technology Index
ASTA	American String Teachers Association
ASTAP	Advanced Statistical Analysis Program (computer programme)
ASTD	American Society for Training and Development
ASTED	Association pour l'Avancement des Sciences et des Techniques de la Documentation (Association for the Advancement of the Science and Technology of Documentation; formerly ACBLF)
ASTI	Applied Science and Technology Index (H.W. Wilson Co.)
ASTIA	Armed Services Technical Information Agency (U.S.; now DDC (1))
ASTRID	Association Scientifique et Technique pour la Recherche en Informatique Documentaire (Belgium)
ASV	Automatic Self Verification (computer term)
ASYVOL	Analyse Synthétique par Vocabulaire Libre (Laval University Library, Quebec)
ATD (1)	Aerospace Technology Division (of LC)

ATD (2)	Association Tunisienne des Documentalistes, Bibliothé-caires et Archivistes (Tunisian Association of Documentalists, Librarians and Archivists)
ATDM	Asynchronous Time-Division Multiplexing (computer term)
ATEC	Agency for Tele-Education in Canada
ATIS	Advanced Thermal Imaging Scanner
AT/L	Advanced Technology/Libraries (periodical)
ATLA	American Theological Library Association
ATLAS (1)	Abbreviated Test Language for All Systems (computer term)
ATLAS (2)	Automatic Tabulating, Listing and Sorting System
ATLIS (1)	Army Technical Libraries and Information Systems (U.S.)
ATLIS (2)	Army Technical Library Improvement Studies (later TISAP; ceased 1974)
ATPI	American Textbook Publishers' Institute
ATRA	American Television and Radio Archives
ATS (1)	Administrative Terminal System (System 360, IBM Corp.)
ATS (2)	American Technical Society
ATSU	Association of Time-sharing Users (U.S.)
AT & T	American Telephone and Telegraph Co.
ATT	Application Transfer Team (of IBM Corp.)
AUA	Association des Universités de l'Atlantique (also known as AAU (2))
AUCC	Association of Universities and Colleges of Canada (Association des Universités et Collèges du Canada)
AUCC/IDO	Association of Universities and Colleges of Canada/ International Development Office
AUCS	Atlantic University Computer Study
AUDACIOUS	Automatic Direct Access to Information with the On-line UDC System (American Institute of Physics Scheme for Nuclear Science)
AUFSC	Association of University Forestry Schools of Canada (also known as AEFUC)

AUL	Assistant University Librarian
AULA	Arab University Library Association (Kuwait)
AUNBT	Association of University of New Brunswick Teachers
AUPELF	Association des Universités Partiellement ou Entièrement de Langue Française (Université de Montreal)
AUPTL	All-Union Patent and Technical Library (U.S.S.R.)
AUSINET	Australian Information Network or Australian Database Network
AUTODOC	Automatic Documentation
AUTOPIC	Automatic Personal Identification Code (of IBM)
AUTOPROMPT	Automatic Programming of Machine Tools
AUTOPSY	Automatic Operating System (of IBM)
AUUA	America's Univac Users Association
A/V	Audio-visual
AVA	Audio-visual Aids
AVC	Alberta Vocational Centre
AV-CIP	Audiovisual Cataloging in Publication
AVDBAD	Association Voltaique pour le Développement des Bibliotheques, des Archives et de la Documentation (Voltan Association for the Development of Libraries, Archives and Documentation, Republic of Upper Volta)
AVG	Audio-Visual Group (Library Association, U.K.)
A-VIS	Audio-visual Information System (U.S. Army)
AVLA	Audio-Visual Language Association (U.K.)
AVLINE	Audio-Visual On-line (of NLM)
AVLS	Audio-Visual Library Services (U.K.)
AVMP	Audiovisual Market Place (publication)
AVS	Audiovisual Section (of LITA)
AVSL	Association of Visual Science Librarians (of UCLA)

AWC	Association for Women in Computing (U.S.)
AWLNET	Area Wide Library Network (U.S.)
AYRES	(IMS Ayer Directory of Publications)
AZABDO	Association Zairoise des Archivistes, Bibliotécaires et Documentalistes (Zairian Association of Archivists, Librarians and Documentalists, Zaire)
BA	Biological Abstracts (U.S.)
BAA	Bibliothèque d'Art et d'Archéologie (France)
BABS	Book Acquisition and Bibliographic Service (of National Book Centre Ltd., Toronto)
BACS	Bibliographic Access and Control System (On-line catalog system of Washington University, School of Medicine
BADADUQ	Banque de Données à Accés Direct de l'Université du Québec (Direct Access to the Data Storage at the Université du Québec)
BAG	Buchhändler-Abrechnungs-Gesellschaft (W.Germany; a book trading agency)
BAI	Biological and Agricultural Index (publication)
BAIE	British Association of Industrial Editors (U.K.)
BAL	Basic Assembler Language (computer term)
BALIS	Bay Area Library and Information System (Oakland, Calif.)
BALLOTS	Bibliographic Automation of Large Library Operations Using a Time-sharing System (of Stanford University)
BALS	Birmingham Association of Library Students (U.K.)
BAMBAM	Bookline Alert: Missing Books and Manuscripts (a database maintained by American Book Prices Current)
BAML	Boston Area Music Libraries
BANQ	Biblionews and Australian Notes and Queries (publication)
BANSDOC	Bangladesh National Scientific and Technical Documentation Centre
BAP	Basic Assembler Program

BAPA	British Amateur Press Association
BAR	Buffer Address Register (computer term)
BARC (1)	Bay Area Reference Center (a cooperative service of public libraries in California)
BARC (2)	Bibliographic and Reference Center (Cornell University)
BARDS	Bucknell Automated Retrieval and Display System (of Bucknell University, Pa.)
BARON)	Business Accounts Reporting Operating Network
BAS (1)	Bibliography of Asian Studies (publication)
BAS (2)	Book Acquisition System (R.R. Bowker Co.)
BAS (3)	Bowker Acquisition System (R.R. Bowker Co.)
BASIC (1)	Beginner's Algebraic Symbolic Interpretive Compiler
BASIC (2)	Beginner's All-purpose Symbolic Instruction Code (computer language)
BASIC (3)	Biological Abstracts Subjects in Context
BASIS (1)	Battelle Automated Search Information System (Battelle Memorial Institute, U.S.)
BA.SIS (2)	Bibliographic Author or Subject Interactive Search (of Nexus)
BASIS (3)	Bulletin of the American Society for Information Science
BASIS-E	Bibliothekarisch-analytisches System zur Informations-Speicherund-Erschliessung (Library Analytical System for Information Storage/Retrieval - Economics, W. Germany)
BASR	Bureau of Applied Social Research (Columbia University, N.Y.)
BASS	Belgian Archives for the Social Sciences
BATAB	Baker & Taylor Automated Buying (computerized ordering system (now defunct)
BATMA	Bookbinding and Allied Trades Management Association (U.K.)
BBC (1)	Basic Bibliographic Citation
BBC (2)	Bliss Bibliographic Classification
B.BIBL	Bachelier en Bibliothéconomie et en Bibliographie
BBIP	British Books in Print (J. Whitaker, U.K.)

BBK	Bibliotechno-bibliograf-icheskaya Klassifikatsiya (Library-bibliographical Classification, U.S.S.R.)
BBLC	Boston Biomedical Library Consortium
BBM	Books-by-Mail
BBN	British Book News (British Council)
BBS (1)	Bulletin Board Service (of Chicago Public Library's North-Pulaski Branch Library service through electronic bulletin board)
BBS (2)	Bulletin Board System (publication, New American Library, N.Y.)
BBTA	British Book Trade Association (Booksellers Association and Publishers Association, U.K.)
BC	Bibliographic Classification (BLISS)
BC2	Bliss Bibliographic Classification - 2nd ed.
BCA	Bliss Classification Association (U.K.)
BCAB	British Computer Association for the Blind (U.K.)
BCAC	Bibliography of Central America and the Caribbean
BCC	British Copyright Council
BCD	Binary-Coded Decimal/Data
BCEI	Bureau Canadien de l'Éducation Internationale (also known as CBIE)
BCIC) BCIT)	British Columbia Institute of Technology
BCL (1)	Books for College Libraries (publication)
BCL (2)	Central Library Processing Service (Amherst, Mass.)
BCLA	British Columbia Library Association
BCLN	British Columbia Library Network
BCLTA	British Columbia Library Trustees Association
BCM	British Catalogue of Music (U.K.)
BCN	Biomedical Communications Network (U.S.)
BCNC	Bibliographic and Communications Network Committee (of NLC (2))

BCP (1)	Bibliothèque Centrale de Prêt (Central Lending Library, France)
BCP (2)	Bibliothèques Centrales de Prêt (Quebec)
BCPL (1)	Baltimore County Public Library (Baltimore, Md.)
BCPL (2)	Basic Computer Programming Language
BCR	Bibliographical Center for Research (U.S.)
BCS (1)	Boeing Computer Services of Canada, Ltd.
BCS (2)	British Computer Society
BCS (3)	Bureau of Ceylon Standards (affiliated with ISO (2))
BCSAA	British Computer Society ALGOL Association (U.K.)
BCSLA	British Columbia School Librarians Association
BCTF	Bibliographic Control Task Force (a project of the Univ. of Missouri)
BCTIC	Biomedical Computing Technology Information Center (U.S.)
BCU	Bibliothèque Cantonale et Universitaire de Lausanne (Switzerland)
BCUC	British Columbia Union Catalogue Project
BDA (1)	Bibliotheek-en Dokumentatieakademie (Library and Documentation Academy, Netherlands)
BDA (2)	Business Data Analysis
BDAM	Basic Direct Access Method
BDC	Binary Decimal Counter (computer term)
BDDR	Bibliotheksverband der Deutsche Demokratische Republik (Library Association of German Democratic Republic; formerly DBV (1))
BDIAC	Battelle Defender Information Analysis Center (Battelle Memorial Institute, U.S.)(now Strategic Technology Office Information Analysis Center)
BDLD	Bookdealer Library Relations (Committee of ALA)
BDLR	Bookdealer-Library Relations Committee (ALA/RTSD/RS)
BDMI	Biographical Dictionaries Master Index

BDMS	Berkeley Data Base Management System (California University)
BDOS	Basic Disk Operating System (computer term)
BEACON	Bibliographic Exchange and Communications Network (of Colorado Academic Libraries Book Processing Center; later CALBPC)
BEAR	Berkeley Elites Automated Retrieval (California University)
BECA	Bureau of Educational and Cultural Affairs (U.S.; now ICA (1) or USICA)
BECEWA	Belgisch Studie-en Documentatiecentrum voor Water (Belgium; also known as CEBEDEAU)
BECLS	Buffalo and Erie County Library System (N.Y.)
BECPL	Buffalo and Erie County Public Library
BEE	Books for Equal Education (U.S.; ceased)
BEEF	Business and Engineering Enriched FORTRAN
BEI	British Education Index (of BSD)
BEIC	Battelle Energy Information Center (Columbus, Ohio)
BEL (1)	Board of Education for Librarianship (U.S.)
BEL (2)	Fort Belvoir Library (U.S. Army)
BELC	Black Employees of the Library of Congress
BELLCAT	(an online catalogue developed by Bell Laboratories Library Network)
BELLREL	Bell Laboratories Library Real Time Loan (U.S.)
BELLS	Buffalo Education Libraries Lighted School Houses
BELLTIP	(Bell Telephone Laboratories - On-line Acquisition and Cataloguing System, U.S.)
BEMA	Business Equipment Manufacturers Association (formerly BEMI; now CBEMA)
BES	Building and Equipment Section (of LAMA)
BESE	Board of Elementary and Secondary Education (La.)
BEST	Business EDP Systems Technique

BETA	Business Equipment Trade Association
BEX	Broadband Exchange (of Western Union)
BF	Bibliotekarforeningen (Association of Librarians, Denmark)
BFI	British Film Institute
b & g	Boys and Girls
BGMI	Biography and Geneology Master Index (replaces BDMI)
BGNS	Begin a Search on Any File (LC's programme)
BGS	Bangladesh Granthagar Samite (Library Association of Bangladesh)
BHI	British Humanities Index (of LA (1))
BI (1)	**Bibliografiska Institutet (Bibliographical Institute, Sweden)**
BI (2)	Bibliographic Instruction
BIA	Braille Institute of America
BIALL	British and Irish Association of Law Librarians (U.K. and Ireland)
BIBCENTER	(Univ. of California Bibliographic Center)
BIBCON	Bibliographic Records Control (of Univ. of California and the California State University)
BIBDES	Bibliographic Data Entry System
BIBLIOFILE	(System providing automation benefits for small libraries) (Information Planning Associates Inc., U.S.)
BIBLIOS	Book Inventory Building and Library Information Oriented System (Orange County Public Library, Calif.)
BIBNET	Bibliographic Network (retrieval system used by various agencies, e.g. OCLC, Inc. 3M Co., etc.)
BIBPRO IV	Bibliography Production (of Informatics, Inc.)
BIC	Books in Canada
BICEPT	Book Indexing with Context and Entry Point from Text

BIDAP	Bibliographic Data Processing Programme
BIDS	Bangladesh Institute of Development Studies
BIE	Books in English (of BSD)
BIEE	British Institute of Electrical Engineers
BIIT	Bureau International d'Information sur le Télécommunications (Switzerland)
BILD	Board of Industrial Leadership and Development (Ontario)
BILG	Building Industry Libraries Group (now Construction Industry Information Group, U.K.)
BILINDEX	(Spanish-English subject heading thesausus)
BIM	British Institute of Management
BINAC	Binary Northrop Automatic Computer
BINET	Bicentennial Information Network (of American Revolution Bicentennial Commission)
BIO	Bedford Institute of Oceanography (N.S.)
BIOS	Basic Input/Output System (computer term)
BIOSIS	Bioscience Information Service (of Biological Abstracts)
BIP	Books in Print (R.R. Bowker Co.)
BIPAD	Bureau of Independent Publishers and Distributors
BIPsubj	Subject Guide to Books in Print
BIRS (1)	Baptish Information Retrieval System (Tenn.)
BIRS (2)	Basic Indexing and Retrieval System
BIRS (3)	British Institute of Recorded Sound
BIS (1)	Bibliographic Instruction Section (of ACRL)
BIS (2)	Brain Information Service (Center for Health Sciences, UCLA)
BIS (3)	British Information Service
BISA	Bibliographic Information on Southeast Asia (of Univ. of Sydney, Australia)

BISAC (1)	Book Industry Study Group (of N.Y. City)
BISAC (2)	Book Industry System Advisory Committee (U.S.)
BI-SAL	Bi-State Academic Libraries (a cooperative project in Iowa)
BISAM	Basic Indexed Sequential Access Method
BISBN	Bibliographic ISBN
BISG	Book Industry Study Group (U.S.)
Bisync	Binary synchronous (an IBM communications protocol)
bit	binary digit (computer term)
B-I-T-S (1)	BIOSIS Information Transfer System
BITS (2)	Business Industry Technology Service (Dayton and Montgomery County Public Library, Ohio)
BIU	Bus Interface Unit (computer term)
BIVES	Bureau d'Information de Voyages et d'Échanges Sociaux (France)
BJRT	Basic Job Readiness Training (a government sponsored programme)
BK	Bibliotekstjanst Katalog (Sweden)
BL	British Library (the new name for British Museum Library organization to unite British Government's diverse libraries into a national library service)
BLAC	Benson Latin American Collection (Univ. of Texas)
BLADE	Basic Literacy for Adult Development (a government sponsored programme)
BLAIS) BLAISE)	British Library Automated Information Service
BLASA	Bantu Library Association of South Africa
BLATT	Bulletin of the Library Association of Trinidad and Tobago
BLBSD	British Library Bibliographical Services Division (also known as BSD)
BLC (1)	Board for Library Co-ordination
BLC (2)	Boston Library Consortium

BLCMP	Birmingham Libraries Co-operative Mechanisation Project (U.K.)
BLEND	Birmingham Loughborough Electronic Network Development
BLET	Bureau of Libraries and Educational Technology (later BLLR; now DLP)
BLib	Bachelor of Librarianship
BLIS (1)	Biblio-Techniques Library and Information System
BLIS (2)	British Librarianship and Information Science (of LA (1))
BLISS	Basic Language for Implementation of System Software
BLISTA	Deutsche Blindenstudienanstalt
BLL	British Library Lending Division (officially BLLD; also known as BLLS)
BLLD	British Library Lending Division (U.K.) (preferred usage is BLLD - also known as BLL,BLLS; formerly LLU, NLLST, NLL and NCL (1))
BLLR	Bureau of Libraries and Learning Resources (Department of Health, Education and Welfare, U.S.; formerly BLET, now DLP)
BLLS	British Library Lending Services (officially BLLD; also known as BLL)
BLM	Basic Language Machine (computer term)
BLOC (1)	Booth Library On-line Circulation (Eastern Illinois State University)
BLOC (2)	British Library Organising Committee (U.K.)
BLOCS	Bucknell Library On-line Circulation System (Bucknell University, U.S.)
BLOWS	British Library of Wildlife Sounds (British Institute of Recorded Sound)
BLPES	British Library of Political and Economic Science (London School of Economics, London University)
BLRDD	British Library Research and Development Department (new name of OSTI)
BLS (1)	Bachelor of Library Science
BLS (2)	Bureau of Labor Statistics (U.S. Dept. of Labor)

BLSOSA	Brighton Library School Old Students Association (U.K.)
BLSRL	British Library Science Reference Library (also known as SRL; formerly NRL (1), NRLSI)
BM	British Museum
BMC (1)	British Museum Catalogue (British Library Reference Division)
BMC (2)	Bubble Memory Controller (computer term)
BMCS	Bibliographic Management Consulting Services
BMD	Biomedical (computer programmmes)
BMDC	Biomedicinska Dokumentationscentralen (Bio-medical Documentation Centre, Karolinska Institute, Sweden)
BMDP	Biomedical Computer Programs
BMI	Book Manufacturing Institute (U.S.)
BML (1)	Branch and Municipal Libraries (of LA (1))
BML (2)	British Museum Library (now part of British Library)
BMLA	Bulletin of the Medical Library Association
BN (1)	Biblioteka Narodowa (The National Library in Warsaw, Poland)
BN (2)	Bibliothèque Nationale (France)
BNA (1)	Biblioteca Nacional de Angola (National Library of Angola)
BNA (2)	Blackwell/North America
B/NA-MARC	BNA MARC
BNB	British National Bibliography
BNB/BLC	BNB/British Library Catalogue
BNBC	British National Book Centre (now British Library Lending Division Gifts and Exchanges Section)
BNB MARC	British National Bibliography MARC
BNC	Bibliothèque Nationale du Canada (also known as NLC (2))
BNCF	Biblioteca Nazionale Centrale-Firenze (National Central Library of Florence)
BNFC	British National Film Catalogue

BNIST	Bureau National d'Information Scientifique et Technique (National Office for Scientific and Technical Information, France)
BNQ	Bibliothèque Nationale du Québec
BNR	Bell Northern Research Network
BNR/ALIRT	BNR/Analytic Library Information Retrieval and Transfer
BNRJ	Biblioteca Nacional do Rio de Janeiro (National Library of Rio de Janeiro)
BoA	Bibliography of Agriculture (CCM Information Corp., U.S.)
BOADICEA	British Overseas Airways Digital Information Computer for Electronic Automation
BOCES	Board of Cooperative Educational Services
BOIM	Basic On-Line Indexing Method (of LC)
BOLD	Bibliographic On-line Library Display (System Development Corp., U.S.)
BOLT	British Columbia Organization of Library Technicians
BOOKLINE	(monograph control and management system of Blackwell Library Systems, Inc.)
BORD	Book Order and Record Document (U.K.)
BOS	Basic Operating System (computer term)
BOT	Beginning of Tape (computer term)
BP and HL	Brown Picton and Hornby Libraries (Liverpool, U.K.)
BP and JCFL	Birmingham Public and Jefferson County Free Library (U.S.)
BPDA	Bibliographic Pattern Discovery Algorithm
BPDC	Book and Periodical Development Council
BPI (1)	Bibliothèque Publique d'Information (Georges Pompidou National Art and Cultural Center, France)
BPI (2)	Business Periodical Index
BPL (1)	Belfast Public Library (Northern Ireland)
BPL (2)	Birmingham Public Libraries (U.K.)
BPL (3)	Boston Public Library

BPL (4)	Brighton Public Library (U.K.)
BPL (5)	Brooklyn Public Library (U.S.)
BPMA	British Printing Machinery Association
BPO	British Post Office
BPP	British Parliamentary Papers
BPPA	Book Publishers' Professional Association
BPR	(American) Book Publishing Record (R.R.Bowker)
BPRA	Book Publishers Representatives Association (U.K.)
BPS (1)	Basic Programming System
BPS (2)	Bibliographic/MARC Processing System (software package for manipulation of MARC format records)
bps (3)	bits per second (computer term)
BPTMA	British Publishers' Traditional Market Agreement
BPWF	Business and Professional Women's Foundation (U.S.)
BQ (1)	Becqueral (SI) (activity of radionuclides)
BQ (2)	Bibliographie du Québec
BRA	British Records Association
BRD	Book Review Digest (H.W. Wilson)
BRI	Book Review Index (Gale Research)
BRIC	Bureau de Recherche pour l'Innovation et la Convergence (France)
BRICS	Black Resources Information Coordinating Services, Inc. (U.S.)
BRIMARC	Brighton/MARC (of Brighton Public Libraries, U.K.)
BRM	Basic Reading Materials (Committee established under the chairmanship of the Adult/Young People's Coordinator)
BROWSER	Browsing On-line with Selective Retrieval (of IBM)
BRS	Bibliographical Retrieval Services (U.S.)
BRT	Bio Research Today (publication)

BRTA	British Regional Television Association
BS	British Standard
BSA	Bibliographical Society of America
BSAM	Basic Sequential Access Method
BSANZ	Bibliographical Society of Australia and New Zealand
BSC	Bibliographical Society of Canada (also known as SBC (2))
B.Sc.B	Baccalauréat en Bibliothéconomie
BSCP	Biological Sciences Communication Project (G. Washington University, U.S.)
BSD	Bibliographical Services Division (British Library; also known as BLBSD)
BSDP	Bibliographic Service Development Program (of CLR)
BSI	British Standards Institution
BSIB	British Society for International Bibliography (merged into Aslib)
BSIC/EFL	Building Systems Information Clearinghouse/Educational Facilities Laboratories Inc., U.S.)
BSLS	Bachelor of Science in Library Science
BSO (1)	Bibliographic Standards Office (of BSD)
BSO (2)	Broad System of Ordering
BSP (1)	Bibliographical Society of the Phillipines
BSP (2)	Burroughs Scientific Processor
BSRA	British Sound Recording Association
BSRIA	Buildings Services Research and Information Association
BSTL	Bibliografické Středisko pro Techickou Literaturu (Bibliographical Centre for Technical Literature, Czechoslovakia)
B&T (1)	Baker & Taylor Co.
BT (2)	Borader Term (in LCSH)
BT (3)	British Telecom

BTAM	Basic Telecommunications Access Method
BTI	British Technology Index (of LA (1))
BTJ	Bibliotekstjänst AB (Sweden)
BTRI	British Theses Retroactive Index (European Bibliographic Center)
BTS	Business Telidon Services (database)
BTSB	Bound to Stay Bound (Books Inc., Ill.)
BTSD	Basic Training for Skills Development Program
BUCCS	Bath University Comparative Catalogue Study (U.K.)
BUCOP	British Union Catalogue of Periodicals (of BSD)
BUFC	British Universities Film Council
BUP	British United Press
BUPCR	Bath University Programme of Catalogue Research (U.K.)
BURISA	British Urban and Regional Information Systems Association (U.K.)
BVD	Belgische Vereniging voor Documentatie (Belgian Association for Documentation; also known as ABD (3))
BYGGDOC	(Swedish Institute of Building Documentation)
BYU Library	Brigham Young University Library
© (1)	Copyright (Universal Copyright Convention)
C (2)	Coulomb (SI) (quantity of electric charge)
CA (1)	Chemical Abstracts (American Chemical Society)
CA (2)	Current Awareness
CAA	Caribbean Archives Association
CAAA	College Art Association of America
CAAE	Canadian Association for Adult Education (also known as ACEA (3))
CAANS	Canadian Association for the Advancement of Netherlandic Studies (also known as ACAEN)
CAAS (1)	Canadian Association for Applied Spectroscopy (now Spectroscopy Society of Canada)

CAAS (2)	Canadian Association of African Studies (also known as ACEA (1))
CAAS (3)	Computer-Assisted Acquisitions System
CAAT	College of Applied Arts and Technology
CAB (1)	Citizen's Advisory Bureau (U.K.)
CAB (2)	Commonwealth Agricultural Bureau (U.K.)
CABS (1)	Committee on Automated Bibliographic Services (of BL)
CABS (2)	Computerized Annotated Bibliography System (Univ. of Alberta)
CABSALA	Central African Branch of the South African Library Association (defunct)
CAC (1)	Chemical Abstracts Condensates (American Chemical Society)
CAC (2)	Current Abstracts in Chemistry (Institute for Scientific Information, U.S.)
CACIC (1)	Chicago Area Computer Information Centers (project of Illinois Regional Library Council)
CAC-IC (2)	Current Abstracts in Chemistry - Index Chemicus (Institute for Scientific Information, U.S.)
CACL	Canadian Association of Childrens Librarians (of CLA)
CACLALS	Canadian Association for Commonwealth Language and Literary Studies (also known as ACELLC)
CACM	Communications of the Association for Computing Machinery
CACon	Chemical Abstracts Condensates (European Space Research Organization Space Documentation Services On-line Version)
CACUL	Canadian Association of College and University Libraries (of CLA; previously also known as ACBCU)
CACUSS	Canadian Association of College and University Student Services (also known as ASECUC)
CAD	Computer-aided Design
CAD/CAM	Computer-aided Design/Computer-aided Manufacturing
CADDE	Canadian Association of Deans and Directors of Education (also known as ACDDE)

CADIG	Coventry and District Information Group (U.K.)
CADO	Central Air Documents Office (U.S.)
CADRE (1)	Collectors, Artists, and Dealers for Responsible Equity (U.S.)
CADRE (2)	Current Awareness and Document Retrieval for Engineers (U.S.)
CAE (1)	Canadian Aviation Electronics
CAE (2)	College of Advanced Education
CAE (3)	Computer-aided Education
CAEO	Coalition of Adult Education Organizations (of ALA)
CAFA	Confederation of Alberta Faculty Associations
CAFB	Certificate d'Aptitude, Fonctions de Bibliothécaire (France)
CAFL	Central Agricultural and Forestry Library (Czecho-slovakia)
CAFRAD	Centre Africain de Formation et de Recherches Administratives pour le Développement (Morocco)
CAGS	Canadian Association of Graduate Schools
CAHSL	Connecticut Association of Health Sciences Libraries (a consortia)
CAHUMC	Commission on Archives and History of the United Methodist Church (U.S.)
CAI	Computer-assisted Instruction
CAIC	Computer-assisted Indexing and Classification
CAIN (1)	Cataloging and Indexing System (National Agricultural Library, U.S.)
CAIN (2)	Cleveland Area Interloan Network (now CAMLS)
CAINT	Computer-assisted Interrogation (of IBM)
CAIP	Computer-assisted Indexing Program (United Nations)
CAIRS	Computer-assisted Information Retrieval System
CAIS (1)	Canadian Association for Information Science (also known as ACSI)
CAIS (2)	Central Abstracting and Indexing Service (of the American Petroleum Institute)

CAISF	Chemical Abstracts Integrated Subject File (American Chemical Society)
CAK	Command Acknowledge (computer term)
CAL (1)	Center for Applied Linguistics (U.S.)
CAL (2)	Central Association of Libraries (a consortium in California)
CAL (3)	Computer-aided Learning
CAL (4)	Confederacy of American Librarians (coined by Michael Gorman in an article, "Toward Bibliographical Control" American Libraries, Nov. 78)
CALA	Chinese American Library Association (U.S.; or Chinese-American Librarians Association)
CALACS	Canadian Association of Latin American and Caribbean Studies
CALAS	Canadian Association of Latin American Studies (also known as ACELA)
CALBPC	Colorado Academic Libraries Book Processing Center (previously BEACON)
CALC	Chicago Academic Library Council
CALIB '83	Conference on College and Academic Library Buildings (New Stanton, Penn., 1983)
CALICO (1)	Columbus Area Library and Information Council of Ohio
CALICO (2)	Computer Assisted Library Instruction Co., Inc. (U.S.)
CALINET	California Library Network (of UCLA)
CALIS	Center for the Advancement of Library and Information Science (City University, N.Y.)
CALL (1)	Canadian Association of Law Libraries (also known as ACBD)
CALL (2)	Current Awareness - Library Literature (periodical, U.S.)
CALLIOPE	Computer Assisted Legislative Liaison: Interactive Online Political Evaluation (developed at the Univ. of Vermont)
CALM (1)	Card and Label Manager (a program written for APPLE II microcomputers)
CALM (2)	Computer-assisted Library Mechanization

CALM (3)	Council of Academic Librarians of Manitoba
CALP	Computer Analysis of Library Postcards (of library buildings)
CALROSA) CALROSEA)	Committee on American Library Resources on South Asia (now CORMOSEA)
CALS	Canadian Association of Library Schools (also known as ACEB)
CALT	Canadian Association of Law Teachers (also known as ACPD)
CALTAC	California Association of Library Trustees and Commissioners
CALUPL	Council of Administrators of Large Urban Public Libraries
CAM (1)	Community Access Module (Univ. of Waterloo's circulation system)
CAM (2)	Computer-aided Manufacturing
CAMESA	Canadian Military Electronics Standards Agency
CAML	Canadian Association of Music Libraries (also known as ACBM)
CAMLS	Cleveland Area Metropolitan Library System (previously CAIN (2))
CAMOL	Computer-assisted Management Learning
CAMP	Cooperative Africana Microform Project (of African Studies Library, Boston University Library)
CAN (1)	Computer Architecture News
CAN (2)	Conservation Administration News (periodical)
CAN'A	Canadiana
CANAC	Catalogage National Centralisé (France)
CANC	Cancel Character (computer term)
CAN/CAT	Canadiana/Cataloguing Subsystem
CANCERLINE	Cancer Information On-line (formerly CCALINE - Cancer Chemotheraphy Abstracts On-line; a database of National Cancer Institute, U.S.)

CANCERLIT	Cancer Literature (of BLAISE)
CANCERPROJ	Cancer Project (of BLAISE)
CANDIS	Canadian Disarmament Information Service
CAN/DOC	Canadian Documents (of NLC (2))
CANEDI	Canadian Education Index
CANFARM	Canadian Farm Management Data System
CANMARC	Canadian Machine Readable Cataloguing
CANMET	Canada Centre for Mineral and Energy Technology
CAN/OLE	Canadian On-line Enquiry (of CISTI; also known as RELAIS)
CANREG	Canadian Register (of Research and Researchers in the Social Sciences)
CAN/SDI	Canadian Selective Dissemination of Information (of CISTI)
CANSIM	Canadian Socio-Economic Information Management System (of Statistics Canada)
CAN/TAP	Canadian Technical Awareness Programme (of CISTI)
CANUC	Canadian National Union Catalogue or Canadian Union Catalogue
CANU:H	Canadian Union Catalogue of Library Materials for the Handicapped
CANUCS	Union List of Serials in the Social Sciences and Humanities held by Canadian Libraries
CANUNET	Canada University Computer Network
CANWIP	(Registry of) Canadian Works in Progress
CAO	(Regional) Committee for Asia and Oceania (of FID)
CAOS	Completely Automated Operational System (of Lockheed on UNIVAC)
CAP (1)	Career Assistance Program and Retraining (of LC)
CAP (2)	Cataloguing in Advance of Publication (of British Library)
CAP (3)	Collection Analysis Project (of ACRL)

CAP (4)   Committee on Automation Planning (of LC)

CAPCON   Capital Consortium Network (Washington, D.C.)

CAPE   Canadian Association of Professors of Education
               (also known as ACPE)

CAPERTSIM   Computer-assisted Program Evaluation Review Technique
               Simulation

CAPL   Canadian Association of Public Libraries (of CLA)

CAPOUG   Capital Osborne Users Group (U.S.)

CAPSA   Canadian Association of Pension Supervisory Authorities

CAPSUL   Computerized Access to Periodicals and Serials (of
               Université Laval, Quebec)

CAPTAIN   Computer-aided Processing and Terminal Access Information
               Network (Rutgers University, U.S.)

CAR (1)   Chemical Abstracts Reviews (American Chemical Society)

CAR (2)   Computer-assisted Retrieval or Computer-assisted
               Microform Retrieval

CARA   Composition Automatique de Repertoires Analytiques
               (Université Laval, Québec)

CARC   Computer-assisted Reference Center

CARD   Compact Automatic Retrieval Device (of MIT)

CARD-A-LERT   (Selective Information Alerting Service for Engineers
               and Scientists, U.S.)

CARDAN   Centre d'Analyses et de Recherches Documentaires
               pour l'Afrique Noire

CARDOSEA   Committee on Archives and Documents of Southeast
               Asia (of AAS (3))

CARDS   Card Automated Reproduction Demand/Distribution
               System (of LC)

CARDSET   (Application of MARC II to build sets of 'cards'
               as output via COM, Information Design Inc., U.S.)

CARE   Computer-Assisted Renewal Education (of Pennsylvania
               University)

CARED   Centre for Applied Research and Engineering Design, Inc.

CARES   Central Advisory Referral Service (New York Metropoli-
               tan Reference and Research Library Agency)

CARI	Chemical Abstracts Reviews Index (American Chemical Society)
CARICOM	Caribbean Community (a bibliography)
CARIS	**Current Agricultural Research Information System (Food and Agriculture Organization)**
CARL (1)	California Academic and Research Libraries (formed with merger of Northern and Southern chapters of ALA and ACRL)
CARL (2)	Canadian Academic Research Libraries
CARL (3)	Canadian Association of Research Libraries (also known as ABRC)
CARL (4)	Colorado Alliance of Research Libraries (a consortia)
CARLIS	Canadian Art Libraries Committee
CARLJS	Council of Archives and Research Libraries in Jewish Studies (U.S.)
CARML	County and Regional Municipality Librarians
CARMOSEA	Committee on Research Materials on Southeast Asia (U.S.; formerly CALROSA and CALROSEA)
CAROL	Circulation and Retrieval On-line (James Cook University, Australia)
CART	Chemical Abstracts Review Titles (American Chemical Society)
CARTI	Chemical Abstracts Review Title Index (American Chemical Society)
CARUP	Caribbean University Press
CAS (1)	Centre for Asian Studies (Univ. of Toronto)
CAS (2)	Certificate of Advanced Study (in library and information science, Univ. of Illinois)
CAS (3)	Chemical Abstracts Service
CAS (4)	Current Awareness Service
CASAA	Canadian Association of Student Awards Administrators
CASA/SME	Computer and Automated Systems Association of the Society of Manufacturing Engineers (U.S.)
CASC	Cooperative Acquisition and Storage Center (in METRO, N.Y.)

CASCADE	Content and Sources of Catalogue Data (for local use; a programme of catalogue research of Bath University, U.K.)
CASCON	Chemical Abstracts Service Condensates (Pittsburgh University)
CASCS	Computer Aided Serials Control System
CASCUM	Classification Analytico-Synthetica Cubana de Medicas (previously ASCOM)
CASDDS	Chemical Abstracts Service Document Delivery Service (of DIALOG)
CASEA (1)	Canadian Association for the Study of Educational Administration
CASEA (2)	Center for the Advanced Study of Educational Administration (Univ. of Oregon)
CASH	Computer-assisted Subject Headings (program of Univ. of California at San Diego)
CASI	Canadian Aeronautics and Space Institute
CASIA	Chemical Abstracts Subject Index Alert (American Chemical Society)
CASIN	Computer-Aided Subject Index (of Food Science and Technology Index)
CAS&ISR	Center for African Studies and Institute for Social Research (Univ. of Zambia)
CASLIS	Canadian Association of Special Libraries and Information Services (of CLA)
CASSI	Chemical Abstracts Service Source Index
CASSIS	Classification and Search Support Information System (an on-line database of U.S. Patent and Trademark Office)
CASSW	Canadian Association of Schools of Social Work (also known as ACESS)
CAST (1)	Center for the Application of Sciences and Technology (Wayne State University, U.S.)
CAST (2)	Clearinghouse Announcements in Science and Technology (Clearinghouse for Federal Scientific and Technical Information, U.S.)
CASTS	Commercial Automation Support of Technical Services (in medium-sized research libraries, an ad-hoc committee on AACR)

CATACEN	Catalogoción Centralizada (Centralized Cataloguing in Columbia; a project)
CATCALL	Completely Automated Technique for Cataloguing and Acquisition of Literature for Libraries
CATED	Centre d'Assistance Technique et de Documentation (France)
CATLA	Chicago Area Theological Library Association
CATLINE	Catalog On-line (National Library of Medicine, U.S.)
CATNIP	Computer-assisted Technique for Numerical Index Preparation
CATNYP	(Carlyle Systems on-line public catalogue installed at the research libraries of NYPL)
CATSPM	Canadian Association of Teachers of Social and Preventive Medicine (also known as ACPMSP)
CATSS	Catalogue Support System (of UTLAS Inc.)
CATSS II	CATSS (2nd version mounted on Tandum hardware)
CATSUP	Catalogue System Update Program (of Carleton University Library, Ottawa)
CATV (1)	Cable Television
CATV (2)	Community Antenna Television
CATVLIB	Cable Library Network
CAUBO	Canadian Association of University Business Officers
CAUCE	Canadian Association for University Continuing Education (also known as AEPUC)
CAUDO	Canadian Association of University Development Officers (also known as ADSDUC)
CAUL	Committee of Australian University Librarians
CAULPS	Charlotte Area Union List of Periodicals and Serials (N.C.)
CAUO	Conseil d'Admission des Universités de l'Ontario (also known as OUCA)
CAURA	Canadian Association of University Research Administrators (also known as ACARU)

CAUSE	College and University System Exchange
CAUSM	Canadian Association of University Schools of Music (also known as ACEUM)
CAUSN	Canadian Association of University Schools of Nursing (also known as ACEUN)
CAUSR	Canadian Association of University Schools of Rehabilitation (also known as ACEUR)
CAUT	Canadian Association of University Teachers (also known as ACPU)
CAUTG	Canadian Association of University Teachers of German (also known as APAUC (1))
CAVAL	Cooperative Action by Victorian Academic Libraries (Australia)
CAVE (1)	Catholic Audio-visual Educators Association (U.S.)
CAVE (2)	Committee Advocating a Voice in Education
CB (1)	Centrale des Bibliothèques (Montreal)
CB (2)	Citizens Band
CB (3)	College Bibliocentre (Toronto)
CBA (1)	Canadian Booksellers Association
CBA (2)	Christian Booksellers Association
CBAC	Chemical-Biological Activities (a database of CAS (3))
CBC (1)	Canadian Broadcasting Corporation
CBC (2)	Children's Book Council
CBC (3)	Colegio de Bibliotecarios Colombianos (Association of Colombian Librarians; now CCB (1))
CBDA	Comissão Brasileira de Documentação Agricola (Brazilian Commission for Agricultural Documentation)
CBE (1)	Competency-Based Education
CBE (2)	Computer-Based Education
CBEL	Cambridge Bibliography of English Literature (publication)
CBEM	Computer-based Educational Material (of LHNCBC)

CBEMA	Computer and Business Equipment Manufacturers Association (previously BEMA and OEMI)
CBHL	Council on Botanical and Horticultural Libraries (U.S.)
CBI (1)	Canadian Business Index
CBI (2)	Confederation of British Industry
CBI (3)	Cumulative Book Index (H.W. Wilson, Co.)
CBIC	Canadian Book Information Centre
CBIE	Canadian Bureau for International Education (also known as BCEI)
CBIP	Canadian Books in Print
CBIS	Campus-Based Information System (Pittsburgh University)
CBISSSH	Committee on Bibliography and Information Service for the Social Sciences and Humanities (of National Library of Canada's Advisory Board Committee)
CBL (1)	Cercle Belge de la Librarie (Belgium Booksellers Association)
CBL (2)	Computer Based Learning
CBL (3)	Cumulative Book List (Whitaker, U.K.)
CBN	Centre Bibliographique National (France)
CBPC	Canadian Book Publishers Council
CBPDC	Canadian Book and Periodical Development Council
CBPE-DDIP	Centro Brasileiro de Pesquisas Educacionais-Divisão de Documentacão e Informacão Pedagógica (Brazilian Center of Educational Research-Department of Ecucational Documentation and Information)
CBPQ	Corporation des Bibliothécaires Professionnels du Québec (also known as CPLQ)
CBR	Centralina Biblioteka Rolnicza (Central Agricultural Library, Poland)
CBRA	Canadian Book Review Annual
CBRS	Computer-based Reference Service (of NLC (2))
CBS (1)	Central Bibliographic System (of LC)
CBS (2)	Columbia Broadcasting System, Inc. (U.S.)

CBSC	Committee on bibliographical Services for Canada (of NLC (2))
CBST	Current Bibliography on Science and Technology (Kagaku Gizyutu Bunkem Sokuho, Japan Information Centre of Science and Technology)
CC	Colon Classification (S.R. Ranganathan)
CCA	Computer Corporation of America
CC:AAM	Committee on Cataloging: Asian and African Materials (of LC)
C-CAD	Center for Computer Assistance to the Disabled (Hurst, Tex.)
CCAUEP	Conseil Canadien des Administrateurs Universitaires en Éducation Physique (also known as CCUPEA)
CCB (1)	Colegio Colombiano de Bibliotecarios (Colombian Association of Libraries; previously CBC (3))
CCB (2)	Command Control Block (computer term)
CCBC	Cooperative Children's Book Center (Wis.)
CCBCS	Canadian Computerized Bibliographic Centre Study (of NLC (2))
CCBSMS	Current Contents- Behavioral, Social and Management Sciences (of ISI (3))
CCC (1)	Canadian Committee on Cataloguing (Comité Canadien de Catalogage)
CCC (2)	Catalog Card Corporation of America (Minneapolis, Minn.)
CCC (3)	Central Classification Committee (of FID)
CCC (4)	Chronological Coverage Code (used by NLC (2))
CCC (5)	Classified Catalogue Code (S.R. Ranganathan, 1958)
CCC (6)	Comité Canadien de Catalogage (Canadian Committee on Cataloguing)
CCC (7)	Copyright Clearance Center (of AAP (2); formerly known as CPC (5))
CCCII	Chinese Character Code for Information Interchange
CC/CP	Current Contents/Clinical Practice (Institute for Scientific Information, U.S.)

CCDA (1)   Commission de Coordination de la Documentation
            Administrative (France)

CC:DA (2)   Committee on Cataloging:Description and Access
            (of RTSD/CCS)

CCDSS   College Canadien des Directeurs de Service de Santé
            (also known as CCHSE)

CCE (1)   Catalog of Copyright Entries

CCE (2)   Collège Canadien des Enseignants (also known as CCT)

CCEB   Conseil Canadien des Écoles de Bibliothécaires
            (also known as CCLS (1))

CCEI   Colorado Committee for Environmental Information

CCF   Common Communication Format (of Unesco)

CCFMC   Center for the Coordination of Foreign Manuscript
            Copying (of LC)

CCG (1)   Computer Communications Group (of Trans Canada
            Telephone System)

CCG (2)   Conforms to Copyright Guidelines

CCH   Commerce Clearing House, Inc.

CCHM   Champaign County Historical Museum (Champaign, Ill.)

CCHSE   Canadian College of Health Service Executives
            (also known as CCDSS)

CCI   Canadian Copyright Institute

CCIP   Conseil Canadien des Ingénieurs Professionels (also
            known as CCPE)

CCIR   Center for Communication and Information Research
            (Univ. of Denver)

CCITT   Comité Consultatif International Télégraphique et
            Téléphonic (Consultative Committee on International
            Telegraph and Telephone)

CCK   Centrale Catalogus voor de Kartografie (Union
            Catalogue for Cartography, Utrecht University,
            Netherlands)

CCL (1)   Concerned California Librarians (coined by Michael
            Gorman in an article "Towards Bibliographic Control",
            American Libraries, Nov. '78)

CCL (2)   Conforms to Copyright Law

CCLC	Cooperative College Library Center (a consortium in Atlanta)
CCLD (1)	Colorado Council on Library Development
CCLD (2)	Commissioner for Education's Committee on Library Development (N.Y.)
CCLIC	Community College Library Consortium (Seattle, Wash.)
CCLM	Coordinating Council of Literary Magazines
CCLN	Council of Computerized Library Networks
CCLO	Coordinating Council of Library Organizations (U.S.)
CCLS (1)	Canadian Council of Library Schools (also known as CCEB)
CCLS (2)	Central Colorado Library System
CCLS (3)	Council of Computerized Library Systems
CCM	Canadian Committee on MARC (Comité Canadien du MARC)
CCMC	Cataloging of Children's Material Committee (of LC)
CCME	Canadian Council of Ministers of Education
CCMIE	(National) Conference on Multicultural and Intercultural Education
CCML	Critical Care Medical Library (database available on BRS of medical text books)
CCNB	Committee for the Coordination of National Bibliographical Control (established by NCLIS, NSF and CLR)
CCNY	College of the City of New York
CCOE	Catalogue Collectif des Ouvrages Étrangers (Union Catalogue of non-French Works, France)
CCOHS	Canadian Centre for Occupational Health and Safety
C-CORE/OEIC	Ocean Engineering Information Centre (of Memorial University, Nfld.)
CCP (1)	Centrale Catalogus van Periodieken (en serie werken in Nederlandse Bibliotheken) (Dutch Union Catalogue of Periodicals and Serials)
CCP (2)	Communications Control Package
CCPE	Canadian Council of Professional Engineers (also known as CCIP)

CCPL (1)	Carroll County Public Library (Westminister, Md.)
CCPL (2)	Cumberland County Public Library
CCPP	Campus Crime Prevention Program (Long Beach, Calif.)
CCQ	Cataloging & Classification Quarterly
CCR (1)	Code of Cataloguing Rules
CCR (2)	Committee on Citation Reform (of AALL)
CCRA	Consumer Communications Reform Act (U.S.)
CCRC	Cataloguing Code Revision Committee (of ALA)
CCRESPAC	Current Cancer Research Project Analysis Center (U.S.)
CCRG	Canadian Classification Research Group (Groupe Canadien pour la Recherche en Classification; of FID/CR)
CCRH	Conseil Canadien de Recherches sur les Humanités (also known as HRCC)
CCRM	Center for Chinese Research Materials (of ARL)
CCRSS	Conseil Canadien de Recherche en Sciences Sociales (also known as SSRCC)
CCRT	Cataloging and Classification Round Table (of CLA (4))
CCRUR	Conseil Canadien de Recherches Urbaines et Regionales (also known as CCURR)
CCS (1)	Cataloging and Classification Section (of RTSD)
CCS (2)	Council of Communication Societies (U.S.)
CCT	Canadian College of Teachers (also known as CCE)
CCTE	Canadian Council of Teachers of English
CCTV	Closed-Circuit Television
CCUBC	Canadian Committee of University Biology Chairmen (also known as CUDBC)
CCUPEA	Canadian Council of University Physical Education Administrators (also known as CCAUEA)
CCURE	Conseil des Centres Universitaires pour la Recherche sur l'Environnement (Council of Centres at Universities for Research on the Environment)
CCURR	Canadian Council on Urban and Regional Research (also known as CCRUR)

CCWI	Collegiate Consortium of Western Indiana
CCY	Coalition for Children and Youth (of ALA)
cd	Candela (SI) (luminous intensity)
CDA	Centrul de Documentare Agricolă (Agricultural Documentation Center, Romania)
CDACL	Career Development and Assessment Center for Librarians (Univ. of Washington, Seattle, Wash.)
CDBCR	Common Data-Base in Computer Readable Form (Chemical Abstracts Service, U.S.)
CDC (1)	Centro de Documentação Cientifica (Scientific Documentation Center, Portugal)
CDC (2)	Control Data Corporation (U.S.)
CDC do IAC	Centro de Documentação Científica do Instituto de Alta Cultura (Portugal)
CDCR	Center for Documentation and Communication Research (Case Western Reserve University, U.S.)
CDDC	Comisión de Documentación Científica (Argentina)
CdesU	Conseil des Universités (Québec) (also known as CofU)
CDF	Catalog Data File (a module of BALLOTS)
CDI (1)	Center for Defense Information (U.S.)
CDI (2)	Comprehensive Dissertation Index (of UMI)
CDIF	Centre de Documentación e Información Educativa (Educational Documentation and Information Center, Mexico)
CDIUPA	Centre de Documentation International des Industries Utilizatrices de Produits Agricoles (International Documentation Center for Industries Utilizing Agricultural Products, France)
CDL	Computer Design Language
CDM	Centrul Documentare Medicală (Medical Documentation Center, Romania)
CDNL	Conference of Directors of National Libraries
CDP	Certificate in Data Processing

CDPL	Central Dallas Public Library
CDS (1)	Cataloging Distribution Service (of LC)
CDS (2)	Centrul de Documentare Stiintifica (Scientific Documentation Centre, Romania)
CDS (3)	Computerized Documentation Service
CDST	Centre de Documentation Scientifique et Technique (France)
CDU	Classification Decimale Universelle (also known as ETO, UDC (1))
CE	Continuing Education (of librarians; a program of ALA)
CEA (1)	Canadian Education Association (also known as ACE (4))
CEA (2)	Cost-Effectiveness Analysis
CEAL	Committee on East Asian Libraries (of AAS (3))
CEAS	Cooperative Educational Abstracting Service (Unesco)
CEBEDEAU	Centre Belge d'Étude et de Documentation des Eaux (Belgium; also known as BECEWA)
CEBFO	Conseil des Enseignants - Bibliothécaires Franco-Ontariens
CEC	Council for Exceptional Children (U.S.)
CECL	Conference of Eastern College Librarians (U.S.)
CECLS	County of Essex Cooperating Libraries System (N.J.)
CED (1)	Capacitance Electronic Disc (videodisc)
CED (2)	Centre pour l'Éducation de Développement (also known as DEC (1))
CEDAF	(Centre for African Studies and Documentation, Belgium)
CEDDA	Center of Experiment Design and Data Analysis (U.S.; of National Oceanic and Atmospheric Administration)
CEDESA	Centre de Documentation Economique et Sociale Africaine (Belgium)
CEDI	Centre Européen de Documentation et d'Information (European Documentation and Information Centre)
CEDIJ	Centre de Recherche et Développement en Informatique Juridique (France)
CEDO	Centre for Educational Development Overseas (U.K.; previously CETO)

CEDOBUL	Centre de Documentation de la Bibliothèque de l'Université Laval (Documentation Centre for the Library of l'Universite Laval, Québec)
CEDOCA	Centre de Documentation Africaine (African Documentation Center, Belgium)
CEDORES	Centre de Documentation et de Recherche Sociales (Belgium)
CEDPA	California Educational Data Processing Association
CEEB	College Entrance Examination Board (U.S.)
CEEFAX	See Facts (a programme of British Broadcasting Corp., also called "dial-a-page"news broadcast)
CEF (1)	Clearinghouse on Educational Facilities (of ERIC)
CEF (2)	Clinton Esses-Franklin (Library) (Plattsburgh, N.Y.)
CEG	Computer Education Group (U.K.)
CEGEP	Colleges d'Enseignement General et Professionel
CEI	Canadian Education Index (also known as RCE)
CEIC	Canada Employment and Immigration Commission
CEIMS	Communications Equipment Information and Modeling System (CACOM Inc., U.S.)
CEIR	Corporation for Economics and Industrial Research (of CDC (2))
CEIS	California Education Information System
CEIST	Centro Europeo Informazioni Scientifiche e Tecniche (Italy)
CEL	Continuing Education in Librarianship Committee (of UBC (2))
CELPLO	Chief Executives of Large Public Libraries of Ontario
CELRF	Canadian Environmental Law Research Foundation
CELRP	College of Education Libraries Research Project (Department of Education and Science, U.K.)
CELS	Continuing Education for Library Staffs in the Southwest (of SLA (4))
CEMA	Colorado Education Media Association

CEMBA	Collection and Evaluation of Materials on Black Americans (of Alabama Agricultural & Mechanical University)
CEMBI	Conference to Explore Machine-Readable Bibliographic Interchange (a group of users and suppliers of MARC which met on several occasions under the sponsorship of CLR)
CEN (1)	Centrale des Bibliothèques (Montreal)
CEN (2)	Comité Européen de Coordination des Normes (European Committee for Standardization)
CENATRA	Centre National d'Assistance Technique et de Recherche Appliquée (Belgium)
CENID	Centro Nacional de Información y Documentación (Chile)
CENTI	Centre pour le Traitement de l'Information (Information Processing Centre, France)
CENTRO	Central New York Library Resources Council
CEP	Caribbean Educational Publications
CERA	Canadian Educational Researchers Association (also known as ACCE)
CERI	Centre for Educational Research and Innovation (Organization for Economic Cooperation & Development)
CERLAL	Centro Regional para el Fomento del Libro en América Latina y el Caribe (Regional Center for the Encouragement of the Book in Latin America and the Caribbean)
CERN	(Organisation Européenne pour la Recherche Nucléaire)
CES	Canadian Ethnology Society
CESPM	Commission de l'Enseignement Supérieur des Provinces Maritimes (also known as MPHEC)
CET	Council for Educational Technology (U.K.; previously NCET)
CETA (1)	Chinese-English Translation Assistance (U.S.; an ad-hoc U.S. Government interagency established to develop translation aids)
CETA (2)	Comprehensive Employment and Training Act (U.S.)
CETIB	Centre de Traitement Informatique des Bibliothèques (France)

CETIS	Centre de Traitement de l'Information Scientifique (European Communities Scientific Information Processing Centre; also called Centre Europeen pour le Traitment de l'Information Scientifique)
CETO	Centre for Educational Television Overseas (U.K.; now CEDO)
CEU	Continuing Education Unit (ACRL's continuing education course units)
CEUCORS	European Center for the Coordination of Research and Documentation in the Social Sciences (Austria)
CFB	Conselho Federal de Biblioteconomia (National Council of Librarianship, Brazil)
CFEE	Canadian Foundation for Economic Education (also known as FCEE)
CFI	Canadian Film Institute (also known as ICF)
CFL (1)	Central Film Library (Central Office of Information, U.K.)
CFL (2)	Consortium of Foundation Libraries
CFL (3)	Council of Federal Libraries
CFP	Canadian Forces Publications (published by the Dept. of Defense)
CFSS	Combined File Search System
CFSTI	Clearinghouse for Federal Scientific and Technical Information (U.S.; formerly OTS; now NTIS)
CFUW	Canadian Federation of University Women (also known as FCFDU)
cg (1)	Centigram (metric) = 10 mg
CG (2)	Computer Graphics
CGE	Canadian General Electric Co. Ltd.
CHAIN	Channeled Arizona Information Network
CHANGE	UTLAS Inc. Users' Group
CHARIBDIS	Chalk River Bibliographic Data Information System (Atomic Energy of Canada Ltd.)
CHC	Cyclohexylamine Carbonate (applied by interleaving books with treated absorbed paper in vapor-phase deacidification - developed by W.H. Langwell, a british chemist, for books and documents)

CHECK	(automatic on-line authority file searching function of WLN)
CHEMCON	Chemical Abstracts Condensates (SDC, on-line version)
CHEMLINE	(on-line chemical dictionary file of BLAISE)
CHEN	Council for Higher Education in Newark (N.J.)
CHEOPS	Chemical Information Systems Operators (now EUSIDIC)
CHERS	Consortium for Higher Education Religious Studies (Ohio)
ChESS	Clearinghouse for Education and Social Studies/Social Science (Educational Resources Information Center, U.S.)
CHILD	Children's Books in Print
CHILD subj	Subject Guide to Children's Books in Print
CHIN (1)	Community Health Information Network (Mount Auburn Hospital, Cambridge, Mass.)
CHIN (2)	Consumer Health Information Network
CHIP	Computer Health Insurance Plan (a maintenance service programme provided by some computer vendors)
CHIPS	Consumer Health Information Program and Services (U.S.)
CHLA (1)	Canadian Health Libraries Association (also known as ABSC)
ChLA (2)	Children's Literature Association (Founded in 1972)
Chpi	Characters per Inch (computer term)
Chps	Characters per Second (computer term)
CHSL	Cleveland Health Sciences Library
CHUHPL	Cleveland Heights - University Heights Public Library
CI (1)	Chain Index
CI (2)	Cumulative Index
CIA	Conseil International des Archives (International Council on Archives)
CIADES	Centro Interamericano de Documentación Económia y Social (Interamerican Center for Economic and Social Documentation, Chile)
CIAE	Canadian Institute for Adult Education (also known as ICEA)

CIAU	Canadian Intercollegiate Athletic Union (also known as USIC)
CIB (1)	Centro de Investigaciones Bibliothecológicas (Librarianship Research Centre, Buenos Aires University, Argentina)
CIB (2)	Citizens Inquiry Branch or Citizens Inquiry Bureau (U.S.)
CIB (3)	Conseil International du Bâtiment pour la Recherche, l'Étude et la Documentation (International Council for Building Research, Studies and Documentation; formerly CIDB)
CIBC	Council for Interracial Books for Children (U.S.)
CIC (1)	Chemical Institute of Canada
CIC (2)	Commonwealth Information Centre (U.K.)
CIC (3)	Community Information Center (U.S.)
CICH	Centro Información Cientifica y Humanistica (Centre for Scientific and Humanistic Information, Mexico)
CICIN	Conference on Interlibrary Communications and Information Networks (Airlie House, Va., 1970)
CICIREPATO	Committee for International Cooperation in Information Retrieval among Examining Patent Officers (also known as ICIREPAT)
CICRIS	Cooperative Industrial and Commercial Reference and Information Service (West London, U.K.; now West London Commercial and Technical Library Service)
CICS	Customer Information Control System (of IBM)
CID (1)	Centre for Information and Documentation (European Communities)
CID (2)	Centro de Información y Documentación (Spain)
CID (3)	Centro de Investigación Documentaria (Argentina)
CIDA (1)	Canadian International Development Agency
CIDA (2)	Centre d'Informatique et Documentation Automatique (France)
CIDA-NGO	Canadian International Development Agency's Non-governmental Organization Division

CIDB	Centre d'Information et de Documentation du Bâtiment (France; now CIB (3))
CIDBEQ	Centre d'Informatique Documentarie pour les Bibliothèques d'Enseignement du Québec
CIDES	Centre d'Information et de Documentation des Sciences Economiques et Sociales (Belgium)
CIDESA	Centre International de Documentation Economique et Sociale Africaine (International Centre for African Social and Economic Documentation, Belgium)
CIDHEC	(Intergovernmental) Centre for Documentation on Housing and Environment (U.N.)
CIDNET	Consortium for International Development Information Network (Univ. of California, Riverside)
CIDNT	Centralny Instytut Dokumentacji Naukowa-Technicznej (Poland; later CIINTE, now Instytut Informacji Naukowej, Technicznej i Ekonomicznej)
CIDOC	**Centro Interamericano de Documentacion (Mexico)**
CIDP	Centre for Parliamentary Documentation (of the Inter-Parliamentary Union, Geneva, Switzerland)
CIDS	Chemical Information and Data System (U.S. Army)
CIDSS	Comité International pour l'Information et la Documentation des Sciences Sociales (also known as ICSSD and ICSSDI)
CIDST	Comité d'Information et de Documentation Scientifiques et Techniques (also known as CSTID)
CIEPS	Centre International d'Enregistrement de Publication en Serie (Unesco) (Information Centre for the Registration of Serial Publication; also known as ISDS-IC)
CIESC	Comparative and International Education Society of Canada (also known as SCECI)
CIF	Central Information File
CIFE	Conseil International pour les Films d'Éducation (also known as ICEF)
CIG (1)	Cataloguing and Indexing Group (of LA (1))
CIG (2)	Coordinate Indexing Group (of Aslib)
CIHM	Canadian Institute for Historical Microreproduction (of NLC; also known as ICMH)

CII	Compagnie Internationale pour l'Informatique
CIINTE	Centralny Instytut Informacji Naukow-Technicznej i Ekonomicznej (Poland; now Instytut Informacji Naukowej, Technicznej i Ekonomicznej, formerly CIDNT)
CIJE	Current Index to Journals in Education (publication of ERIC)
CILA (1)	Centro Interamericano de Libros Academicos
CILA (2)	(International Community of Booksellers Association) (also known as IASV; ICBA)
CIM (1)	Computer Input from Microfilm or Computer Input Microfilm
CIM (2)	Computer-Integrated Manufacturing
CIMCOM	Computer-Integrated Manufacturing and Communication (U.S.)
CIMS	Customer Information Management System (of Cataloging Distribution Service of LC)
CIN (1)	Chemical Industry Notes (a Chemical Abstract service)
CIN (2)	Cooperation Information Network
CIN (3)	Cooperative Information Network (of Stanford University Libraries
CINAHL	Cumulative Index to Nursing and Allied Health Literature (a DIALOG database)
CINCH	Computerized Information Network for Community Health (City University of New York)
CINDA	Computer Index to Automated Data (Centre de Compilation de Donnèes Neutroniques, France)
CINDAS	Center for Information and Numerical Data Analysis and Synthesis (of Purdue University)
CINFAC (1)	Counterinsurgency Information Analysis Center (American University, Washington, D.C.)
CINFAC (2)	Cultural Information Analysis Center (American Institute for Research)
CINL	Cumulative Index to the Nursing Literature (U.S.)
CINTE	Centrum Informacji Naukowej Technicznej i Ekonomicznej (Centre of Scientific, Technical and Economic Information, Poland)

CIOA	Center for Information on America (U.S.)
CIOCS	Communications Input/Output Control System
CIP (1)	Cataloging-in-Publication
CIP (2)	Community Information Project (American Academy Library, U.S.)
CIPC	Centro Información de Politica Cientifica y Tecnologica (Centre for Information in Political Science and Technology, Mexico)
CIPP	Context, Input, Process, Product (Ohio State University Evaluation Center)
CIPS	Canadian Information Processing Society (also known as ACI)
CIR	Consortium for Information Resources (of several hospital libraries in Mass.)
CIRAS	Census Information Retrieval and Analysis System (U.K.)
CIRC (1)	Central Information Reference and Control (U.S. Department of Defense)
CIRC (2)	Circulation Input Recording Centre (Colo.)
CIRC (3)	Colorado Instruments Inc. Circulation System (U.S.)
CIRCA	Computerized Information Retrieval and Current Awareness
CIRF	Centre International d'Information et de la Recherche sur la Formation Professionnelle (of ILO)
CIRK	Computing Technology Center Information Retrieval from Keywords (Union Carbide Corp., U.S.)
CIRS	Community Information and Referral Service (of MPL (1))
CIS (1)	Cable Information Services (Connecticut State Library)
CIS (2)	Catalog Information Service
CIS (3)	Cataloging-in-Source
CIS (4)	Center for Information Services (Akron University, Ohio)
CIS (5)	Chemical Information System
CIS (6)	Community Information Section (of PLA (6))

CIS (7)	Community Information Specialist
CIS (8)	Congressional Information Service, Inc. (U.S.)
CIS (9)	Cue Indexing System
CIS (10)	Current Information Selection (of IBM)
CISAC	Confédération Internationale des Sociétés d'Auteurs et Compositeurs (International Confederation of Societies of Authors and Composers, France)
CISCO	Committee for Intersociety Cooperation (U.S. Library Societies)
CIS/CONG H	Congressional Information Service/Congressional Hearings
CISE	Colleges, Institutes and Schools of Education (Group of LA (1))
CISI (1)	Centre for Inventions and Scientific Information (Czechoslovakia)
CISI (2)	Compagnie Internationale de Service et Informatique
CIS/Index	Congressional Information Service/Index to Congressional Publications and Public Laws
CISIR	Ceylon Institute of Scientific and Industrial Research
CISRC	Computer and Information Science Research Center (Ohio State University)
CISSIG	Cataloguing and Indexing Systems Special Interest Group (Art Libraries Society, U.S.)
CISTI	Canada Institute for Scientific and Technical Information (of National Research Council; formerly National Sciences Library; also known as ICIST)
CISTIP	Committee on International Scientific and Technical Information Programs (of Commission on International Relations (NAS/NRC), U.S.))
CIT (1)	California Institute of Technology
CIT (2)	Cancer Information Thesaurus
CIT (3)	Center for Information Technology (of Stanford University)
CITE (1)	Computerized Information Transfer in English (of NLM)
CITE (2)	Consolidated Index of Translations into English (of Chicago University and SLA (6))

CITE (3)	Current Information Tapes for Engineers (Engineering Index, U.S.)
CITE (4)	Current Information Transfer in English (of NLM)
CIU	Computer Interface Unit
CJCLS	Community and Junior College Libraries Section (of ACRL; formerly ACRL/JCLS)
CJIS	Criminal Justice Information Systems (U.S.)
CJK	Chinese, Japanese, Korean (system) (a cooperative project of RLG and LC; also known as RLG/CJK)
CJP	Cooperative Journal Program (of IUC)
CKC	Consultants Keyword Clearing House (a section of American Libraries LEADS)
cl	Centilitre (metric) = 10 ml
CLA (1)	California Library Association
CLA (2)	Canadian Library Association (previously also known as ACB (2))
CLA (3)	Canadian Linguistic Association
CLA (4)	Catholic Library Association (U.S.)
CLA (5)	Chinese Librarians Association (U.S.)
CLA (6)	Colorado Library Association
CLA (7)	Comision Latinamericana de la Federation Internacional de Documentacion (Brazil)
CLA (8)	Commonwealth Library Association (officially COMLA)
CLA (9)	Connecticut Library Association
CLABC	Congregational Libraries Association of British Columbia or Congressional Libraries Association of British Columbia
CLADES	Centro Latino Americano de Documentacion Economica y Social (Chile) (Latin-American Center for Economic and Social Documentation - United Nations Economic Commission for Latin America)
CLAE	Council of Library Association Executives (Ohio)
CLAH	Conference on Latin American History

CLAIM	Center for Library and Information Management (Loughborough University of Technology, Leicester, U.K.)
CLAIMS/CHEM	Class Code, Assignee, Index, Method Search-Chemistry (IFI Plenum Data Co. Arlington, Va.)
CLAIMS/GEM	Class, Code, Assignee, Index, Method Search - General, Electrical, Mechanical (IFI Plenum Data Co. Arlington, Va.)
CLAM	Consortium of Library Automation in Mississipi
CLAN (1)	California Library Automation Network
CLAN (2)	Cooperative Library Action for New South Wales
CLANN	College Libraries Activities Network in New South Wales
CLASP	Central Massachusetts Library Administration Project
CLASS (1)	California Library Authority for Systems and Services
CLASS (2)	Centralized Library Automation System (Iowa State Travelling Library)
CLASS (3)	Current Literature Alerting Search Service (Biological Abstracts)
CLASS (4)	Current Literature Awareness Service Series (of ERIC)
CLCM	Cooperating Libraries of Central Maryland
CLD	Central Library and Documentation (Branch, International Labour Office)
CLDI	Conseil de Leadership et de Développement Industriel (Ont.)
CLE	Continuing Librarians Education
CLEA	Canadian Library Exhibitors' Association
CLEAR	Center for Labor Education and Research (Univ. of Colorado)
CLEI	Center for Libraries and Education Improvement (U.S.)
CLEN	Continuing Library Education Network (of AALS (1), ceased 1975)
CLENE	Continuing Library Education Network and Exchange (U.S.)
CLENERT	Continuing Library Education Network and Exchange Round Table

CLEOPATRA	Comprehensive Language for Elegant Operating System and Translator Design (programming language)
CLEP	College Level Examination Program (U.S.)
CLEPR	Council on Legal Education for Professional Responsibility (U.S.)
CLEWS	Classified Library Employees of Washington State
CLIC (1)	Canadian Law Information Council
CLIC (2)	Committee on Library Cooperation (San Diego, Calif.)
CLIC (3)	Community Library Information Center (Prince George's County Library System, Md.)
CLIC (4)	Cooperating Libraries in Claremount (a consortium in California)
CLIC (5)	Cooperating Libraries in Consortium (Minn.)
CLICC	Cooperative Libraries in Central Connecticut
CLIMBS	Countway Library Medical Bibliographic Service (Harvard University)
CLINK	Coal Information Network of Kentucky
CLINPROT	Clinical Cancer Protocols (of BLAISE)
CLIP (1)	College Library Information Packets (of ACRL)
CLIP (2)	Compiler Language for Information Processing (of SDC (2))
CLIP (3)	Coordinated Library Information Program, Inc. (Madison, Wis.)
CLIR	Clearinghouse for Library and Information Resources (now includes CLIS (2))
CLIS (1)	Central Library and Information Services (Commonwealth Scientific & Industrial Research Organization, Australia)
CLIS (2)	Clearinghouse on Library and Information Sciences (of ERIC; now incorporated in CLIR)
CLIS (3)	Computer Library Services Inc.(Mass.)
CLJ	Canadian Library Journal
CLL	Cornell Law Library

CLMC	Canadian Learning Materials Centre
CLN	Cooperative Library Network (U.S.)
CLO	Centrum voor Literatuuronderzoekers (Centre for Information Specialists, Netherlands)
CLOSSS	Check List of Social Science Serials (Bath University Library, U.K.)
CLOUT	Concerned Librarians Opposing Unprofessional Trends (a group in Orange County, Calif.)
CLPS	Central Library Processing Service (Mass.)
CLR	Council on Library Resources (U.S.)
CLRU	Cambridge Language Research Unit (U.K.)
CLS (1)	Children's Libraries Section (of CLA (4))
CLS (2)	Classification of Library Science (Classification Research Group, U.K.; also known as LSC (2))
CLS (3)	Clear Screen Instruction (computer term)
CLS (4)	College Libraries Section (of ACRL)
CLS (5)	Coordinated Library System (N.M.)
CLS (6)	Cumann Leabharlanne na Scoile (Irish Association of School Librarians)
CLSB	California Library Services Board
CLSD	Collaborative Library Systems Development Project (of Chicago, Columbia and Stanford Universities)
CLSI	CL Systems, Inc. (also known as Computer Library Services, Inc.)
CLSR	Computer Law Service Reporter
CLSS	Canadian Library Science Society (publishes journal which succeeds Canadian Library Progress)
CLSU	Cooperative Library Service Unit (of Connecticut, a multitype cooperative)
CLT	Communications Line Terminal
CLTA	Canadian Library Trustees Association (of CLA)
CLUNY	Cooperating Libraries of Upper New York

CLW	College of Librarianship, Wales
CM (1)	Cartographic Materials
cm (2)	Centimetre (metric) = 10 mm
CMA (1)	Chemical Market Abstracts (Predicasts Inc., U.S.)
CMA (2)	Colleges of Mid-America Inc. (S.D.)
CMC	Computers in the Media Center
CMCP	Catalog Maintenance and Card Production
CMDP	Cooperative Media Development Program (of NMAC)
CMEA	Council for Mutual Economic Assistance (Moscow)
CMEC	Council of Ministers of Education, Canada (Conseil des Ministres de l'Éducation, Canada)
CMI	Computer-Managed Instruction
CML (1)	Central Music Library (Westminster Public Library, U.K.)
CML (2)	Clinical Medical Librarian
CMLA	Canadian Music Library Association
CMLE	Central Minnesota Libraries Exchange
CMLEA	California Media and Library Educators Association
CMOD	Customer Must Order Direct
CMP	Catalog Management and Publication Division (of LC)
CMRLS	Central Massachusetts Regional Library System
CMS (1)	Canadian Micrographics Society
CMS (2)	Conversational Monitor System (computer term)
CMS (3)	Coordinierte Management Systeme (Frankfurt, W.Germany)
CMU	Carnegie-Mellon University (U.S.)
CNBH	Conseil National des Bibliothèques d'Hôpitaux (National Council of Hospital Libraries, Belgium)
CNC	College of New Caledonia (B.C.)
CNDP	Centre National de Documentation Pédagogique (France)

CNDST	Centre National de Documentation Scientifique et Technique (National Centre for Scientific and Technical Documentation, Belgium; also known as NCWTD)
CNI	Canadian News Index
CNIB	Canadian National Institute for the Blind
CNIDST	Comité National de l'Information et de la Documentation Scientifique et Technique
CNK	Common Noun Keyword
CNLA	Council of National Library Associations (U.S.; also known as CNLS; now CNLIA)
CNLIA	Council of National Library and Information Associations (previously known as CNLA, CNLS)
CNLIA/JCCC	CNLIA Joint Committee on Cataloging and Classification Codes
CNLIA/JCCPI	CNLIA Joint Committee on Copyright Practice and Implementation
CNLS	Council of National Library Associations (U.S.; also known as CNLA; now CNLIA)
CNPITC	China National Publishing Industry Trading Corp.
CNRC	Conseil National de Recherches du Canada (also known as NRC (2) and NRCC)
CNRS	Centre National de la Recherche Scientific (France)
CNT	Cumulated New Titles (of ISDS)
COA	Committee on Accreditation (of ALA)
COAM	Customer Owned and Maintained
CO-ASIS	Central Ohio Chapter of ASIS
COAU	Conseil Ontarien des Affaires Universitaires (also known as OCUA)
COBICIL	Cooperative Bibliographic Center for Indiana Libraries
COBIGO	Comité de Coordination des Bibliothèques Gouvernementales du Québec
COBOL	Common Business Oriented Language (computer language)
COBRA	Collaboration for Bibliographic Records in Art (a programme of Worldwide Books and Boston Public Library)

COBSA	Computer Service Bureau Association (U.K.)
COBSI	Council on Biological Sciences Information (U.S.)
COCOSEER	Coordinating Committee for Slavic and East European Library Services
CODAP	Client-Oriented Data Acquisition Program (U.S.)
CODASYL	Conference on Data Systems Languages
CODATA	Committee on Data for Science and Technology (International Council of Scientific Unions)
CODE (1)	Commission on Declining Enrolment (in the schools of Ontario)
CODE (2)	Coordinated Delivery (system) (South Central Research Library Council, N.Y.)
CODE (3)	Council of Drama in Education
CODEN	(a set of five letter codes for the titles of scientific and technological periodicals & monographs)
CODEX	Collection of Documents Extremely Handy
CODIE	Community Outreach through Direct Information Exchange (computer system in PPLD, Colorado Springs)
CODOC	Cooperative Documents Project (of OULCS)
CODSULI	Conference of Directors of State Libraries of Illinois
COfU	Council of Universities (Quebec) (also known as CdesU)
COGEODATA	Committee on Storage, Automatic Processing and Retrieval of Geological Data
COGO	Coordinate Geometry (computer language)
COHD	Copyright Office History Document (of LC)
COHM	Copyright Office History Monograph (of LC)
COI	Central Office of Information (U.K.)
COIN (1)	Central Ohio Interlibrary Network
COIN (2)	Centralny Osrodek Informacji Normalizacyjnej (Information Centre for Standardization, Poland)
COIN (3)	Cobol Indexing and Maintenance Package (National Computing Centre, U.K.)
COIN (4)	Coordinated Occupational Information Network (a microform database)

COINS (1)	Computer and Information Sciences
COINS (2)	Copyright Office In-Process System (of LC)
COINS (3)	(International Symposium on) Computer and Information Science
COINT	Communication and Information Technology (a multidisciplinary approach)
COL	Computer Oriented Language
COLA (1)	Committee on Library Automation (ISAD's Discussion Group)
COLA (2)	Cooperation in Library Automation (of LASER (2))
COLASL	Compiler Los Alamos Scientific Laboratories (a computer language)
COLBAV	Colegio de Bibliotecónomos y Archivistas de Venezuela (Association of Venezuelan Librarians and Archivists)
COLOG	Chicago Online Users Group
COLONET	Colorado Library Network
COLT	Council on Library Technology or Council on Library/Media Technology Assistants (U.S.)
COM	Computer Output Microfilm (Microfiche/Microform)
COMARC	Cooperative Machine-Readable Cataloging (of LC)
COMBAT	Committee on Standards for Bibliographic Output Formats
COMCAT	COM Catalogue
COMECON	Council for Mutual Economic Assistance
COMEINDORS	Composite Mechanized Information and Documentation Retrieval System
COMIT	Computer Language of MIT
COMLA	Commonwealth Library Association (also known unofficially as CLA (8))
COMLIP	Community Media Library Program (Columbia University School of Library Service, U.S.)
COMLOS	Committee on Multitype Organizations Systems (of LA (2))
COMM	Communications Information (a database)

COM-O-LIB	(Newsletter of Community College Libraries in Ontario)
COMP	Computer Output Microfilm Peek-a-boo
COMPAC	Computer Program for Automatic Control
COMPACS	Computer Output Microforms Program and Concept Study
COMPACT (1)	Compatible Algebraic Compiler and Transfer (computer term)
COMPACT (2)	Computerization of World Facts (Stanford Research Institute, U.S.)
COMPASS	Computer Assisted Search Service (a Cornell University Library Service)
COMPENDEX	Computerized Engineering Index (U.S.)
COMPFILE	Complement File (of NLM)
COMSAT	Communications Satellite Corporation (U.S.)
COMSTAC	Commission on Standards and Accreditation of Services for the Blind (U.S.)
COMTEC (1)	Computer Micrographics and Technology
COMtec (2)	Computer Micrographics Technology
COMUT	Programa de Comutacao Bibliográfica (created in 1981 and is cosponsored by the Brazilian Ministry of Education and Culture and the National Board for Scientific and Technological Development)
CONACYT	Consejo National de Ciencia y Tecnología (Mexico)
CONCORD/LIB	Cooperative Ontario Committee on Research & Development in Libraries
CONDOC	Consortium to Develop On-line Catalog (at the Univ. of Notre Dame Libraries)
CONDUIT	(Experimentation in the transportation of computer-based curriculum materials - Dartmouth College, N.C.; Oregon State University; Iowa University; Texas University)
CONICET	Consejo Nacional de Investigaciones Científicas y Técnicas (National Council for Scientific and Technical Research, Argentina)
CONICYT	Comisión Nacional de Investigación Científica y Tecnológica (National Commission for Scientific and Technological Research, Chile)

CONLIS	Committee on National Library/Information Systems (U.S.)
CONSAL	Conference/Congress of Southeast Asian Librarians (U.S.)
CONSALD	Committee on South Asia Libraries and Documentation (of LC)
CONSER	Conversion of Serials or Consolidation of Serials (a project of CLR; a shared database in machine-readable format)
CONSUL	Council of New England State University Librarians
CONTACT	(a human service information and referral agency, U.S.)
CONTU	National Commission on New Technological Uses of Copyrighted Works (U.S.)
CONVAL	Connecticut Valley Libraries
COO	Committee on Organization (of ALA)
COOKI	Coordinated Keysort Index
COP (1)	Canadian Official Publications (collection in NLC)
COP (2)	Committee on Planning (of ALA)
COPANT	Pan American Standards Coordinating Committee
COPAR	Committee for the Preservation of Architectural Records (National Clearinghouse for Information Concerning Architectural Records, U.S.)
COPDOP	Committee on the Processing Departments Orientation Program (of LC)
COPES	Committee on Program Evaluation and Support (of ALA)
COPES/PBA	COPES Planning and Budget Assembly
COPI	Committee on Policy Implementation (of ALA)
COPIC	Computer Program Information Centre (European Communities; now European Computer Program Information Centre)
COPICS	Copyright Office Publication and Interactive Cataloging System (of LC)
COPNIP	Committee on Pharmacomedical Nonserial Industrial Publications (of SLA (6))
COPOL	Council of Polytechnic Librarians (U.K.; also known as CPL (4))

COPUL	Council of Prairie University Libraries
CORAL (1)	Computer On-Line Real-Time Applications Language
CORAL (2)	Council of Research and Academic Libraries (Univ. of Texas)
CORD	Committee on Research in Dance (George Washington University, U.S.)
CORKS	Computer-oriented Record Keeping System (Central Institute for the Deaf, U.S.)
CORLS	Central Ontario Regional Library System
CORMOSEA	Committee on Research Materials on Southeast Asia (a committee of AAS (3))
CORSAIR	Computer Oriented Reference System for Automatic Information Retrieval (Forsvarets Forskningsansalt, Sweden)
COSAL	Congress of Southeast Asian Librarians
COSAP	Cooperative On-Line Serials Acquisition Project (U.S.)
COSATI	Committee on Scientific and Technical Information (Federal Council on Science and Technology, U.S.)
COSBA	Computer Services and Bureaux Association (U.K.)
COSEBI	Corporacion de Servicios Bibliotecarios (Puerto Rico)
COSERV	National Council for Community Services to International Voters
COSI	Committee on Scientific Information (U.S.)
COSLA	Chief Officers of State Library Agencies (of ALA)
COSLINE	Council of State Library Agencies in the Northeast (of New England States)
COSMEP	Committee of Small Magazine Editors and Publishers (U.S.)
COSMIC	Computer Software Management and Information Center (Georgia University, U.S.)
COSMOS	County of San Mateo Online System (U.S.)
COSTAR	Conversational On-line Storage and Retrieval
COSTI	Centre for Scientific and Technological Information (National Council for Research and Development, Israel)

COSWL	Committee on the Status of Women in Librarianship (of ALA)
COU	Council of Ontario Universities (also known as CUO)
COWL	Council of Wisconsin Libraries
CP	Command Processor (computer term)
CPA (1)	Chemical Propulsion Abstracts (John Hopkins University, U.S.)
CPA (2)	Critical Path Analysis (management term)
CPAA	Current Physics Advance Abstracts (American Institute of Physics)
CPB	Corporation for Public Broadcasting (U.S.)
CPBX	Computerized Private Branch Exchange (U.S.)
CPC (1)	Card Programmed Calculator (computer term)
CPC (2)	Carolina Population Center (a library database)
CPC (3)	Cataloging Policy Committee (of CTRLN)
CPC (4)	Central Pennsylvania Consortium
CPC (5)	Copyright Payments Center (name changed to CCC (7))
CPDA	Council for Periodical Distributors Association
CPI (1)	Canadian Periodical Index
CPI (2)	Central Patents Index (Derwent Publications, U.K.)
CPI (3)	Chemicals and Petroleum Magnetic Tape Database (International Systems Inc., U.S.)
CPI (4)	Current Physics Information (American Institut of Physics)
CPIA	Chemical Propulsion Information Agency (John Hopkins University, U.S.)
CPIC	Charged Particles Information Center (U.S. Atomic Energy Commission)
CPL (1)	Chicago Public Library
CPL (2)	Commonwealth Parliamentary Library (Australia)
CPL (3)	Council of Planning Librarians (U.S.)

CPL (4)	Council of Polytechnic Librarians (U.K.; also known as COPOL)
CPLI	Catholic Periodical and Literature Index (publication of CLA (4))
CPLQ	Corporation of Professional Librarians of Quebec (also known as CBPQ)
cpm (1)	Cards per minute (computer term)
CP/M (2)	Control Program for Microcomputers (operating system)
CPM (3)	Critical Path Method (management term)
CPM (4)	Current Physics Microform (of American Institute of Physics)
CPOMR	Computerized Problem-Oriented Medical Record (of Univ. of Vermont)
CPPA	Canadian Periodical Publishers' Association
CPPBS	Conseil Pédagogique Provincial des Bibliothèques Scolaires du Nouveau-Brunswick
cps	Cards per Second (computer term)
CPT	Current Physics Titles (of American Institute of Physics)
CPU	Central Processing Unit (Core of a computer containing the circuits required to interpret and execute programmed instructions)
CR	Carriage Return Character (computer term)
CRAM	Card Random Access Memory (computer term)
CRC (1)	Cataloguing Rules Committee (Library Association Cataloguing and Indexing Group, U.K.)
CRC (2)	Chapter Relations Committee (of ALA)
CRC (3)	Communications Research Centre
CRC (4)	Composing Reducing Camera (of UMI)
CRC (5)	Cyclic Redundancy Check
CRCD	Canadian Rehabilitation Council for the Disabled
CRCD(C)	Collège Royal des Chirurgiens Dentistes du Canada (also known as RCD(C))

CRCRC	Computing Reviews Category Revision Committee
CRD (1)	Congressional Reference Division (of LC)
CRD (2)	Conseil de Recherches pour la Défense (also known as DRB)
CRDI	Centre de Recherches pour le Développement International
CRDSD	Current Research and Development in Scientific Documentation (of NSF)
CRE	Cooperative Reference Exchange (of LC)
CREA	Congressional Research Employees Association (U.S.)
CREAC	Conseil de la Recherche en Économie Agricole du Canada (also known as AERCC)
CREATE	Center for Research and Evaluation in Applications of Technology in Education (U.S.)
CRECORD	Congressional Record On-Line (Capitol Services Inc., U.S.)
CREDO	Centre for Curriculum Renewal and Educational Development Overseas (U.K.)
CREE	Centre for Russian and East European Studies (at Univ. of Toronto)
CREF	College Retirement Equities Fund (U.S.)
CREPUQ	Conférence des Recteurs et des Principaux des Universités du Québec (also known as CRPQU)
CRESS	Computerized Reader Enquiry Service System
CREW	Continuous Review, Evaluation, and Weeding
CRG (1)	Classification Research Group (U.K.)
CRG (2)	Council of Regional Groups (of RTSD)
CRI	Current Research and Development in Israel (of COSTI)
CRIARL	Consortium of Rhode Island Academic and Research Libraries
CRIB	Computerized Resources Information Bank (U.S. Geological Survey)
CRIS (1)	Combined Retrospective Index Sets (index to book reviews in scholarly journals, 1886-1974, Carrolton Press, Arlington, Va.)

CRIS (2)	Command Retrieval Information System
CRIS (3)	Current Research Information System (U.S. Department of Agriculture)
CRISP	Catalogued Resources and Information Survey Programmes (College of Librarianship, Wales)
CRISPE	Computerized Retrieval Information Service on Precision Engineering (Cranfield Institute of Technology, U.K.)
CRIU	Centre de Recherches et d'Innovation Urbaines (Université de Montréal)
CRL (1)	Center for Research Libraries (U.S.)
CRL (2)	Certified Record Librarian (U.S.)
CRL (3)	Certified Reference Librarian (U.S.)
CRL (4)) C&RL)	College and Research Libraries (periodical)
CRL (5)	Council on Library Resources
CRLC	Capitol Region Library Council (Hartford, Conn.)
CRM (1)	Cataloging and Records Maintenance
CRM (2)	Conseil de Recherches Médicales (also known as MRC)
CRMA	City and Regional Magazine Association (U.S.)
CRMC(C)	Collège Royal des Médecins et Chirurgiens du Canada (also known as RCPS(C))
CRML	Connecticut Regional Medical Library
CRO (1)	Cathode Ray Oscilloscope
CRO (2)	Copyright Receipt Office (of BSD)
CROSS	Computerized Rearrangement of Special Subjects or Computerized Rearrangement of Subject Specialists
CRP	Composition Reduction Printing
CRPQU	Conference of Rectors and Principals of Quebec Universities (also known as CREPUQ)
CRRC	Cataloguing Rules Revision Committee (of LA (1))
CRS	Congressional Research Service (of LC; previously LRS)

CRSG	Classification Research Study Group
CRT (1)	Cathode Ray Terminal or Cathode Ray Tube
CRT (2)	Copyright Royalty Tribunal (U.S.)
CRUS	Centre for Research on User Studies (Univ. of Sheffield, U.K.)
CRYSIS	Correctional Records Information Systems (U.S.)
CSA	Canadian Standards Association
CSAL	Congress of Southeast Asian Librarians
CSAS	Canadian Society for Asian Studies (also known as ACEA (2))
CSB	Cataloging Service Bulletin (of LC)
CSBS	Canadian Society of Biblical Studies (also known as SCEB)
CSC (1)	Computer Science Corp. (U.S.)
CSC (2)	Computer Search Center (Illinois Institute of Technology Research Center)
CSCS	California State College, Stanislaus
CSCSB	California State College, San Bernadino
CSD	Children's Services Division (of ALA; now ASLC)
CSDA	Central States Distributors Association (book distributors, U.S.)
CSE	Computer Science and Engineering
CSEA	Canadian Society for Education Through Art (also known as SCEA)
CSF (1)	Canada Studies Foundation (also known as FEC)
CSF (2)	Central Serials File
CS/HI	Computer Software/Hardware Index
CSI	Chemical Substructure Index (of ISI (3))
CSID	Centro de Servicius de Informacion y Documentacion (Mexico)
CSIN	Chemical Substances Information Network

CSIR (1)	Council for Scientific and Industrial Research (South Africa)
CSIR (2)	Council of Scientific and Industrial Research (India)
CSIRO	Commonwealth Scientific and Industrial Research Organisation (Australia)
CSISRS	Cross Section Information Storage and Retrieval System (National Neutron Cross Section Center, U.S.)
CSL (1)	Comparative Systems Laboratory (Case Western Reserve University, U.S.)
CSL (2)	Computer Simulation Language
CSL (3)	Connecticut State Library
CSL (4)	Conseil Supérieur du Livre
CSLA (1)	Canadian School Library Association (of CLA)
CSLA (2)	Church and Synagogue Library Association (U.S.)
CSLA (3)	Connecticut School Library Association
CSLDB	California Spanish Language Data Base
CSLDIS	Centre for the Study of Librarianship, Documentation and Information Sciences (Yugoslavia)
CSLS	China Society of Library Science
CSMA	Carrier Sense Multiple Access Collision Detection (computer term)
CSMA/CD	Carrier Sense Multiple Access with Collision Detection
CSMP	Continuous System Modeling Program (computer language)
CSN	Canadiana Serial Number
CSP	Control Switching Point (computer term)
CSPC	Central Science and Patent Collection (of BLSRL)
CSR	Central Serials Record
CSRA	Canadian Semiotics Research Association (also known as ACRS)
CSRC	Chicano Studies Research Center (of UCLA)

CSRL   Center for the Study of Rural Librarianship (Clarion
              State College, Penn.)

CSRU   Chemical Society Research Unit (U.K.; now UKCIS)

CSRUIDR   Chemical Society Research Unit in Information
              Dissemination and Retrieval (U.K.)

CSS (1)   Circulation Service Section (of LAMA)

CSS (2)   Computer System Simulator

CSSA   Canadian Social Science Abstracts (of York University)

CSSDA   Council on Social Science Data Archives (U.S.)

CSSE   Canadian Society for the Study of Education (also
              known as SCEE)

CSSHE   Canadian Society for the Study of Higher Education
              (also known as SCEES)

CSSL   Continuous Systems Simulation Language (computer
              language)

CSTI (1)   Centre of Scientific and Technological Information
              (National Council for Research and Development,
              Israel)

CSTI (2)   Council of Scientific and Technical Institutes (U.K.)

CSTID   Committee for Scientific and Technical Information
              and Documentation (European Communities; also known
              as CIDST)

CSTV   Controlled Scan Televideo (application of video
              technology tested in a library environment by FLNPP)

CSUC   California State University and Colleges

CSULB   California State University at Long Beach

CT   Chemical Titles (American Chemical Society)

CTA   Canadian Telebook Agency

CTAVI   Centre Technique Audiovisual International (International
              Audiovisual Centre, Belgium)

CTB   Centre de Techniques Bibliographiques (Tunisia)

CTC   Centrale Technische Catalogus (Union Catalogue on
              Science and Technology, Delft University of Technology,
              Netherlands)

CTCL	Community and Technical College Libraries Section (of CACUL)
CTF	Canadian Teachers' Federation (also known as FCE)
CTFE	Colleges of Technology and Further Education (sub-section of the University and Research Section of LA (1))
CTHB	Chalmers Tekniska Högskolas Bibliotek (Library of Chalmers University of Technology, Sweden)
CTI (1)	Classified Titles Index (of ISDS)
CTI (2)	Computer Translation Inc. (U.S.)
CTIAC	Concrete Technology Information Analysis Center (Mass.)
CTIC	Cable Television Information Center (advisory group created by Ford and Markle Foundations, U.S.)
CTLS	Cumberland Trail Library System (U.S.)
CTS	Computer Training Services, Inc. (U.S.)
CTSS	Compatible Time-Sharing System
CU	Conseil des Universités (Council of Universities)
CUAC	Cartographic Users Advisory Council (U.S.)
CUASA	Carleton University Academic Staff Association
CUBE	Cooperating Users of Burroughs Equipment
CUBG	College and University Booksellers Group (Booksellers Association, U.K.)
CUBI	Centro Nazionale per il Catalogo Unico delle Biblioteche Italiane (Italy)
CUCCA	Canadian University and College Counselling Association (also known as ACCUC)
CUDBC	Comité Universitaire des Directeurs de Biologie du Canada (also known as CCUBC)
CUDOS	Comprehensive University of Dayton On-line Information Services
CUFC	Consortium of University Film Centers (U.S.)
CUG	Closed User Group

CUL	Cambridge University Library (U.K.)
CULP	California Union List of Periodicals
CULS (1)	College and University Library Section (of CLA (4))
CULS (2)	College and University Library Section (of NYLA)
CULSA	Cornell University Libraries Staff Association
CUMARC	Cumulated Machine Readable Cataloguing
CUMREC	College and University Machine Records Conference (U.S.)
CUMWA	Consortium of Universities of the Washington Metropolitan Area (Washington, D.C.)
CUNY	City University of New York
CUO	Conseil des Universités de l'Ontario (also known as COU)
CUP (1)	Canadian University Press (also known as PUC)
CUP (2)	College and University Publishers (U.K.)
CUPE	Canadian Union of Public Employees
CURE	Citizens United for Responsible Education
CURLS	College, University and Research Librarians (ceased)
CUS	Commission des Universités de Saskatchewan (also known as SUC (1))
CUSIP	Committee on Uniform Security Identification Procedures
CUSLS	College, University and Seminary Libraries Section (of CLA (4))
CUSO	Canadian University Service Overseas (also known as SUCO)
CUSS (1)	Computerized Uniterm Search System (Dames & Moore, U.S.)
CUSS (2)	Cooperative Union Serials System (of OULCS)
CUTA	Chama Cha Ukutubi, Tanzania (Tanzania Library Association)
CV	Centrale Vereninging voor Openbare Bibliotheken (Central Association for Public Libraries, Netherlands)

CVA	Committee for the Visual Arts (N.Y.)
CVCC	Canadian Videotex Consultative Committee (set up by the Department of Communications)
CVCN	Collegiate Video Counselling Network
CVLG	Central Vancouver Librarians Group (started in 1973 amongst the special libraries in downtown area and VPL Science and Business Divisions)
CWA (1)	Canada Water. Waste Resources Document Reference Centre
CWA (2)	Communications Workers of America
CWIAU	Canadian Women's Intercollegiate Athletic Union (also known as USIF)
CWILS	Connecticut Women in Libraries
CWIT	Concordance Words in Titles
C W MARS	Central Western Massachusetts Automated Resource Sharing
CWONC	Canadian Women of Note, Computerized (biographies of 1000 Canadian women into a computerized database)
CWP	Circulation Working Party (Aslib Computer Applications Group, U.K.; now Acquisitions, Cataloguing and Circulation Working Party)
CWRL	Case Western Reserve University Libraries (Ohio)
CWRU	Case Western Reserve University (formerly WRU)
CYASS	Children's and Young Adult Services
CyLA	Ceylon Library Association
D-A (1)	Decision-Analyst
DA (2)	Direct Access
DA (3)	Dissertation Abstracts (UMI; also known as DAI)
DAA	Dictionary of Architectural Abbreviations, Signs and Symbols (New York: Odyssey Press, 1965)
DAACUG	Duncan Area Atari Computer Users Group (U.S.)
DAB	Dictionary of American Biography

DAC	Digital-to-Analog Circuit (computer term)
DACOM	Datascope Computer Output Microfilmer
DAD	Digital Audio Disc
DAFT	Digital Analogue Function Table (computer term)
dag	Dekagram (metric) = 10 g
DAI	Dissertation Abstracts International (UMI; also known as DA (3))
DAIRI	Dissertation Abstracts International Retrospective Index (of UMI)
DAIRS	Dial Access Information Retrieval System (Shippensburg State College, Pa.)
DAIS (1)	Doctor of Arts in Information Science
DAIS (2)	Document Analysis and Information System (Michigan University)
dal	Dekalitre (metric) = 10 l
dam (1)	Dekametre (metric) = 10 m
DAM (2)	Direct Access Method (computer term)
DAMSEL	Data Management System and Econometric Language
DANBIF	Danske Boghandleres Importørforening (Danish Book-sellers Import Association, Denmark)
DAR	Daily Activity Report (produced by computer, usually for library circulation operations)
DARE (1)	Data Retrieval System for the Social and Human Sciences (Unesco)
DARE (2)	Documentation Automated Retrieval Equipment
DARPA	Defense Advanced Research Projects Agency (U.S.)
DASD	Direct-Access Storage Devices
DATACOM	Data Communications (a global network)
DATALIB	(a shared acquisitions and cataloguing System operated by Sigma Data Computing Corp;, Silver Spring, Md.)
DATA Line	Dial a Teacher Assistance Line (a reference service)
DATAPAC network	(a commercial interconnection between the TransCanada Network and the Telenet in U.S.)

DATE	Dial Access Technical Education (of IEEE)
DATRAN	Data Transmission Company (U.S.)
DATRIX	Direct Access to Reference Information - Xerox Service (UMI)
DAVI	Department of Audiovisual Instruction (of NEA; now AECT)
DAX	Data Acquisition and Control
DB (1)	Danmarks Biblioteksforening (Danish Library Association)
DB (2)	Decibel
DB (3)	Deutsche Bibliothek (W. Germany)
DBA (1)	Database Administration (of UTLAS Inc.)
DBA (2)	Data Base Administrator
DBA (3)	Documentation, Bibliothèques, Archives (Unesco; also known as DLA (4))
DBAM	Data Base Access Method
DB Bih	Drustro Bibliotekara Bosne i Hercegovine (Library Association of Bosnia and Herzegovina, Yugoslavia)
DBDL	Data Base Definition Language
DBI	Deutsche Bibliotheksinstitut (German Library Institute, Berlin)
DBM	Database Management
DBMC	Database Management Control (of UTLAS Inc.)
DBMS (1)	Database Management Section (of UTLAS Inc.)
DBMS (2)	Database Management System
DPB	Data Base Processor
DBPH	Division for the Blind and Physically Handicapped (of LC)
DBRO/DORLS	Directeurs des Bibliothèques Régionales de l'Ontario (also known as DORLS)
DBS (1)	Dominion Bureau of Statistics (now Statistics Canada)

DBS (2) Društvo Bibliotekarjev Slovenije (Society of Librarians in Slovenia, Yugoslavia)

DBV (1) Deutscher Bibliotheksverband (East Germany; now BDDR)

DBV (2) Deutscher Buchereiverband e.V. (German Library Association, W. Germany)

DC Decimal Classification or Dewey Classification (also known as DDC (2))

DCA (1) Digital Communications Associates, Inc.

DCA (2) Digital Computer Association (U.S.)

DCB Dictionary of Canadian Biography

DCC Descriptive Cataloging Committee (of ALA)

DCD Decimal Classification Division (of LC)

DCE Data Circuit-terminating Equipment (computer term)

DCEPC Decimal Classification Editorial Policy Committee (of RTSD)

DCIST Directory of Computerized Information in Science and Technology (Science Associates/International Inc., U.S.)

DCLA District of Columbia Library Association

DCLC District of Columbia Library Council

DCPL District of Columbia Public Library

DCRT Division of Computer Research and Technology (of National Institute of Health, Public Health Services, U.S.)

DCTL Direct Coupled Transister Logic (computer term)

DDC (1) Defense Documentation Center (U.S.; formerly ASTIA and DTIC)

DDC (2) Dewey Decimal Classification (also known as DC)

DDD Database Design and Development (of UTLAS Inc.)

DDI Direct Dial In (computer term)

DDL Data Definition Language (computer language)

DDN Digital Data Network

DDP	Distributed Data Processor
DDR	Dynamic Device Reconfiguration (computer term)
DDS	Dataphone Digital Service (communication service of Bell System)
DDT	Dynamic Debugging Tool (computer term)
DE	Disk Emulator (computer term)
DEACON	Direct English Access and Control (computer term; General Electric Co., U.S.)
DEAF	Deaf Environment Action Force
DEC (1)	Development Education Centre (also known as CED (2))
DEC (2)	**Digital Equipment Computer Users Society**
DECADE	DEC's Automatic Design System
DECCA	Decentralized Cataloguing Project of Det Kongelige Bibliotek, Copenhagen
DECUS	Digital Equipment Corporation Users Society
Del	Delete Character (computer term)
DEM	Demodulator (computer term)
DEMA	Data Entry Management Association (U.S.)
DENDRAL	(a system developed at the Stanford Heuristic Programming Project)
DEP	Database Enhancement Program (of UTLAS Inc.)
DES	Department of Education and Science (U.K.)
DESIDOC	Defence Scientific Information and Documentation Centre (India)
DET	Division of Educational Technology (of OLLR)
DETAB	**Decision Tables (computer language)**
DEU	Duplicates Exchange Union (of RTSD)
DEUCE	Digital Electronic Universal Calculating Engine (computer term)
DEVSIS	Development of Sciences Information System (a project of IDRC, ILO, OECD, UDDP and Unesco)

DEZ Diethyl Zinc (vapor) (developed by LC for deacidification of books)

DF Documentation Française (France)

DFL Display Formatting Language (computer language)

Dfs Dataflow Systems Inc. (U.S.)

DFT Discrete Fourier Transform

dg Decigram (metric) = 100 mg

DGD Deutsche Gesellschaft für Dokumentation (German Society for Documentation, W. Germany)

DGES Direction Générale de l'Enseignement Supérieur, Québec (also known as DHEQ)

DGRST Délégation Générale a la Recherche Scientifique et Technique (France)

DHEQ Directorate of Higher Education, Quebec (also known as DGES)

DHEW Department of Health, Education and Welfare (U.S.; also known as HEW)

DIALOG (Lockheed's Computerized Information System)

DIANE Direct Information Access Network for Europe (of EURONET)

DIAOLS Defense Intellegence Agency On-line Information System (U.S.)

DICOM Diagnosing Individual Competence on Microfiche (program from Eastman Kodak Co., U.S.)

DIDACTA (International Educational Materials Fair, Basel, Switzerland)

DIF Drug Information Fulltext (a database file of American Society of Hospital Pharmacists)

DILS Dataskil Integrated Library System

DIMDI Deutches Institut für Medizinische Dokumentation und Information (German Institute for Medical Documentation and Information in Cologne, W. Germany)

DIMECO Dual Independent Map Encoding (File of the Counties of the U.S. Laboratory for Computer Graphics and Spatial Analysis, Harvard University)

DIN	Deutsches Institut für Normung (W. Germany)
DIODE	Digital Input/Output Display Equipment
DIP	Dual-Inline Package (computer term - switches on the computer circuit board)
DIRAC	Direct Access (Stanford University, U.S.)
DIRLINE	Directory of Information Resources Online (NLM's system for accessing NRC data)
DIRR	(International Road Research Documentation (of OECD) (also known as IRRD)
DIRS	DIMDI Information Retrieval Service
DIS (1)	Drug Information Sources (of SLA (6))
DIS (2)	Dynamic Information Systems Inc. (U.S.)
DISC (1)	Divisional Interests Special Committee (formed 1974 to represent common interests of ALA Divisions, ceased 1979)
DISC (2)	Drug Information Service Center (Univ. of Minnesota)
DISCUS	Institute of Library Research (of UCLA)
DISISS	Design of Information in the Social Sciences (Univ. of Bath, U.K.)
DK	Dezimal Klassifikation (UDC (1))
dl	Decilitre (metric) = 100 ml
DLA (1)	Delaware Library Association
DLA (2)	Delhi Library Association (India)
DLA (3)	Division of Library Automation (of Univ. of Calif.)
DLA (4)	Documentation, Libraries and Archives (Directorate of Unesco ; also known as DBA)
DLAI	Documentation, Library and Information Infrastructures (Unesco)
DLIMP	Descriptive Language for Implementing Macro-Processors (programming language)
DLP	Division of Library Programs (of OLLR; formerly BLLR and BLET)
DLQ	Drexel Library Quarterly

DLR	Dominion Law Reports (of QL systems)
DLS	Department of Library Studies (Univ. of West Indies, Kingston, Jamaica)
DLSEF	Division of Library Services and Educational Facilities (U.S. Office of Education)
dm	Decimetre (metric) = 100 mm
DMA (1)	Data Management Association (U.S.)
DMA (2)	Direct Memory Access (computer term)
DMARC	DOBIS MARC
DMIC	Defense Metals Information Center (Ohio)
DML (1)	Data Management Language
DML (2)	Data Manipulation Language
DMM	Digital Multimeter (computer term)
DMOT	DMARC Out
DMS (1)	Data Management System
DMS (2)	Display Management System
DNA	Deutscher Normenausschuss (German Standards Association, W. Germany)
DNB (1)	Deutsche Nationalbibliographie (E. Germany)
DNB (2)	Dictionary of National Biography
DOBIS	Dortmunder Bibliothekssystem (Dortmund Bibliographic Information System)
DOC	(Federal) Department of Communication
DOCA	Documentation Automatique (Automatic Documentation; section of CETIS)
DOCEX	Document Expediting (program of Update Publications)
DOCHSIN	District of Columbia Health Science Information Network
DOCTOR	Dictionary Operation and Control for Thesaurus Organization (of JICST)
DOD (1)	Directory of Directories (an annotated guide to Business and Industrial Directories)

DOD (2)	Documents on Documents (collection; contains publications which originate in various states in the administration of state documents depository programs, U.S.)
DOE	Department of Energy (U.S.)
DOE-RECON	(Bibliographic On-line Information Retrieval System, U.S.)
DOLARS	Disk On-line Accounts Receivable System
DOMSAT	Domestic Satellite
DORLS	Directors of Ontario Regional Library Systems (Directeurs des Bibliothèques Régionales de l'Ontario)
DOS	Disc Operating System (of IBM)
DOZI-CIINTE	Czialowy Ośrodek Zagadnién Informacyjnch Centralnego Instytutu Informacji Naukowo-Technicznej i Ekonomicznej (Branch Center on Information Problems at the Central Institute for Scientific, Technical and Economic Information, Poland)
DP	Data Processing
DPA (1)	Diary Publishers Association (U.K.)
DPA (2)	Domestic Policy Association (U.S.)
DPB	Department of Printed Books (of R & D)
DPED	Data Processing for Education (publication)
DPL (1)	Dallas Public Library
DPL (2)	Denver Public Library
DPL (3)	Detroit Public Library
DPL/DMA	Data Processing Librarians and Documentation Managers Association (U.S.)
DPLS	Division of Public Library Services
DPMA	Data Processing Management Association
DPPH	Division for the Blind and Physically Handicapped (of LC; now NLS/BPH)
DPRC	Direction and Planning Review Committee (of ALA)
DPS (1)	Data Processing System
DPS (2)	Document Processing System (of IBM)

DRA	Data Research Associates (St. Louis, Mo.)
DRACON	Drug Abuse Communications Network (N.Y.)
DRAT	Disaster Recovery Assistance Team (program of Wyoming State Library)
DRAW	Direct-Read-After-Write (a technique employed to create optical disc)
DRB	Defence Research Board (also known as CRD (2))
DRCOG	Denver Regional Council of Governments
DRCS	Dynamically Redefinable Character Set (computer term)
DREA	Defence Research Establishment Atlantic
D-REF	Data Reference (a database of Water Resources Document Reference Centre, Canada. Dept. of Fisheries and the Environment, Inland Waters Directorate)
DRI	Data Resources, Inc.
DRIS	Diagnostic Radiology Information System (Arkansas University)
DRL	Data Retrieval Language
DRS	Document Retrieval System
DRTC	Documentation Research and Training Centre (Bangalore, India)
DRUGDOC	(Selective Dissemination of Information Service, Excerpta Medica Foundation, Netherlands)
DS	Data Set
DSB	Deutsche Staatsbibliothek (German State Library, W. Germany)
DSDD	Double-sided Double Density (Disk drives)
DSE	Data Set Extention
DSI (1)	Diffusion Sélective de l'Information (Selective dissemination of information)
DSI (2)	Division of Science Information (U.S.)
DSIR	Department of Scientific and Industrial Research (U.K., New Zealand, etc.)
DSIS (1)	Defence Scientific Information Service

DSIS (2)	Directorate of Scientific Information Services (Defence Research Board)
DSNA	Dictionary Society of North America (formerly SSDL)
DSS (1)	(Canadian Government Publications Catalogued)
DSS (2)	Decision Support System
DSS (3)	DIALOG Statistical Service
DTB	Dansk Tekniske Bibliotek (Danish Technological Library)
DTE	Data Terminal Equipment
DTIC	Defence Technical Information Center (now DDC (1))
DTIE	Division of Technical Information Extension (U.S. Atomic Energy Commission; now Technical Information Center)
DTL (1)	Desk Top Library
DTL (2)	Diode-Transistor Logic (computer term)
DTO	Dansk Teknisk Oplysningstjeneste (Danish Technical Information Service)
DTUC	David Thompson University Centre (B.C.)
DUALabs	Data Use and Access Laboratories (U.S.)
DUET	Distance University Education Via Television (a programme of Mount St. Vincent University, N.S.)
DVEB)	Deutscher Verband Evangelischer Büchereien (German Association of Protestant Libraries, W. Germany)
DVT	Deutscher Verband Technische-Wissenschaftlicher Vereine (Federation of Technical Scientific Associations, W. Germany)
DWG	DOBIS Working Group
DX	Duplex (computer term)
DYNAMO	(a digital simulation program of MIT)
DYNIX	(an on-line integrated system, North Provo, Utah)
DYSTAL	Dynamic Storage Allocation Language (computer language)

EAI	Electronic Associates, Inc.
EALA	East African Library Association
EALS	East African Literature Service (Kenya, Tanzania, Uganda)
EAM	Electronic Accounting Machine
EANDC	European-American Nuclear Data Committee
EAPH	East African Publishing House (Nairobi)
EASL	East African School of Librarianship (Uganda)
EAX	Electronic Automatic Exchange
EB	Encyclopaedia Britannica
EBAD	École de Bibliothécaires, Archivistes et Documentalistes (School of Librarians, Archivists and Documentalists, Senegal)
EBC	European Bibliographic Centre
EBCDC	Extended Binary-Coded Decimal Interchange Code (computer term; also known as EBCDIC, EBDIC)
EBCDIC	Extended Binary-Coded Decimal Interchange Code (also known as EBCDC, EBDIC)
EBDIC	Extended Binary-Coded Decimal Interchange Code (also known as EBCDC, EBCDIC)
EBEC	Encyclopaedia Britannica Educational Corporation
EBIG	Economics and Business Information Group (Aslib)
EBP	Early British Periodicals (of UMI)
EBSS	Education and Behavioral Science Section (of ACRL)
EBU	European Broadcasting Union (Switzerland)
EC (1)	Editorial Committee (of ALA)
EC (2)	Encyclopedia Canadiana
ECA	Educational Centres Association (U.K.)
ECAP	Electronic Circuit Analysis Program (computer language)
ECAP II	Electronic Circuit Analysis Program II (computer language)
ECARBICA	East and Central African Regional Branch of the International Council on Archives

ECB	Educational Computer Board
ECCL	Erie City and County Library
ECDOC	European Commission Documentation (Brussels, Belgium)
ECEA	Exceptional Child Education Abstracts (of Council for Exceptional Children, Reston, Va.)
ECER	Exceptional Child Education Resources (Va.)
ECIS	European Communities Information Service (U.K.)
ECL	Emitter-coupled Logic (computer term)
ECMA	European Computer Manufacturers Association
ECOL	Environmental Conservation Library (Minneapolis, Minn.)
ECRL	Eastern Caribbean Regional Library (Trinidad)
ECSLA	East Central State School Libraries Association (Nigeria)
ECSSID	European Conference on Social Science Information and Documentation (Moscow, U.S.S.R., 1977)
ECT	Environmental Control Table
ECU	East Carolina University
EDA	Educational Development Association (U.K.)
EDAC	Error Detection and Correction (computer term)
EDC (1)	Education Development Center, Inc. (Mass.)
EDC (2)	European Documentation Centre (European Communities)
EDCOM	Educational Computing Network
EDGE	Electronic Data Gathering Equipment
EDIAC	Electronic Display of Indexing Associations and Content (Documentation Inc., U.S.)
EDIC (1)	Educational Delivery through Interactive Computing (of AHEC)
EDIC (2)	Engineering Data Identification and Control (U.S.)
EDICT	Engineering Departmental Interface Control Technique
EDIS	Engineering Data Information System (Howard Research Corp., U.S.)

EDITOR	(a programme written for on-line cataloguing (of BLAISE))
EDITS	Educators Information Technology System (InTech. Corp., Penn.)
EDP (1)	Educational Data Processing
EDP (2)	Electronic Data Processing
EDPAC	(a package of five computer programs)
EDRS (1)	Engineering Data Retrieval System
EDRS (2)	ERIC Document Reproduction Service (U.S.)
EDS	Energy Data System
EDSAC	Electronic Delay Storage Automatic Calculator (a first generation computer)
EDSTAT (1)	Educational Statistics (of National Center for Educational Statistics of HEW)
EDSTAT (2)	Educational Statistics Information Access Service
EDUCOM	Educational Communication (Interuniversity Communication Council, U.S.)
EDUNET	(an educational computer services network created under the auspices of the Planning Council on Computing in Education and Research)
EDVAC	Electronic Discrete Variable Automatic Computer (a first generation computer)
EEA	Educational Exhibitors Association (U.K.)
EEB	Enosis Ellenon Bibliothekarion (Greek Library Association; also known as GLA (3))
EEC	European Economic Community
EEL	East End Literacy Program (started in 1978, Ont.)
EEMCT	Encyclopedia of Educational Media Communications and Technology
EEO	Equal Employment Opportunity (U.S.)
EEOC	Equal Employment Opportunity Commission (U.S.
EEPROM	Electrically Erasable Programmable Read-only Memory (computer term)

EFLA	Educational Film Library Association (U.S.; previously known as EFLIC)
EFLIC	Educational Film Library Lending Committee (U.S.; now EFLA)
EFT	Electronic Funds Transfer (computer term used in banking industry)
EFVA	European Foundation of Visual Aids (U.K.)
E & G	Exchange and Gift Division (of LC)
EGIS	Executives Guide to Information Sources (Gale Research)
EGLI	Essay and General Literature Index (H.W. Wilson)
EI	Engineering Index (U.S.)
EIA (1)	Electronic Industries Association
EIA (2)	Energy Information Administration (of U.S. Dept. of Energy)
EIBM	Escuela Interamericana de Biblioteconomica (Colombia)
EIC (1)	Engineering Information Center (U.S.)
EIC (2)	Environmental Information Center (U.S.; previously known as Energy Information Center)
EID	Environmental Information Division (U.S.)
EIES	Electronic Information Exchange System (of New Jersey Institute of Technology)
EIN	European Informatics Network
EIRMA	European Industrial Research Management Association
EIS (1)	Economic Information Systems, Inc. (U.S.)
EIS (2)	Educational Institute of Scotland
EIS (3)	Environmental Impact Statement(s) (an ILL service at the Northwestern University Library)
EISO	Educational Information System of Ontario (an on-line search service through OISE, produces material through ONTERIS Project)
EJIC	Education and Job Information Center (N.Y.)
EK	Einheitsklassifikation (Unified classification, W. Germany)

EKI	Electronic Keyboarding, Inc. (U.S.)
EKU	Eastern Kentuky University
EL	English Language (cataloguing of BSD)
ELA (1)	Edmonton Library Association
ELA (2)	Electronic Library Association (of ALA)
ELA (3)	Ethiopian Library Association
ELBS	English Language Book Society (U.K.)
ELD	Edge Lit Display (computer term)
ELHILL	(Information Retrieval Software used by BLAISE)
ELIRT	Environmental Laboratories Information Retrieval Technique
ELIS	Encyclopaedia of Library and Information Science (Marcel Dekker, U.S.)
ELMIG	Electronic Library Membership Initiative Group (of ALA)
ELMS	Exploratory Library Management System (IBM)
ELPS	English Literary Periodicals (of UMI)
ELSEGIS	Elementary and Secondary Education General Information Survey
EM	Excerpta Medica (Amsterdam)
EMA	Equipment Market Abstracts (a database of PREDICASTS, Cleveland, Ohio)
EMAC	Educational Media Association of Canada
EMBASE	Excerpta Medica Online
EMC (1)	Educational Media Council
EMC (2)	Encyclopedia of Music in Canada (Encyclopédie de la Musique au Canada)
EMCOM	Educational Media Catalogs on Microfiche (publication)
EMF	Excerpta Medica Foundation (Netherlands)
EMIC	Environmental Mutagen Information Center (U.S. Atomic Energy Commission)

EMIE (1)	Educational Media Institute Evaluation (project of NEA)
EMIE (2)	Ethnic Materials Information Exchange (of ALA)
EMIETF	Ethnic Materials Information Exchange Task Force (N.Y.)
EMILS	Electric Memory Integrated Library System (a mini-computer based system of Electric Memory Inc.)
EMIS	Effluent Management Information System (Development Sciences Inc., U.S.)
EMMA	Extra-MARC Material (of BLAISE)
EMOL	Excerpta Medica On-Line (Netherlands)
EMPIS	Engineering Materials and Processes Information Service (of General Electric Co.)
EMRIC	Educational Media Research Information Center (U.S.)
EMRLS	East Midlands Regional Library System (U.K.)
EMS (1)	Early MARC Search (of LC)
EMS (2)	Electronic Mail System
EMSC	Educational Media Selection Centers (U.S.)
ENDS	European Nuclear Documentation System (Euratom)
ENERGYLINE	Energy Online (database of EIC (2))
ENIAC	Electronic Numerical Integrator and Calculator (first large scale computer built, 1946)
ENSB	Ecole Nationale Supérieure de Bibliothécaires (France)
ENVIROBIB	Environmental Periodicals Bibliography (code name for the indexed bibliographic material available through DIALOG)
ENVIRON	Environmental Information Retrieval On-line (of Environmental Protection Agency, U.S.)
EOF	End of File (computer term)
EOLS	Eastern Ontario Library System (also known as EORLS)
EORLS	Eastern Ontario Regional Library System (also known as EOLS)
EOS	Electonic Office Systems

EPA	Environmental Protection Agency (U.S.)
EPB (1)	Electronic Publishing and Bookselling (periodical)
EPB (2)	Environmental Periodicals Bibliography (ABC-Clio, Inc.)
EPC (1)	Editorial Policy Committee (of Decimal Classification)
EPC (2)	Editorial Processing Centres (provides links between several electronic scientific journals)
EPC (3)	European Patent Convention
EPDA	Education Professions Development Act (U.S.)
EPFL	Enoch Pratt Free Library (John Hopkins University, U.S.)
EPIC	Electronic Properties Information Center (of CINDAS)
EPIE	Educational Products Information Exchange (Idaho State University)
EPIS	Extramural Programs Information System (of NLM)
EPL (1)	Edmonton Public Library (Alta.)
EPL (2)	Everett Public Library (Wash.)
EPLA	East Pakistan Library Association (defunct)
EPO	European Patent Office
EPROM	Erasable Programmable Read-only Memory (computer term)
EPSILON	Evaluation of Printed Subject Indexes by Laboratory Investigation (College of Librarianship, Wales)
EPSS	Experimental Packet Switching System (computer term)
ERA (1)	Engineering Research Associates
ERA (2)	Equal Rights Amendment (U.S)
ERA (3)	European Research Associates (Belgium)
EREP	Environmental Recording, Editing and Printing Program
ERI	Econometric Research Inc. (U.S.)
ERIC	Educational Resources Information Center (U.S. Office of Education)
ERIC/AE	ERIC Clearinghouse on Adult Education (Syracuse University, U.S.)

ERIC/C	ERIC/Central (U.S.)
ERIC/CAPS	ERIC Clearinghouse on Counselling and Personnel Services (also known as ERIC/CG)
ERIC/CEC	ERIC Clearinghouse on Exceptional Children (also known as ERIC/EC)
ERIC/CEF	ERIC Clearinghouse on Educational Facilities (Wisconsin University, U.S.)
ERIC/CEM	ERIC Clearinghouse on Educational Management (also known as ERIC/EA)
ERIC/CG	ERIC Clearinghouse on Counselling and Personnel Services (also known as ERIC/CAPS)
ERIC/ChESS	ERIC Clearinghouse for Social Studies or Social Science Education (also known as ERIC/SO)
ERIC/CLIS	ERIC Clearinghouse on Library and Information Sciences (now ERIC/IR)
ERIC/CLL	ERIC Clearinghouse on Languages and Linguistics
ERIC/CRESS	ERIC Clearinghouse on Rural Education and Small Schools (New Mexico State University)
ERIC/CRIER	ERIC Clearinghouse on Retrieval of Information and Evaluation on Reading (Indiana University)
ERIC/CS	ERIC Clearinghouse on Reading and Communication Skills (also known as ERIC/RCS)
ERIC/CUE	ERIC Clearinghouse on Urban Education (also known as ERIC/UD)
ERIC/EA	ERIC Clearinghouse on Educational Management (also known as ERIC/CEM)
ERIC/EC	ERIC Clearinghouse on Exceptional Children (also known as ERIC/CEC)
ERIC/ECE	ERIC Clearinghouse on Elementary and Early Childhood Education (also known as ERIC/PS)
ERIC/EM	ERIC Clearinghouse on Educational Media and Technology (merged with ERIC/CLIS in 1974 to form ERIC/IR)
ERIC/EMT	ERIC Clearinghouse on Educational Media and Technology (Stanford University; now ERIC/IR)
ERIC/FL	ERIC Clearinghouse on Languages and Linguistics (also known as ERIC/CLL)

ERIC/HE	ERIC Clearinghouse on Higher Education
ERIC/IR	ERIC Clearinghouse on Information Resources (ASIS and Stanford University; formerly ERIC/CLIS, ERIC/EM, ERIC/EMT)
ERIC/IRCD	ERIC Information Retrieval Center on the Disadvantaged (Columbia University, U.S.)
ERIC/JC	ERIC Clearinghouse on Junior Colleges
ERIC/PS	ERIC Clearinghouse on Elementary and Early Childhood Education (also known as ERIC/ECE)
ERIC/RC	ERIC Clearinghouse on Reading and Communication Skills (also known as ERIC/CS)
ERIC/SE	ERIC Clearinghouse for Science, Mathematics and Environmental Education (also known as ERIC/SMEAC)
ERIC/SMEAC	ERIC Clearinghouse for Science, Mathematics and Environmental Education (also known as ERIC/SE)
ERIC/SO	ERIC Clearinghouse for Social Studies or Social Science Education (also known as ERIC/ChESS)
ERIC/SP	ERIC Clearinghouse on Teacher Education
ERIC/TM	ERIC Clearinghouse on Tests, Measurements, and Evaluation
ERIC/UD	ERIC Clearinghouse on Urban Education (also known as ERIC/CUE)
ERISTAR	Earth Resources Information Storage, Transformation, Analysis and Retrieval (of Auburn University for National Aeronautics and Space Administration, U.S.)
ERPLS	Eastern Regional Public Library System (Mass.)
ERT	Exhibits Round Table (of ALA)
ESANET	European Space Agency Network
ESCI	Environmental Science Citation Index (Johnson Associates Inc., U.S.)
ESDAC	European Space Data Center (W. Germany)
ESEA	Elementary and Secondary Education Act (U.S.)
ESI	Environmental Science Index (of Environment Information Center, U.S.)

ESIC	Environmental Science and Information Center (U.S. Atomic Energy Commission)
ESIT	Egyptian Society for Information Technology
ESL	Engineering Societies Library (U.S.)
ESLA	Egyptian School Library Association
ESRIN	European Space Research Institute (Italy)
ESRO-SDS	European Space Research Organization - Space Documentation Service
ESS	Electronic Switching System (computer term)
ESTC	Eighteenth-Century Short-Title Catalogue (of British Library)
ESTC/NA	North American (part of ESTC Project)
ESTEC	European Space Research and Technology Center (Netherlands)
ETC	European Translations Centre (Deft, Netherlands)
ETIC	English Teaching Information Centre (U.K.)
ETIS-MARFO	European Economic and Technical Information Service in Machine Readable Form
ETO	(Universal Decimal Classification, Hungary) (also known as CDU, UDC (1))
ETV	Educational Television
ETVO	Educational Television Branch of Ontario
ETX	End of Text
EUDISED	European Documentation and Information Systems of Education
EUMC	Entr'aide Universitaire Mondiale du Canada
EURATOM	Organisation Atomique Européenne
EURIM	European Conference on Research into the Management of Information Services and Library Services (also called European Conference on Research into Management of Information)
EUROCOMP	European Computing Congress

EURODOC	(Joint Documentation Service of European Space Research Organization, Eurospace and European Launcher Development Organization
EURONET	European Information Retrieval Service (also called European On-line Retrieval Service, European Communities)
EURONET-DIANE	EURONET-Direct Information Access Network
EUSIDIC	European Association of Scientific Information Dissemination Centres (formerly CHEOPS)
EUSIREF	European Referral Service (of EUSIDIC)
EVIMEC	Eastern Virginia Medline Consortium
EVR	Electronic Video Recording
EWA	Education Writers Association (U.S.)
EXCP	Execute Channel Programmes (computer term)
F	Farad (SI) (electric capacitance)
FABS	Formulated Abstracting (Linguistic Documentation Centre (Univ. of Ottawa)
FACT (1)	Fuel Abstracts and Current Titles
FACT (2)	Fully Automated Cataloguing Technique (Library Micrographic Services Inc., U.S.)
FAHSLN	Flint Area Health Science Library Network (Mich.)
FAIR	Fast Access Information Retrieval (of Biomedical Engineering, U.K.)
FAIRS (1)	Federal Aviation Information Retrieval System (U.S.)
FAIRS (2)	Fully Automatic Information Retrieval System
FALA	Federation of Asian Library Associations (later AFLA)
FAM	Fortran Assembly Program
FAME	Florida Association for Media in Education
FAMIS	Financial and Management Information System (U.S. Dept. of the Navy)
FAN	Foreign Acquisition Newsletter (of ARL, ceased 1980)

FAO	Food and Agriculture Organisation (of U.N.)
FAP	Financial Analysis Program
FAPUQ	Fédération des Associations de Professeurs d'Université du Québec
FAST	(Lists produced by Univ. of Toronto COM catalogue – full bibliographic record, authors, subjects, and titles)
FASTCAT	Fast Catalog (of LC)
FAUL	Five Associated University Libraries (in New York) (Buffalo, Rochester, Syracuse, Cornell and Binghamton)
FAUST	Folkebibliotekernes Automation System (Public libraries computerization system, Denmark)
FAXPAK	(a Facsimilie Communication Network of ITT)
FBON	Fundamental'naya Biblioteka Obstichestrennykh Nauk (Fundamental Library of Social Sciences, U.S.S.R.)
FBR (1)	Forskningsbiblioteksrådet (Council of Research Libraries, Sweden)
FBR (2)	Full Bibliographic Record
FCBG	Federation of Children's Book Groups (U.K.)
FCC	Federal Communications Commission (U.S.)
FCE	Fédération Canadienne des Enseignants (also known as CTF)
FCEE	Foundation Canadienne d'Éducation Économique (also known as CFEE)
FCFDU	Fédération Canadienne des Femmes Diplômées des Universités (also known as CFUW)
FCPL	Fairfax County Public Library
FCRDE	Foundation Canadienne de Recherche du Droit de l'Environnement
FCU	Federal Credit Union (of LC)
FD	Full Duplex (computer term; also known as FDX)
FDM	Frequency Division Multiplexing (computer term)
FDTF	Federal Documents Task Force (of GODORT)

FDX	Full Duplex (computer term; also known as FD)
FEBAB	Federação Brasileira de Associações de Bibliotecários (Brazilian Federation of Associations of Librarians)
FEBAB/CBDJ	FEBAB/Comissão Brasileira de Documentação Jurídica (FEBAB Committee of Legal Documentation, Brazil)
FEC	Fondation d'Études du Canada (also known as CSF (1))
FEDLINET	Federal Library and Information Network (now FEDLINK)
FEDLINK	Federal Library and Information Network (of LC; previously FLECC; also known as FEDLINET and FEDNET)
FEDNET	Federal Library and Information Network (now FEDLINK)
FEMA	Federal Emergency Management Agency (U.S.)
FF	Flip-Flop (computer term)
FFS (1)	Formatted File System (computer term)
FFS (2)	Frequently-Found Substructures (Institute for Scientific Information, U.S.)
FFSL	Fédération Française de Syndicats de Libraires (France)
FIAB	Fédération Internationale des Associations de Bibliothécaires (also known as IFLA)
FIAF	Fédération Internationale des Archives du Film (Belgium; also known as IFFA)
FIAI	Fédération Internationale des Associations d'Instituteurs (International Federation of Teachers' Associations
FIBP	Federazione Italiana delle Biblioteche Popolari (Federation of Italian Public Libraries)
FID	Fédération Internationale de la Documentation (International Federation of Documentation; formerly IID and IIB)
FIDAC	Film Input to Digital Automatic Computer (Georgetown University, U.S.)
FID/CAO	FID Commission for Asia and Oceania
FID/CCC	FID Central Classification Committee (for the development of UDC (1))
FID/CLA	FID Comision Latinoamericana (Regional Commission for Latin America)

FID/CNC	FID Canadian National Committee
FID/CR	FID Committee on Classification Research
FID/DC	FID Committee on Developing Countries
FID/DT	FID Committee on the Terminology of Information and Documentation
FID/ET	FID Committee on Education and Training
FID/II	FID Committee on Information for Industry
FIDJC	Fédération Internationale des Directeurs de Journaux Catholiques (International Federation of Directors of Catholic Publications, France)
FID/LD	FID Committee on Linguistics in Documentation
FID/MSR	FID Committee on Mechanical Storage and Retrieval
FID/OM	FID Committee on Operational Machine Techniques and Systems
FID/RI	FID Committee on Research on the Theoretical Basis of Information
FID/RRS	FID Research Referral Service
FID/TD	FID Committee on Training of Documentalists
FID/TM	FID Committee on Theory and Methods of Systems, Cybernetics and Information Networks
FID/TMO	FID Committee on Theory, Methods and Operations of Information Systems and Networks
FIFO	First-in-first-out (computer term)
FIInfSc	Fellow of the Institute of Information Scientists (U.K.)
FILA	Federation of Indian Library Associations (previously known as NACILA)
FILLS	Fast Interlibrary Loans and Statistics (IBM-PC software for interlibrary loans developed by the library at MacNeal Memorial Hospital in Berwyn, Ill.)
FILMNET	Film Users Network
FIND/SVP	(Information on demand service of SVP network)
FIP	Fédération Internationale des Phonothèques (International Federation of Record Libraries)

FIPP   Fédération Internationale de la Presse Periodique (International Federation of the Periodical Press, France)

FIPS   Federal Information Processing Standards (U.S.)

FIPSCAC   Federal Information Processing Standards Coordinating and Advisory Committee (U.S.)

FIPSE   Funds for the Improvement of Post-Secondary Education (of ACRL)

FIRL   Faceted Information Retrieval for Linguistics

FIRST (1)   Fast Interactive Retrieval System Technology

FIRST (2)   Federal Information Research Science and Technology Network (Committee on Scientific and Technical Information, U.S.)

FISCAL   Fee-based Information Service Centers in Academic Libraries (U.S.)

FIT   Fédération Internationale des Traducteurs (International Federation of Translators)

FIU   Federation of Information Users (U.S.)

FIUC   Fédération Internationale des Universités Catholiques (also known as IFCU)

FIZ   Fachinformationszentrum Technik (Information Centre for Technical Services in Frankfurt)

FJCC   Fall Joint Computer Conference

FLA (1)   Federal Librarians Association (U.S.)

FLA (2)   Fellow of the Library Association (U.K.)

FLA (3)   Fiji Library Association

FLA (4)   Florida Library Association

FLA (5)   Foothills Library Association

FLAA   Fellow of the Library Association of Australia

FLAI   Fellow of the Library Association of Ireland

FLASH   (a list of Australian subject headings, 1981)

FLC   Federal Library Committee (of LC)

FLECC   Federal Libraries Experiment in Cooperative Cataloging (now FEDLINK)

FLIC (1)	Film Library Information Council (U.S.)
FLIC (2)	Film Library Intercollege Cooperative (Penn.)
FLICC	Federal Library and Information Center Committee (U.S.; previously called FLC)
FLIN	Florida Library Information Network
FLIP	Film Library Instantaneous Presentation
FLIRT	Federal Librarians Round Table (of ALA; now FLRT)
FLIS	Faculty of Library and Information Science (e.g. of the Univ. of Toronto)
FLNPP	Federal Network Prototype Project
FLOP (1)	Floating Octal Point (computer term)
FLOP (2)	Foreign and International Official Publications (collection in NLC)
FLORIDA COMCAT	Florida Computer Catalog of Monographic Holdings
FLP	Free Library of Philadelphia
FLRT	Federal Librarians Round Table (of ALA; previously FLIRT)
FLS	Faculty of Library Science
FLSAA	Faculty of Library Science Alumni Association (of Univ. of Toronto)
FM	Frequency Modulation
FMFP	Farm Machinery and Food Processing Information (database)
FMQ	Fichier MARC Québecois
FMS	Fortran Monitor System
FNBC	Fédération Nationale des Bibliothèques Catholiques (Belgium)
FNBFA	Federation of New Brunswick Faculty Associations
FNIC	Food and Nutrition Information and Educational Materials Center (of NAL)
FNL	Friends of National Libraries (U.K.)
FNZLA	Fellow of the New Zealand Library Association

FOBID	Federatie van Organisaties op het Gebiej van het Bibliotheek-, Informatie- en Documentatiewezen (Federation of Organizations in Library, Information and Documentation Services, Netherlands)
FOCAS	Firm Order Control and Selection (of Richard Abel Co.)
FOF	Facts on File
FOI	Freedom of Information (1st part of Access to Information, Act - Canada)
FOIA	Freedom of Information Act (U.S.)
Fol	Folio (book size)
FOL USA	Friends of Libraries USA
FOPW	Federation of Organizations for Professional Women
FORE	Foundation of Record Education (of AMRA)
Formac	Formula Manipulation Compiler (computer language)
FORMS	File Organization Modeling System (Planning Research Corp., U.S.)
FORTRAN	Formula Translation (computer language)
FOSDIC	Film Optical Sensing Device for Input to Computers
FOSE	Federal Office Systems Expo (U.S.)
FPAP	Floating Point Array Processor (computer term)
FPC	Forest Press Committee (a committee for the revision of DDC (2))
FRD	Federal Research Division (of LC)
FRED	Front End for Databases
FREES	File Retrieval and Editing Systems (Text Systems Inc., (U.S.)
FRF	Freedom to Read Foundation (also known as FTRF)
FRINGE	Film and Report Information Generator
FROM	Field Programmable Read Only Memory (computer term)
FSAIS	Federation of Science Abstracting and Indexing Services (U.S.)

FSALA	Fellow of the South African Library Association
FSFA	Federation of Specialised Film Associations (U.K.)
FSPD	Faculty and Staff Program Development Office (South Campus Miami-Dade Community College)
FSTA	Food Science and Technology Abstracts (of IFIS)
FTE	Full Time Equivalent
FTET	Full Time Equivalent Terminals
FTIR	Fourier Transform Infrared Spectrophotometry
FTRF	Freedom to Read Foundation (of ALA; also known as FRF)
FTS	Federal Telecommunications System (U.S.)
FTU	First Time Use (initial use by a library of a record located in the utility's database and not input by the library)
FVRL	Fraser Valley Regional Library (B.C.)
FVRLS	Fort Vancouver Regional Library System (Vancouver, Wash.)
FY	Financial Year or Fiscal Year
FYI	For Your Information
G	Gram (metric) = 1,000 mg
GAC (1)	Geographic Area Code (MARC format developed by LC)
GAC (2)	Government Advisory Committee (on Internal Book and Library Programs (U.S.))
GALA	Graphic Arts Literature Abstracts (Graphic Arts Research Center, Rochester Institute of Technology, Rochester, N.Y.)
GAO	(U.S.) General Accounting Office (Washington, D.C.)
GAP	General Assembly Program (computer term)
GARC	Graphic Arts Research Center (U.S.)
GARE	Guidelines for Authority and Reference Entries (of LC)
GARP	Global Atmospheric Research Program (Switzerland)

GASP	General Activity Simulation Program (computer term)
GATD	Graphic Analysis of Three-dimentional Data
GATTIS	Georgia Institute of Technology Technical Information Service (U.S.)
GB (1)	Gigabit (10^9 bits)
GB (2)	Gigabyte (10^9 bytes)
GBDL	Gesellschaft für Bibliothekswesen und Dokumentation des Landbauses (Association of Librarianship and Documentation in Agriculture, W. Germany)
GBIL	Gosudarstvennaya Biblioteka SSR Imeni V I Lenina (Leninstate Library, U.S.S.R.; also known as GBL)
GBL	Gosudarstvennaya Ordena Lenina Biblioteka SSR Imeni V.I. Lenina (also known as GBIL)
GBRLS	Georgian Bay Regional Library System
GCIS	Georgia Career Information System (statewide computer based service that provides career decision-making information, description of 245 separate occupations, programs, etc., U.S.)
GCLC	Greater Cincinnati Library Consortium
GDB	Gesellschaft für Dokumentation und Bibliographie (Austrian National Library)
GDBMS	Generalized Data Base Management Systems
GDL	Genesee District Library (Flint, Mich.)
GDNS	Government Data Network System
GE	General Electric Corp.
GEBO	General Egyptian Book Organization
GECOS	General Electric Comprehensive Operating System
GED	General Educational Development (a method for preparing high school dropouts for GED high school equivalency test, U.S.)
GEIS	General Electric Information Service
GEMS	Government Electronic Message Service
GENDA	General Data Analysis and Simulation

GEOREF	World Geographic Reference System (U.S.)
GEOSCAN	(database operated by the Canadian Centre for Geoscience Data, Energy, Mines and Resources, Canada)
GESYDAMS	Groupe d'Exploitation des Systèmes de Documentation Automatisés en Médecine et en Sciences (Laval University, Quebec)
GFF	Generalized Facet Formula (Colon Classification)
GIBUS	Groupe Informatistique de Bibliothèques Universitaires et Spécialisées (France)
GID	Gesellschaft für Information und Dokumentation (Documentation and Information Society, Frankfurt)
GIDEP	Government-Industry Data Exchange Program (U.S.)
GIFI	General Information File Interrogation (computer term)
GIGO	Garbage In, Garbage Out (computer term)
GILA	Government of India Librarians Association
GIM	Generalized Information Management System
GIPSY	General Information Processing System (U.S. Geological Survey)
GIRL	Generalized Information Retrieval Language (Defense Nuclear Agency, U.S.)
GIRU	Graphic Information Research Unit (of Royal College of Arts, U.K.)
GIS	Generalized Information System
GITIS	Georgia Institute of Technology (School of) Information Sciences (U.S.)
GJP	Graphic Job Processor (computer term)
GK 3	General Catalogue of Printed Books, 3rd ed. (of BL)
GLA (1)	Georgia Library Association
GLA (2)	German Library Association
GLA (3)	Greek Library Association (also known as EEB)
GLA (4)	Guyana Library Association
GLEIS	Great Lakes Environmental Information Sharing (previously IPAHGEIS)

GLIN   Georgia Library Information Network

GLIS   Geac Library Information System

GLISA   Graduate Library Institute for the Spanish Speaking
            Americans

GLMD   Georgia Library Media Department

GLS (1)   General Library System (e.g. of Univ. of Wisconsin-
            Madison)

GLS (2)   Graduate Library School (of Univ. of Chicago)

GMD   General Material Designation (used in descriptive
            cataloguing, AACR2)

GMIS   Government Management Information Sciences (U.S.)

GMP   **Guide to Microforms in Print** (publication)

GOAST   Geac Office Automation System

GOD   Great Online Database

GODORT   Government Documents Round Table (of ALA)

GODORT FDTF GODORT Federal Document Task Force (Working Group on
            Bibliographic Control)

GODORT IDTF GODORT International Documents Task Force

GODORT LDTF GODORT Local Documents Task Force

GODORT   GODORT Machine-Readable Government Information
MRGITF   Task Force

GODORT SDTF GODORT State Documents Task Force

GODORT SLDTF GODORT State and Local Documents Task Force

GPA   Geophysical Abstracts (U.S. Geological Survey)

GPIB   General Purpose Interface Bus (computer term used
            for inter-unit communications in micros)

GPNITL   Great Plains National Instructional Television
            Library (U.S.)

GPNTB   Gosudarstrennaya Publichnaya Nauchno-teknicheskaya
            Biblioteka SSSR (State Public Scientific and Technical
            Library, U.S.S.R.)

GPNY   Gay Presses of New York

GPO	Government Printing Office (U.S.)
GPO MARC	Government Printing Office MARC (U.S.)
GPSDIC	General Purpose Scientific Document Image Code (U.S.)
GPSS	General Purpose Systems Simulator (computer language)
GRACE	Graphic Arts Composing Equipment (of NLM)
GRA & I	Government Reports Announcements & Index (publication)
GRANTS	Foundation Grants Index (Foundation Center, N.Y.)
GRIPHOS	General Retrieval and Information Processing for Humanities-Oriented Studies (of New York University)
GRISA	(Group for Research on Automatic Scientific Information, Euratom)
GROVE 5	Grove's Dictionary of Music and Musicians (5th ed., 1954)
GROVE 6	The New Grove Dictionary of Music and Musicians (6th ed., 1980)
GRTA	Government Reports Topical Announcements (of NTIS)
GSAM	Generalized Sequential Access Method
GSIS	Group for Standardization of Information Services (U.S.)
GSLIS	Graduate School of Library and Information Science
GTA	Government Telecommunications Agency
GTDI	United Nations Trade Data Interchange Directory
GTE	General Telephone and Electronics
GTIS	Gloucestershire Technical Information Service (U.K.)
GUIDE	Guidance of Users of Integrated Data Processing Equipment
GUIM	Gold Unit Initiator Module (a file transfer module of the Université de Québec)
GULP	General Utility Library Programs
GURM	Gold Unit Responder Module (a file transfer system of NLC)
GWP	Graphics Working Party (Library Association Media Cataloguing Rules Committee, U.K.)

Gy   Gray (SI) (absorbed dose of ionising radiation)

GZS   Gesamtverzeichnis der Zeitchriften und Serien (Union
            catalogue of periodical and serial holdings, W. Germany)

H   Henry (SI) (inductance)

HA (1)   Historical Abstracts (ABC-Clio, Inc.)

HA (2)   History and Allied Subjects

HABS   Human Relations Area Files Automated Bibliographic
            System (of Yale University, U.S.)

HADIS   Huddersfield and District Information Service (U.K.)

HALDIS   Halifax and District Information Service (U.K.)

HAMIC   Health and Medical Information Cooperative (of Southern
            Maine)

HAM-TMCL   Houston Academy of Medicine-Texas Medical Center
            Library

HAPI   Hispanic American Periodicals Index (UCLA Latin American
            Center Publications (of Univ. of Calif.)

HARFAX   (an industry database, a subsidiary of Harper & Row
            Inc. on NEXIS)

HARLIC   Houston Area Research Library Consortium

HASL   Hertfordshire Association of Special Libraries (U.K.)

HASP   High Level Automatic Scheduling Program (computer term)

HATRICS   Hampshire Technical Research, Industrial and Commercial
            Service (U.K.)

HAVOC   Humberside Audio-visual Catalogue (U.K.)

HAYSTAQ   Have You Stored Answers to Questions? (of National
            Bureau of Standards, U.S.)

HBD   Hrvatsko Bibliotekarsko Društvo (Association des
            Bibliothécaires de Croatie; Croation Library Association,
            Yugoslavia)

HBR   Harvard Business Review (periodical)

HCL   Hennepin County Library (U.S.)

HCLS   Health Care Libraries Section (of ASCLA)

HCTLDS   Hungarian Central Technical Library and Documentation
            Center (Hungary)

HCUA	Honeywell Computer Users Association
HD	Half Duplex (computer term; also known as HDX)
HDAM	Hierarchical Direct Access Method (computer term)
HDI	Historical Documents Institute (U.S.)
HDLC	High-Level Data Link Control (computer term)
HDX	Half Duplex (computer term; also known as HD)
HEA	Higher Education Act (U.S.)
HECUS	Higher Education Center for Urban Studies (Conn.)
HEEP	Health Effects of Environmental Pollution (Abstracts on) (Biosciences Information Service of Biological Abstracts and NLM)
HEGIS	Higher Education General Information Survey (of USOE)
HEIAC	Hydraulic Engineering Information Analysis Center (U.S.)
HEIAS	Human Engineering Information Analysis Service (Mass.)
HELAS	Higher Education Library Advisory Service (N.Y.)
HELIN	Higher Education Library Information Network (of Univ. of Rhode Island)
HELP (1)	Health Education Library Program (of Carnegie Public Library, Pittsburgh, Pa.)
HELP (2)	Heckman's Electronic Library Program (Ind.)
HELP (3)	Help Extend Libraries to People with Handicaps
HELPIS	Higher Education Learning Programmes Information Service (publication of NCET)
HERMAN	Hierarchical Environmental Retrieval for Management Access and Networking (of Biologica Information Service)
HERO	Historical Evaluation and Research Organization (Va.)
HERTIS	Hertfordshire Technical Library and Information Service (U.K.)
HEW	Health, Education and Welfare (Department of, U.S.; also known as DHEW)
HF	High Frequency

hg	Hectogram (metric) = 100 g
HICLASS	Hierarchical Classification
HILC	Hampshire Inter-library Center (U.S.)
HILOW	Health and Information Libraries of Westchester (N.Y.)
HIPO	Hierarchy Plus Input-Process-Output (computer term)
HIRA	Health Instructional Resources Association (Mich.)
HIS (1)	Honeywell Information Systems
HIS (2)	Hospital Information System
HISARS	Hydrological Information Storage and Retrieval System (of Noth Carolina State University)
HISP	Health Information Sharing Project (in Syracuse and Onondaga Counties, N.Y.)
HISTLINE	History of Medicine Online (of NLM)
HITCH	Health Information to Community Hospitals (program of Norris Medical Library of UCLA)
hl	Hectolitre (metric) = 100 l
HLA (1)	Halifax Library Association (N.S.)
HLA (2)	Hawaii Library Association
HLAS	Handbook of Latin American Studies (publication of LC's Hispanic Division)
HLL	High-Level Language (computer term)
HLPE	Hospital, Library and Public Employees Union (U.S.)
hm	Hectometre (metric) = 100 m
HMSO	Her/His Majesty's Stationery Office (U.K.)
HOLSA	Health Oriented Libraries of San Antonio (Tex.)
HOLUG	Houston Online Users Group (Tex.)
HOP	Headings Only Product (a by product of computer run against UTLAS Inc. authority file, showing the linkages created by the authority records)
HOQ	Hansard Oral Questions (of QL Systems; also known as HQO)

HOTShops	Hands-on Technology Shops
HP	Hewlett-Packard
HPB	Hand Printed Books Project (Machine-readable Bibliographic Records Project, Univ. of Western Ontario)
HPCI	Himpunan Pustakawan Chusus Indonesia (Indonesian Association of Special Librarians)
HPL	Houston Public Library (Tex.)
HQE	Hansard Question Écrites (of QL Systems; also known as HWQ)
HQO	Hansard Question Orale (of QL Systems; also known as HOQ)
HRAF	Human Relations Area Files (of Yale University, U.S.)
HRCC	Humanities Research Council of Canada (also known as CCRH)
HRIS	Highway Research Information Service (of NRC (3))
HRLSD	Health and Rehabilitative Library Services Division (of ALA; formerly AHIL, now part of ASCLA)
HRLSD/ LSBPHS	HRLSD Library Services to the Blind and Physically Handicapped Section (now ASCLA/LSBPHF)
HRLSD/LSPS	HRLSD Library Services to Prisoners Section (now ASCLA/LSPS)
HRN	Human Resources Network (Pa.)
HS	History Section (of RASD)
HSL	Highway Safety Literature (of National Highway Traffic Safety Administration, Washington, D.C.)
HSLMIP	Health Sciences Library Management Intern Program (U.S.)
HSLS	High School Libraries Section (of CLA)
HSN	(Illinois Dept. of Mental Health and Development Disabilities Library Services Network)
HSRC	Health Sciences Resource Centre (of CISTI)
HSRT	Health Sciences Round Table (of CLA (4))
HSSI	Humanities and Social Sciences Index (of Blackwell Ltd.)

HT	Horizontal Tab (computer term)
HTH	Host Terminal Handlers
HULTIS	Humberside Libraries Technical Interloan Scheme (U.K.; formerly Hull Technical Interloan Scheme)
HUMARIS	Human Resources Information System
HUMRRO	Human Resources Research Organization (Va.)
HURI	Harvard Ukranian Research Institute (Mass.)
HWQ	Hansard Written Questions (of QL Systems; also known as HQE)
HYK	Helsingin Yliopiston Kirjasto (Helsinki University Library)
Hz	Hertz (SI) (frequency)
I & A	Abstracting and Indexing (also known as A & I)
IAA	International Aerospace Abstracts (American Institute of Aeronautics & Astronautics, N.Y.)
IAALD	International Association of Agricultural Librarians and Documentalists
IABF	International Antiquarian Book Fair
IABLA	Inter-American Bibliographical and Library Association
IAC (1)	Information Access Company (U.S.)
IAC (2)	Information Analysis Centre
IAC (3)	International Communication Agency (U.S.; previously USIA)
IACB	International Advisory Committee on Bibliography (of Unesco; now IACBDT)
IACBDT	International Advisory Committee on Bibliography, Documentation and Terminology (of Unesco; previously IACB)
IACDT	International Advisory Committee for Documentation and Terminology (Unesco)
IACOD	International Advisory Committee on Documentation, Libraries and Archives

IAD (1)	Integrated Automatic Documentation
IAD (2)	International Association of Documentalists and Information Officers (also known as AID (3))
IADIS	Irish Association for Documentation and Information Services
IADLA	International Association for the Development of Documentation, Libraries and Archives in Africa (also known as AIDBA)
IAEA	International Atomic Energy Agency (Vienna, Austria)
IAG	International Applications Group (of IFIP)
IAIMS	Integrated Academic Information Management System (of NLM)
IAL	International Algebraic Language
IALL	International Association of Law Libraries
IALPS	Inter Active Library Processing System (of H.C.E. Library Automation System, Fort Worth, Tex.)
IAMC	Institute for the Advancement of Medical Communications (U.S.)
IAMCR	International Association for Mass Communication Research (Switzerland)
IAME	Illinois Association for Media in Education
IAML	International Association of Music Librarians (also known as AIBM,IVM, IVMB)
IAMLANZ	International Association of Music Librarians, Australia/ New Zealand Branch
IAMSLIC	International Association of Marine Science Libraries and Information Centers
IANL	International Association of National Librarians
IAO	Insurers' Advisory Organization (formerly Canadian Underwriters' Association)
IAOL	International Association of Orientalist Librarians
IAP	Information Analysis Products (of ERIC)
IARD	Information Analysis and Retrieval Division (American Institute of Physics)

IASA	International Association of Sound Archives
IASC (1)	Indexing and Abstracting Society of Canada (also known as SCAD)
IASC (2)	International Association for Statistical Computing
IASL (1)	Illinois Association of School Librarians
IASL (2)	International Association of School Librarianship (Univ. of Western Michigan)
IASLIC	Indian Association of Special Libraries and Information Centres
IASP	International Association of Scholarly Publishers (Univ. of Toronto)
IASSA	Institute of Archival Science for Southeast Asia (Malasia)
IASSIST	International Association for Social Science Information Service/Systems and Technology
IASV	Internationale Arbeitsgemeinschaft von Sortiments-buchhändler-Vereinigungen (International Community of Booksellers Associations; also known as ICBA, CILA (2))
IATL	International Association of Theological Libraries
IATLIS	Indian Association of Teachers of Library Science
IATUL	International Association of Technological University Libraries
IAU	International Association of Universities (also known as AIU)
IAVA	Industrial Audio-Visual Association (U.S.)
IAVRS	International Audiovisual Resource Service (Unesco)
IBBD	Instituto Brasileño de Bibliografia e Documentação (Brazilian Institute of Bibliography and Documentation)
IBBY	International Board on Books for Young People (also known as IBBYP)
IBBYP	International Board on Books for Young People (also known as IBBY)
IBD	International Book Distributors Ltd. (U.K.)
IBDI	International Bureau of Documentation and Information of Sport

IBE	International Bureau of Education (Unesco)
IBFD	International Bureau of Fiscal Documentation
IBI	Intergovernmental Bureau for Informatics (U.S.)
IBICT	Instituto Brasileiro de Informaçao em Ciencia e Tecnologia (Rio de Janeiro, Brazil)
IBID	International Bibliography, Information, Documentation (R.R. Bowker, U.S.)
IBI/ICC	IBI International Computation Centre (Italy; also known as ICC (3))
IBIS	International Book Information Service (U.K.)
IBM	International Business Machines Corp. (U.S.)
IBM PC	IBM Personal Computer
IBR	Institute for Behavioral Research (York University)
IBS	Informationsbanken System (W. Germany)
IBSAT	Indexing by Statistical Analysis Techniques
IBSR	Interactive Bibliographic Search and Retrieval
IBY	International Book Year (Unesco)
IBZ	Internationale Bibliographie der Zeitschriftenliteratur (W. Germany)
IC (1)	Index Chemicus (of ISI (3))
IC (2)	Integrated Circuit (computer term)
IC (3)	International Centre (of ISDS)
ICA (1)	International Communications Agency (U.S.; formerly BECA and USIA; also known as USICA)
ICA (2)	International Communications Association (Tex.; previously NSSC)
ICA (3)	International Council of Archives (also called International Council on Archives)
ICADI	Inter-American Centre for Agricultural Documentation and Information (Inter-American Institute of Agicultural Sciences)
ICAI	Institute for Computer-Assisted Information (U.S.)

ICAITI	Instituto Centro Americano de Investigacion y Technologia Industrial (Central American Institute of Research and Industrial Technology, Guatemala)
ICBA	International Community of Booksellers Associations (also known as CILA (2), IASV)
ICBY	International Council on Books for Young People
ICC (1)	Inter Company Comparisons (U.K.) (an information database about British companies)
ICC (2)	International Children's Centre
ICC (3)	International Computation Center (Italy; also known as IBI/ICC)
ICCA	International Conference on Computer Applications (in developing countries, held at Asian Institute of Technology, Bangkok)
ICCC (1)	International Cataloging Consultation Committee (of LC)
ICCC (2)	International Conference on Computer Communications (Washington, D.C.)
ICCP (1)	Institute for Certification of Computer Professionals (U.S.)
ICCP (2)	International Conference on Cataloguing Principles (Paris, 1961)
ICCR	Indian Council of Cultural Relations (U.S.)
ICE	In Circuit Emulator (computer term)
ICEA	Institut Canadien d'Éducation des Adultes (also known as CIAE)
ICEF	International Council for Educational Films (also known as CIFE)
ICES	Integrated Civil Engineering System (computer language)
ICF	Institut Canadien du Film (also known as CFI)
ICFES	Instituto Colombiano para el Fomento de la Educacion Superior
ICG	Institute for Graphic Communication (U.S.)
ICHSANA	International Congress of Human Sciences in Asia and North Africa

ICIA	International Communications Industries Association (U.S.; formerly NAVA)
ICIC	International Copyright Information Centre (Unesco)
ICIM	(International Council of Museums) (also known as ICOM)
ICIP	International Conference on Information Processing
ICIREPAT	International Cooperation in Information Retrieval among Examining Patent Offices (Switzerland; also known as CICIREPATO)
IC/ISDS	International Center/ISDS
ICIST	Institut Canadien de l'Information Scientifique et Technique (also known as CISTI)
ICL (1)	International Computers Ltd.
ICL (2)	Irish Central Library for Students (also known as ICLS)
ICLEBC	Institute of Continuing Library Education of British Columbia
ICLG	International and Comparative Librarianship Group (of LA (1))
ICLS	Irish Central Library for Students (also known as ICL (2))
ICLTN	Interagency Council on Library Tools for Nursing (U.S.)
ICMH	Institut Canadien de Microreproduction Historiques (also known as CIHM)
ICO	International Congress of Orientalists
ICOM	International Council of Museums (also known as ICIM)
ICON	(a microcomputer developed by CEMCORP for the Ontario Ministry of Education)
ICONCLASS	Iconography Classification (Netherlands)
ICOSAL	Idaho Council of State Academic Libraries
ICOT	Institute for New Computer Generation Technology (also known as INCOGT)
ICP	Interlibrary Cooperative Project
ICPL	Iowa City Public Library
ICPSR	Inter-University Consortium for Political and Social Research (Univ. of Michigan)

ICR	International Council for Reprography
ICRDB	International Cancer Research Data Bank Program (U.S.)
ICRS	Index Chemicus Registry System
ICSED	(International Standard Classification of Education Unesco) (also known as ISCED)
ICSI	International Conference on Scientific Information (Washington, D.C., Nov. 1958)
ICSSD	International Committee for Social Science Information and Documentation (also known as CIDSS and ICSSDI)
ICSSDI	International Committee for Social Sciences Documentation and Information (Paris; also known as CIDSS and ICSSD)
ICST	Institute for Computer Science and Technology (U.S.)
ICSTI	International Centre of Scientific and Technical Information (U.S.S.R.)
ICSU	International Council of Scientific Unions (Paris)
ICSU-AB	International Council of Scientific Unions Abstracting Board (of IFLA)
ICU	International Christian University (Japan)
IDC (1)	Information Dynamics Corporation (U.S.)
IDC (2)	Interactive Data Corporation (U.S.)
IDC (3)	International Data Corporation
IDC (4)	International Documentation in Chemistry
IDC (5)	Internationale Dokumentations-gesellschaft für Chemie (W. Germany)
IDC-KTHB	Royal Institute of Technology Library (Sweden)
IDDS	International Digital Data Service
IDEA	Inductive Data Exploration and Analysis
IDEEA	Information and Data Exchange Experimental Activities (U.S. Army)
IDEP	International Data Exchange Program (U.S.)
IDI	International Labour Documentation (of ILO)
IDICT	Intituto de Documentación e Información Científica y Técnica (Cuba)

IDIOT	Instrumentation Digital On-line Transcriber
IDIS	Iowa Drug Information Service (Univ. of Iowa)
IDL & RS	International Data Library and Reference Service (now SRCDL)
IDP	Institute of Data Processing (U.K.)
IDRC	International Development Research Centre
IDRS	Inter-Departmental Reference Service (Univ. of Philippines, Manila)
IDS (1)	Integrated Data Store (computer term)
IDS (2)	Interlibrary Delivery Service (Penn.)
IDST	Information and Documentation in Science and Technology
IDT	Institutul Central de Documentare Technica (Central Institute for Technical Documentation, Rumania)
IDTF	International Documents Task Force (of GODORT)
IEAB	Internacia Esperanto - Asocio de Bibliotekistoj (International Association for Esperanto-Speaking Librarians)
IEALC	Inland Empire Academic Libraries Cooperative (of Univ. of Calif. at Riverside)
IEC	Information Exchange Centre (of CISTI)
IEEE	Institution of Electrical and Electronics Engineers (U.S.)
IEEE-CS	IEEE-Computer Society
IEIC	Iowa Educational Information Center (Univ. of Iowa)
IEMA	Iowa Educational Media Association
IEN	(Xerox) Information Exchange Network (U.S.)
IEPRC	International Electronic Publishing Research Centre
IF	Intellectual Freedom (Committee of CLA)
IFAC	International Federation of Automatic Control
IFC	Intellectual Freedom Committee (of ALA)
IFCU	International Federation of Catholic Universities (also known as FIUC)
IFD	International Federation for Documentation (also known as FID)

IFFA	International Federation of Film Archives (Belgium; also known as FIAF)
IFFS	International Federation of Film Societies (U.K.)
IFIP	International Federation for Information Processing
IFIPS	International Federation of Information Processing Societies
IFIS	International Food Information Service
IFLA	International Federation of Library Associations and Institutions (also known as FIAB)
IFLP	Index to Foreign Legal Periodicals (of AALL)
IFORS	International Federation of Operational Research Societies
IFRT	Intellectual Freedom Round Table (of ALA)
IGAEA	International Graphic Arts Education Association (U.S.)
IGB	Internationale Germanistische Bibliographie (publication)
IGC	Institute for Graphics Communication (U.S.)
IGOs	International Intergovernmental Organizations
IGSS	International Graduate Summer School (in Librarianship and Information Science)
IGSWWBN	Idaho Grade Schools World Wide Bibliographic Network
IGY	International Geophysical Year
IHEC	Indiana Higher Education Commission
IIA	Information Industry Association (U.S.)
IIASA	International Institute for Applied Systems Analysis
IIB	Institut International de Bibliographie (later IID; now FID)
IIC	International Institute of Communications (Italy)
IICS	Institut Indo-Canadien Shastri (also known as SICI)
IID	Institut International de Documentation (formerly IIB; now FID)
IIE	Institute of International Education (U.S.)
IIF	Information Item File

III	Information International, Inc.
IIMP	Information Industry Market Place (publication, R.R. Bowker)
I Inf Sc	Institute of Information Scientists (U.K.; also known as IIS (2))
IIRS (1)	Institute for Industrial Research and Standards (of ISO (2))
IIRS (2)	International Information Retrieval Service (Netherlands)
IIS (1)	Index to International Statistics (U.S.)
IIS (2)	Institute of Information Scientists (U.K.; also known as I Inf Sc)
IITRI	Illinois Institute of Technology Research Institute
ILA (1)	Idaho Library Association
ILA (2)	Illinois Library Association
ILA (3)	Indian Library Association or All-India Library Association
ILA (4)	Indiana Library Association
ILA (5)	Iowa Library Association
ILA (6)	Iranian Library Association
ILA (7)	Israel Library Association
ILAB	International League of Antiquarian Booksellers (U.K.)
ILACS	Integrated Library-administration and Cataloguing System (Unilever, Netherlands)
ILEA	Inner London Education Authority (U.K.)
ILIC	International Library Information Center (GSLIS, Univ. of Pittsburgh)
I-LITE	Iowa Library Information Teletype Exchange
Ill (1)	Illustration (s)
ILL (2)	Interlibrary Loan (also known as ILLO)
ILLC	International Library to Library Project (of MLA (7))
ILLIAC	Illinois Automatic Computer
ILLINET	Illinois Library and Information Network

ILL ME	Interlibrary Loan Micro Enhancer (of OCLC Inc.)
ILLMESS	Interlibrary Loans Batch Messaging (Ont.)
ILLO	Interlibrary Loan (also known as ILL (2))
ILLS	Interlibrary Loan System
ILO	International Labour Organisation (of U.N.)
ILP	Index to Legal Periodicals (H.W. Wilson Co.)
ILR	Institute of Library Research (Univ. of Calif.)
ILRC	Illinois Regional Library Council
ILS	Integrated Library System
ILSUS	Integrated Library System Users Society (U.S.)
ILTA (1)	Illinois Library Trustee Association
ILTA (2)	Indiana Library Trustee Association
IMAC	Illinois State Library Microfilm Automated Catalog
IMC (1)	International Information Management Congress
IMC (2)	International Micrographic Congress
IMCE	International Meeting of Cataloguing Experts (Copenhagen, 1969)
IMDS	International Microform Distribution Service
IME	Information Management Education
IME&C	Information Management Exposition & Conference (N.Y.)
IMG	Informational Media Guaranty (U.S. Book Trade)
IMI	Iowa-Missouri-Illinois Library Consortium
IMIA	International Medical Informatics Association
IML	Instructional Media Laboratory (Univ. of Wisconsin)
IMNC	International MARC Network Committee (formerly IMNS:SC)
IMNS	International MARC Network Study
IMNS:SC	International MARC Network Study Steering Committee (now IMNC)

IMO	International MARC Office
IMP (1)	Index of Mathematical Papers (of AMS (1))
IMP (2)	International MARC Project
IMPA	International Personnel Management Association
IMP-BL	International MARC Project - British Library
IMP-DB	International MARC Project - Deutsche Bibliothek
IMPRESS	Interdisciplinary Machine Processing for Research and Education in Social Sciences (Dartmouth College, N.H.)
IMPRINT	Imbricated Program for Information Transfer
IMRADS	Information Management, Retrieval and Dissemination System
IMS (1)	Information Management System
IMS (2)	Instructional Management System
IMSA	International Management Systems Association (now Internet-International Management Systems Association)
IMSL	International Mathematical and Statistical Library
IMULS	Intermountain Union List of Serials (Hayden Library, Arizona State University)
INB	Indian National Bibliography
INCINC	International Copyright Information Center (Franklin Book Programs Inc., U.S.)
INCIRS	International Communication Information Retrieval System (Florida University)
INCLUDE	Implementing New Concepts of the Library for Urban Disadvantaged Ethnics (Cleveland Public Library, U.S.)
INCOGT	Institute for New Computer Generation Technology (also known as ICOT)
INCOLSA	Indiana Cooperative Library Services Authority
INC's	(Local) Information Network Centers (a plan of Massachusetts Board of Library Commissioners)
IndAct	Index de l'Actualité
INDIRS	Indiana Information Retrieval System

INDIS   Industrial Information System (United Nations Industrial Development Organization)

INEL   International Network of Emerging Libraries (U.S.)

iNET   Intellegent Network (a cooperative project involving several Canadian institutions, coordinated by NLC and mounted by the Computer Communications Group of the Trans Canada Telephone System)

INFAS   Institut für Angewandte Sozialwissenschaft (Institut for Applied Social Sciences in Bonn, W. Germany)

INFCO   Information Committee (of ISO (2))

INFO/DOC   (a source of U.S. Government publications, documents, and reports - Washington, D.C.)

INFOL   Information Oriented Language (of CDC (2))

INFONET   Information Network

INFORMS   Information Organization Reporting and Management System

INFOSERV   (Faxon's online database of new serial titles)

INFOTERM   International Information Centre for Terminology (Vienna, Austria)

INFRAL   Information Retrieval Automatic Language (programming language)

INFROSS   Information Requirements of the Social Science (U.K.)

INFUT   Information Utility (project) (Case Western Reserve University, U.S.)

INI   Institute Nazionale de l'Informazione (National Institute of Information, Italy)

INIBON   Institut Nacnoj Informacii i Fundamental'naja Biblioteka po Obsscestvennym Naukam (Institute of Scientific Information and Main Library of the Social Sciences, U.S.S.R.)

INII   Italian National Information Institute

INION   Institut Naučnoj Informacii po Obščestvennym Naukam Akademii Nauk S.S.S.R. (Institute of Scientific Information on Social Sciences of the U.S.S.R. Academy of Science, Moscow)

INIS   International Nuclear Information System (of International Atomic Energy Agency, Vienna, Austria)

INKA	Informationszentrum Karlsruhe (Information Centre Karlsruhe)
INLE	Instituto Nacional del Libro Espanol (Spain)
INNOVACQ	(multi-processor, micromomputer-based acquisitions system developed by Innovative Interfaces of Berkeley, Calif., utilized by UTLAS Inc.)
INP	In-process
INPADOC	International Patent Documentation Centre
INRDG	Institut National de Recherches et de Documentation (Guinea)
INRS	Institut National de Recherche Scientifique (Quebec)
INSAF	Interim Name Source Authority File (of UTLAS Inc., later became SHARAF)
INSDOC	Indian National Scientific Documentation Centre (India)
INSEE	Institut National de la Statistique et des Études Économiques (France)
INSERM	Institut National de la Santé et de la Recherche Medicale (France)
INSPEC	Information Service for the Physics and Engineering Communities (U.K.)
INSPEL	International Newsletter of Special Libraries (of IFLA)
INSTARS	Information Storage and Retrieval Systems
INTAMEL	International Association of Metropolitan City Libraries (U.K.)
INTD	Institut National de Techniques de la Documentation (France; also known as AINTD)
INTECH	Integrated Technologies (U.S.)
INTELSAT	International Telecommunications Satellite Consortium (U.S.)
INTERLIB	(governmental libraries cooperative (U.K.))
INTER MARC	International MARC
INTIME	Interactive Textual Information Management Experiment (of IBM)
INTREX	Information Transfer Experiments (of MIT)

INWATS	Inward Wide Area Telephone Service
I/O	Input/Output (computer term)
IOB	Inter-Organization Board for Information Systems and Related Activities (of U.N.)
IOCS	Input-Output Control System (computer term)
IOD	Information on Demand, Inc. (Berkeley, Calif.)
IOL	Institute of Librarians (India)
IOLS	Integrated Online Library Systems
IOM	Institute of Office Management
IOP (1)	Input-Output Processor (computer term)
IOP (2)	Institute of Printing (U.K.)
IPA (1)	Information Planning Associates Inc. (U.S.)
IPA (2)	Information Processing Architecture
IPA (3)	Information Processing Association (Israel)
IPA (4)	International Pharmaceutical Abstracts (publication)
IPA (5)	International Publishers Association
IPAD	Integrated Program for Aerospace-Vehicle Design
IPAHGEIS	Inter-Professional Ad Hoc Group for Environmental Information Sharing (U.S.; now GLEIS)
IPARA	International Publishers Advertising Representatives Association (U.K.)
IPC (1)	Information Processing Code
IPC (2)	International Patent Classification
IPDA	International Periodical Distributors Association
IPFW	Indiana University-Purdue University at Fort Wayne
IPG	Information Policy Group (of OECD)
IPI (1)	Ikatan Pustakawan Indonesia (Indonesian Library Associ Association)
IPI (2)	International Press Institute
IPI/MIS	International Press Institute/Management and Information System

IPL	Information Processing Language
IPLO	Institute of Professional Librarians of Ontario (ceased)
IPL-V	Information Processing Language V
IPPEC	Inventaire Permanent des Périodiques Étrangers en Cours (Union catalogue of current foreign periodicals, France)
IPS (1)	Information Providers (organization in U.K., provides information on Prestel: Videotex Service)
IPS (2)	International Publications Service
IPSJ	Information Processing Society of Japan
IPTC	International Press Telecommunications Committee (U.K.)
IQ	InfoQuest (of UTLAS Inc.; a microcomputer-based online public access catalogue for small libraries, operating on IBM-PC)
IQCC	Internetwork Quality Control Council (of OCLC Inc.)
I & R (1)	Information and Referral (Services, U.S.)
IR (2)	Information Retrieval
IRA	International Reading Association
IRADES	Istituto Ricerche Applicate Documentazione e Studi (Italy)
IRANDOC	Iranian Documentation Centre
IRAS	Information Retrieval Advisory Services Ltd. (U.K.)
IRC	International Relations Committee (of ALA)
IRCS	International Research Communications System (U.K.)
IRE	Institute of Radio Engineers
IREBI	Indice de Revistas de Bibliotecologia (Spain and Argentina)
IRFs	Information Retrieval Facilities (of CCBCS)
IRG	Inter-Record Gap (computer term)
IRGMA	Information Retrieval Group of the Museums Association (U.K.)

IRIA (1)	Infra Red Information Analysis (Center) (Michigan University)
IRIA (2)	Institute de Recherche d'Informatique et d'Automatique/ d'Automatisme (France)
IRIS (1)	Institute's Retrieval-of-Information Study (of OISE)
IRIS (2)	International Research Information Service (American Foundation for the Blind)
IRL	Information Retrieval Language or Index Retrieval Language
IRLA (1)	Independent Research Libraries Association (U.S.)
IRLA (2)	Information Retrieval and Library Automation (Lomond Systems Inc., U.S.)
IRLBPH	Illinois Regional Library for the Blind and Physically Handicapped
IRLC	Illinois Regional Library Council
IRMA	Information Revision and Manuscript Assembly
IRMS	Information Retrieval and Management System (of IBM)
IRO	International Relations Office (of ALA)
IRON	Information Resources of Nevada (publication)
IROS	Instant Response Ordering System (of Bro-Dart, Inc.)
IRP (1)	Information Resources Press (U.S.)
IRP (2)	Institut de Recherches Politiques
IRPP	Institute for Research on Public Policy
IRRD	International Road Research Documentation (of OECD; also known as DIRR)
IRRL	Information Retrieval Research Laboratory (of Univ. of Illinois)
IRRT	International Relations Round Table (of ALA)
IRS (1)	Information Retrieval Service/System
IRS (2)	Internal Revenue Service (U.S.)
IRS (3)	International Referral System (U.N.'s Environmental Programme)
IRSC	International Research Society for Children

IRT	Institute of Reprographic Technology
IRUC	Information and Research Utilization Center (in Physical Education and Recreation for the Handicapped, U.S.)
ISA (1)	Information Science Abstracts (publication)
ISA (2)	Information Services Association (U.K.)
ISA (3)	International Federation of National Standardizing Association
ISA (4)	International Standards Association
ISA (5)	Irregular Serials and Annuals (publication)
ISAD	Information Science and Automation Division (of ALA; now LITA)
ISAM	Index Sequential Access Matter/Method
ISAN	International Standard Authority Numbers
ISAR	Information Storage and Retrieval
ISAS	Information Science and Automation Section (of LITA)
ISBD	International Standard Bibliographical Description
ISBD (A)	ISBD for Antiquarian Books
ISBD (A/V)	ISBD for Audiovisual Materials
ISBD (CM)	ISBD for Cartographic Materials
ISBD (CP)	ISBD for Component Parts
ISBD (G)	ISBD - General
ISBD (M)	ISBD for Monographic Publications
ISBD (MRF)	ISBD for Machine-readable Files
ISBD (NBM)	ISBD for Non-Book Materials
ISBD (PM)	ISBD for Printed Music
ISBD (S)	ISBD for Serials
ISBN	International Standard Book Number
ISBS	International Scholarly Book Services (U.S.)

ISCED   International Standard Classification of Education
            (Unesco) (also known as ICSED)

ISCF   International Standard Control Form

ISCG   Information Services Coordinating Group (of CLA)

ISCI   Information Systems Consultants, Inc. (Bethesda, Md.)

ISCU   International Council of Scientific Unions

ISD   Information Services Division (of Honeywell Corp.)

ISDG   Information Science Discussion Group (U.K.)

ISDS   International Serials Data System (of UNISIST)

ISDS-IC   ISDS - International Centre (Unesco) (also known as
            CIEPS)

ISER   Institute of Social and Economic Research (U.S.)

ISFL   International Scientific Film Library (Belgium)

ISI (1)   Indian Standards Institution

ISI (2)   Information Sciences Institute (Southern California
            University)

ISI (3)   Institute for Scientific Information (U.S.)

ISI (4)   Israel Standards Institute

ISIC   International Standard Industrial Classification (of U.N.)

ISIN   Indiana Seminar on Information Networks (held 1971)

ISIP   Internacionalna Stalna Ižlozba Publikacija (International
            Permanent Exhibition of Publications, Zagreb University,
            Yugoslavia)

ISIRI   Institute of Standards and Industrial Research of Iran

ISIS (1)   Integrated Set of Information Systems (also known as
            Integrated Scientific Information Systems, ILO)

ISIS (2)   International Science Information Service (U.S.)

ISLA   Iowa Small Libraries Association

ISLIC   Israel Society of Special Libraries and Information
            Centres (also known as ASMI)

ISLT   Information Science Languages Test (College of Librarian-
            ship, Wales)

ISMEC	Information Services in Mechanical Engineering (Institute of Electrical Engineers, U.K.)
ISO (1)	Information Systems Office (of LC)
ISO (2)	International Standards Organization (also called International Organization for Standardization)
ISODATA	Iterative Self-Organizing Data Analysis Technique
ISODOC	International Centre for Standards in Information and Documentation (of ISO (2))
ISONET	ISO Information Network (of ISO (2))
ISORID	International Information System on Research in Documentation (Unesco)
ISO/TC	International Organization for Standardization/Technical Committee (Geneva, Switzerland)
ISPL	Instruction Set Processor Language (computer language)
ISPs	Information Service Providers (participants in the iNET Trials)
ISR (1)	Index to Scientific Reviews (of ISI (3))
ISR (2)	Information Storage and Retrieval
ISRD	Information Storage, Retrieval and Dissemination
ISRS	Information Storage and Retrieval Systems
ISS	Information Systems Specialists Office (of LC)
ISSC	International Social Science Council (Paris, France)
ISSMB	Information Systems Standards Management Board
ISSN	International Standard Serial Number
IST	Industrielle - Services Techniques, Inc. (a firm with whom UTLAS Inc. is negotiating agreement for services in Quebec)
ISTA	Information Sciences, Technologies and Activities
ISTC	Institute of Scientific and Technical Communicators (U.K.)
ISTIC	Institute of Scientific and Technical Information of China (Beijing)
ISTIM	Interchange of Scientific and Technical Information in Machine Language

IS & TP	Index to Scientific and Technological Proceedings
ISVD	Information System for Vocational Decisions (Harvard University, U.S.)
IT	Internal Translator (computer term)
ITAC	International Target Audience Code (of IFLA)
ITAL	Information Technology and Libraries (periodical of LITA; previously known as JOLA)
ITCA	Inter-American Technical Council of Archives
ITE	Institute of Telecommunications Engineers
ITF	Interactive Terminal Facility (computer term)
ITI	Information Transform Industries (newly formed consulting firms at California)
ITIRC	IBM Technical Information Retrieval Centre (of IBM)
ITSS	International Travelling Summer School (of AAL)
ITT	International Telephone and Telegraph Corp. (U.S.)
ITU	International Telecommunications Union
ITVA	International Television Association
IUBP	Inter-University Borrowing Project (of OULCS: also called Inter-University Borrowing Plan)
IUC	Interuniversity Council (of North Texas area)
IUL (1)	Indiana University Libraries
IUL (2)	Information Utilization Laboratory (Pittsburgh University)
IUPUI	Indiana University - Purdue University at Indianapolis
IUS	Information Unlimited Software
IUTS	Inter-University Transit System (Inter-library loan service between a number of universities in Ontario)
IVLS	Illinois Valley Library System
IVM) IVMB)	Internationale Vereinigung der Musikbibliotheken (also known as AIBM, IAML)
IWG	International Writers' Guild

IWP	International Word Processing Association (U.S.; also known as IWPA)
IWPA	International Word Processing Association (U.S.: also known as IWP)
IWWG	International Women's Writing Guild (U.S.)
IWY	International Women's Year
IYC	International Year of the Child
IYDP	International Year of Disabled Persons (1981)
IYL	International Youth Library
IZI	Internationales Zentralinstitut für das Jugend-und Bildungsfernsehen
J	Joule (SI) (energy, work, quantity of heat)
JAALD	Japanese Association of Agricultural Librarians and Documentalists (Japan)
JAC	Joint Advisory Committee (on Non-book materials, composed of representatives from ALA, CLA, AECT and the Education Media Association of Canada)
JACKPHY	Japanese, Arabic, Chinese, Korean, Persian, Hebrew, and Yiddish (minimal-level cataloguing at LC)
JACS	Journal Article Copy Service (of NTIS)
JAKIS	Japanese Keyword Indexing Simulation
JAL	Journal of Academic Librarianship
JALA	Joint Acquisitions List for Africana (Bimonthly, of Herskovits Library of African Studies)
JAMA	Journal of the American Medical Association
JAMAL	Jamaican Movement for the Advancement of Literacy
JAMASS	Japanese Medical Abstract Scanning System (International Medical Information Centre, Japan)
JANET	Just Another Network (of Univ. of Waterloo, Ont.)
JANUS	(a new programme to provide searching of the MARC database)
JAS	Journal Access Service (of CRL (1))

JASIS	Journal of the American Society of Information Science
JBI	Jugoslovenski Bibliografiski Institut (Yugoslav Bibliographic Institute, Yugoslavia)
JCAH	Joint Commission on the Accreditation of Hospitals
JCCC	Joint Committee on Cataloging and Classification Codes (also known as CNLIA/JCCC)
JCCPI	Joint Committee on Copyright Practice and Implementation (also known as CNLIA/JCCPI)
JCEB	Joint Council on Educational Broadcasting (now JCET)
JCET	Joint Council on Educational Telecommunications (U.S.; formerly JCEB)
JCIT	Jerusalem Conference on Information Technology (1971)
JCL	Job-Control Language (programming language)
JCLS	Junior College Libraries Section (of ACRL)
JCMST	Journal of Computers in Mathematics and Science Teaching
JCP	Joint Committee on Printing (of U.S. Congress)
JCR	Journal Citation Reports (of ISI)
JCTND	Jugoslovenski Centar za Tehničku i Naučno Dokumentaciju (Yugoslavia)
JCULS	Joint Committee on the Union List of Serials (sponsored by NLC)
JDS	Job Diagnostic Survey
JEIPAC	JICST Electronic Information Processing Automatic Computer (Japan Information Centre of Science and Technology)
JEL	Journal of Education for Librarianship
JERK	Journal of Easily Repressed Knowledge
JGE	Journal of General Education
JIBF	Jerusalem International Book Fair
JICST	Japan Information Centre of Science and Technology (Nihon Kagaku Gizyutu Zyoho Senta)
JICTAR	Joint Industry Committee for Television Advertising Research (U.K.)

JIS	Japanese Industrial Standard
JLA (1)	Jamaica Library Association
JLA (2)	Japan Library Association
JLA (3)	Jewish Librarians Association
JLA (4)	Jordan Library Association
JLH	Journal of Library History
JMRT	Junior Members Round Table (of ALA)
JNUL	Jewish National and University Library (Israel)
JOIN	Journals Online Interactive Network (educational package of AHEC)
JOLA	Journal of Library Automation (of ISAD; now ITAL)
Joss	JOHNNIAC Open Shop System (computer language)
Jovial	Jules Own Version of International Algebraic Language (computer language)
JPRS	Joint Publications Research Service (U.S.)
JPTC	Japan Publications Trading Company
JSA	Japanese Standards Association (Japan)
JSC	Joint Steering Committee (of AACR II)
JSCAACR	Joint Steering Committee for Revision of the Anglo-American Cataguing Rules
JSCLCBS	Joint Standing Committee on Library Cooperation and Bibliographic Services (of Library Associations of Malaysia and Singapore)
JSLS	Japan Society of Library Science
JUBIUNA) JUBUNA)	Junta de Bibliotecas Universitarias Nacionales Argentinas (Argentina)
JUL	Joint University Libraries (in Tenn., defunct)
JUPCON	Jos University Planning Consultants (Nigeria)
JURIS (1)	Justice Retrieval and Inquiry System (Dept. of Justice, U.S.)
JURIS (2)	Juristisches Informationssystem (Judicial Information System, Bonn, W. Germany)

K (1)	Kelvin (SI) (thermodynamic temperature)
K (2)	Kilo
K (3)	1,000 or 1,024 (=2^{10}) (refers to computer storage capacity)
KASC	Knowledge Availability Systems Center (Pittsburgh University, U.S.)
Kb (1)	Kilobit (10^3 bits)
KB (2)	Kilobyte (10^3 bytes)
KBF	Kommunale Bibliotekarers Forening (Municipal Librarians Association, Norway)
Kc (1)	Kilocycle
KC (2)	Kyle Classification
KCLA	Kerala College Librarians' Association (India)
KCLS	King County Library System (Seattle, Wash.)
KCPL	Kansas City Public Library
KDEM	Kurzweil Data Entry Machine
KENCLIP	Kentucky Cooperative Library Information Project
KETAL	Kalamazoo (et al.) Library Consortium (Mich.)
Kg	Kilogram (Metric) = 1,000 g
KGCLIS	Kentucky Governor's Conference on Libraries and Information Services
KHz	Kilohertz (10^3 cycles/sec)
KIC	Kansas Information Circuit (consortium, Kansas State Library)
KINKLE	(The Complete Encyclopedia of Popular Music and Jazz, 1900-1950)
KIP	Knowledge Industry Publications (also known as KIPI)
KIPI	Knowledge Industry Publications Inc. (U.S.; also known as KIP)
KISS	Keep It Simple Sir/Stupid
KIT	Key Issues Tracing System (a current affairs database created from the New York Times and other publications)

KKL	Kirjastonhoitajien Keskusliitto - Bibliotekariernas Centralförbund r.y.(Central Federation of Librarians, Finland)
Kl	Kilolitre (Metric) = 1,000 l
KLA (1)	Kansas Library Association
KLA (2)	Karachi Library Association (Pakistan)
KLA (3)	Korean Library Association (South Korea; also known as Tohyop)
KLIC	Key Letter in Context
KLSS	Korean Library Science Society (also known as KLOSS)
km	Kilometre (Metric) = 1,000 m
KMK	Könyvtártudományi és Módszertani Központ (Centre for Library Science and Methodology, National Széchenyi Library, Hungary)
KNB	Kenya National Bibliography
KNLS	Kenya National Library Service
KNOGO/ALS	(a library theft detection system combining automated circulation control developed by Knogo Corp., Hicksville, N.Y.)
KOLSS	Korean Library Science Society (also known as KLSS)
KOMRML	Kentucky, Ohio, Michigan Regional Medical Library
KORSTIC	Korean Scientific and Technological Information Centre
KPIC	Key Phrase in Context
KRI	King Research Inc. (U.S.)
KRM (1)	Kids' Riddle Month (in Portland, Ore.)
KRM (2)	Kurzweil Reading Machine (device manufactured by Kurzweil Computer Company, Cambridge, Mass. which turns print into synthesized speech)
KRN	Knight-Ridder Newspapers, Inc.
KS	Kent Study (of cost-benefit model of some critical library operations)
KSR	Keyboard Send-Receive (computer term)
KSU	Kansas State University

KTHB	Kungliga Tekniska Högskolans Bibliotek (Royal Institute of Technology Library, Sweden)
KULSAA	Karachi University Library Science Alumni Association (Pakistan)
KW	Kilowatt (10^3 watts)
KWAC	Key Word and Context
KWADE	Keyword as a Dictionary Entry (of IBM)
KWIC	Key Word in Context
KWINDEX	Key Word Index (Golden Gate Systems, U.S.)
KWIP	Key Word in Permutation
KWIT	Key Word in Title
KWOC	Key Word Out of Context
KWOT	Key Word Out of Title
KWUC	Keyword and Universal Decimal Classification
l	Litre (Metric) = 1,000 ml
LA (1)	Library Association (formerly LAUK)
LA (2)	Library Automation
LAA (1)	Library Assistants' Association (U.K.; now AAL)
LAA (2)	Library Association of Alberta
LAA (3)	Library Association of Australia (previously AIL (2))
LAB	Library Association of Barbados
LA/BL	Library Association/British Library Committee (of AACR2)
LAC (1)	Library Advisory Council (Dept. of Education and Science, U.K.)
LAC (2)	Library Association of China (Taiwan)
LACAP	Latin American Cooperative Acquisitions Project
LACASIS	Los Angeles Chapter of ASIS
LACOIN	Lowell Area Council on Inter Library Networks (Mass.)

LACoPL	Los Angeles County Public Library (System)
LACPL	Los Angeles County Public Library
(LA)CUNY	City University of New York Librarians Association (also called Library Association of the City University of New York)
LAD	**Library Administration Division** (of ALA; now LAMA)
LADG	Library Automation Discussion Group
LADLE	Librarians' Anti-Defamation League (U.K.)
LADSIRLAC	Liverpool and District Scientific, Industrial and Research Library Advisory Council (U.K.)
LAG (1)	Librarians' Automation Group (Australia)
LAG (2)	Library Action Group (U.K.)
LAI	Library Association of Ireland (Cumann Leabharlann na h Eireann)
LAIS	Library Acquisitions Information System (Library Automation, Research and Consulting Association, U.S.)
LAL	Latin American Library (of Oakland Public Library)
LALR	Lookahead LR (Left-to-Right, Rightmost) (computer term)
LALS	Libraries and the Learning Society (of ACRL)
LAMA	Library Administration and Management Association (of ALA; previously LAD)
LAMA BES	LAMA Buildings and Equipment Section
LAMA CCS	LAMA Circulation Services Section
LAMA LOMS	LAMA Library Organization and Management Section
LAMA PAS	LAMA Personnel Administration Section
LAMA PRS	LAMA Public Relations Section
LAMA SASS	LAMA Systems and Services Section
LAMA SS	LAMA Statistics Section
LAMBDA	Local Access to and Management of Bibliographic Data and Acquisitions System (of SOLINET)
LAMP (1)	Library Additions and Maintenance Program (of Honeywell Corp.)

LAMP (2)   Library Resources in Literature, Art, Music, Philosophy
            (Jackson State College, U.S.)

LAMP (3)   Literature Analysis of Microcomputer Publications
            (periodical)

LAMSAC   Local Authorities Management Services and Computer
            Committee (U.K.)

LAN   Local Area Network

LANAC   Lawyers Alliance for Nuclear Arms Control, Inc. (U.S.)

LANCET   Library Association National Council for Educational
            Technology (U.K.)

LANS   Local Area Networks

LAO   Library Association of Ottawa (also known as ABO (2))

LAOSA   Librarianship and Archives Old Students' Association
            (London University, U.K.)

LAPC   Library Automation Planning Committee (of the Library
            Association of China)

LAPL (1)   Library Association Publishing Ltd. (U.K.)

LAPL (2)   Los Angeles Public Library

LAPT   Library Acquisitions: Practice and Theory (periodical)

LAQ   Library Administration Quarterly

LAR (1)   Library Association Record (U.K.)

LAR (2)   Linear Associative Retrieval

LARC (1)   Library Automatic Recognition Computer

LARC (2)   Library Automation Research and Consulting Association
            (U.S.; now Library Information Science Division of the
            World of Information Systems Exchange)

LARC (3)   Library Automation Research Communications Association
            (merged with WISE)

LARC (4)   Livermore Automatic Research Computer

LARITA   Lewis Audiovisual Research Institute and Teaching
            Archive (Univ. of Arizona)

LARSIS   Library Association Reference, Special and Information
            Section (U.K.)

LAS (1)	Library Access System (of IBM)
LAS (2)	Library Association of Singapore (also known as PPS)
LASER (1)	Light Amplification by Stimulated Emission of Radiation
LASER (2)	London and South Eastern Library Region (U.K.; formerly SERB, SERLB and LUC)
LASERCAT	(a videodisk data storage system providing links between CLSI and UTLAS Inc.)
LASIE	Library Automated Systems Information Exchange (Australia)
LASL (1)	London Association of Special Librarians (Ont.)
LASL (2)	Louisiana Association of School Librarians
LASL Library	Los Alamos (N.M.) Scientific Laboratory Library
LASP	Linked Authority System Project (a cooperative project funded by Council on Library Resources to implement a shared LC, RLG and WLN authority files)
LASRG	Library Association Sound Recordings Group (U.K.; now Audiovisual Group) (also known as SRG)
LASSA	Learning and Study Skills Association (Ont.)
LASSOS	Library Automation System and Services Options Study (of R & D)
LATT	Library Association of Trinadad and Tobago
LAUK	Library Association of the United Kingdom (now LA (1))
LAVC	Los Angeles Valley College
LAWNET	Law Network (of Univ. of Florida Law Library)
LB	Line Buffer (computer term)
LBDQ	Leader Behavior Description Questionnaire
LBI	Library Binding Institute (U.S.)
LBPL	Long Beach Public Library
LC	Library of Congress (U.S.)
LCA	Library Club of America (ceased)

LCB	Line Control Block (computer term)
LCC	Library of Congress Classification
LCCC	Library of Congress Computer Catalog
LCCN	Library of Congress Catalog Card Number
LCD (1)	Library of Congress' Depository Cards
LCD (2)	Liquid Crystal Display (computer term)
LCD (3)	List of Chosen Descriptors
LCF	Librarians' Christian Fellowship (U.K.)
LC/FARA	Folklife and Ethnolomusicology Archives and Related Collections in the United States and Canada (of LC)
LCGC	Library Council of Greater Cleveland
LCIB	Library of Congress Information Bulletin
LCLA	Lutheran Church Library Association
LCME	Liaison Committee on Medical Education (to accredit U.S. and Canadian Medical Schools)
LCMS	Library Collection Management System (of UTLAS Inc. introduced in 1979, now ceased)
LCNHWR	Library of Congress Name Headings with Reference
LC-NRC	Library of Congress - National Referral Center (for Science and Technology)
LCOMM	Library Council of Metropolitan Milwaukee
LCPA	Library of Congress Professional Association
LCRI	Library of Congress Rule Interpretations (of AACR II)
LCS (1)	Library Collection Service (of TSI)
LCS (2)	Library Control/Computer System (of Univ. of Illinois)
LCS (3)	Library Control System (OSU's computerized circulation system)
LCSH	Library of Congress Subject Headings
LD	Livres Disponibles (French books in print)
LDC (1)	Library Development Consultants (Washington, D.C.)

LDC (2)	Library Documentation Centre
LDMS	Library Data Management System (of Univ. of Chicago Library)
LDTF	Local Documents Task Force (of GODORT)
LDX	Long Distance Xerox
LEADER	Lehigh Automatic Device for Efficient Retrieval (Lehigh University, U.S.)
LEADS (1)	Library Employment and Development for Staff (job advertisements in American Libraries (periodical))
LEADS (2)	Library Experimental Automated Demonstration System (Or.)
LEAP	Library Exchange Aids Patrons (a cooperative program of libraries in Connecticut)
LEARN	Librarians in Education and Research in the Northeast (U.S.)
LED (1)	Library Education Division (of ALA; now SCOLE)
LED (2)	Light-Emitting Diode
LEEP	Library Education Experimental Project (Syracuse University, U.S.)
LEG	Library Education Group (of LA(1))
LENDS	Library Extends Catalog Access and New Delivery System (of Georgia Institute of Technology)
LEPU	Library Education and Personnel Utilization (of ALA)
LERLS	Lake Erie Regional Library System
LERO	Library Environmental Resource Office (of LC)
LES	Library Education Section (of CLA (4))
LETIS	Leicestershire Technical Information Service (U.K.)
LEXIS	(an on-line legal text storage system of Mead Technology Laboratories, N.Y.)
LF	Low Frequency
LFPL	Louisville Free Public Library
LGIO	Local Government Information Office (U.K.)
LHF	Library Holdings Format (of UTLAS Inc.)

LHNC) LHNCBC)	Lister Hill National Center for Biomedical Communications (of NLM)
LHRT	Library History Round Table (of ALA)
LHS	Library History Seminar
LHTN	Library Hi Tech News (periodical)
LIAS (1)	Library Automation with an Integrated Design
LIAS (2)	Library Information Access System (Pennsylvania State University Libraries)
LIB CAT	Library Catalog (software)
LIBCON	Library of Congress (usually refers to LIBCON database)
LIBER	Ligue des Bibliothèques Européennes de Recherche (European Association of Research Libraries)
LIBEX	Bureau for International Library Staff Exchange (a three year experiment in coordinating library exchanges between Britain and U.S., Canada, France and Federal Republic of Germany, program of British Library Association)
LIBGIS	Library General Information Survey (of NCES)
LIBIS	Leuvens Integraal Bibliotheek Systeem (of Leuven Library in Belgium)
LIBLIT	Library Literature (periodical)
LIBNAT	Library Network Analysis Theory (of TLA (2))
LIBRIS (1)	Library Information Service (of Baker & Taylor Co.)
LIBRIS (2)	Library Information System (National Online Computer System, Sweden)
LIBRUNAM	(pilot system implemented by CONACYT for multinational transfer of bibliographic information)
LIBSAC	(Australian-based integrated system, utilized at Acadia University, Wolfville, N.S.)
LIBSAC/PAM	LIBSAC Public Access Method (Acadia University, Wolfville, N.S. - online catalogue)
LIB SIM	Library Simulation Model (Wayne State University, U.S.)
LIBTRAD	Library and Book Trade Relations Working Party (U.K.)
LICOSH	Library of Congress Subject Headings (database)

LIFO	Last-in-First-out (computer term)
LILIBU	Lista de Libros para Bibliotecas Universitarias (Select list of Latin American university libraries)
LILMIG	Library & Information Literature Membership Initiative Group (of ALA)
LILRC	Long Island Library Resources Council (U.S.)
LINC (1)	Libraries for Nursing Consortium (Boston, Mass.)
LINC (2)	(Memphis' I & R Service)
LINCS	Language Information Network Clearinghouse System (U.S.)
LINGUA	Linguistic Analysis
Link (1)	(Information and Referral Service in North York, Ont.)
LINK (2)	Lambeth Information Network (U.K.)
LINOSCO	Libraries of North Staffordshire and South Cheshire in Cooperation (U.K.)
LINX	(a network of F.W. Faxon Co.)
LION	Libraries Online Inc. (a network in Conn.)
LIONS	Library Information and Online Network (of N.Y. Public Library; previously SADPO)
LIP	London International Press (U.K.)
LIP Service	Library Instruction Program (for undergraduate students at OSU)
LIRAC	Library and Information Retrieval Applications Centre
LIRES-MC	Literature Retrieval System, Multiple Searching - Complete Text (Institute of Paper Chemistry, U.S.)
LIRT	Library Instruction Round Table (of ALA)
LIS (1)	Library and Information Science
LIS (2)	Library Information Service (of Univ. of Illinois Library Research Center)
LIS (3)	Lockheed Information Systems (U.S.)
LISA (1)	Library and Information Science Abstracts (of LA (1) and Aslib)
LISA (2)	Library Information Systems Analysis

LISA (3)	Local Integrated Software Architecture
LISDA	Library and Information Services Development Act (previously LSCA)
LISE	Libraries of the Institutes and Schools of Education (U.K.)
LISI	Library Interface Systems Inc. (U.S.)
LIS/MEX	Library and Information Science Meetings Exchange (of Massachusetts Bureau of Library Extention)
Lisp	List Processing (computer language)
LIS/PX	Library and Information Service Program Exchange (of GLIS, Univ. of Arizona)
LISR	Line Information Storage and Retrieval (of NASA)
LISSA	Librarians Serving San Antonio (Tex.)
LISST	Library and Information Science Scholarship Today (Maryland University, U.S.; now LIST (1))
LIST (1)	Library and Information Science Today (periodical; previously LISST)
LIST (2)	Library Information Service for Teesside (Middlesbrough, U.K.)
LISTS	Library Information System Time-sharing
LITA	Library Information and Technology Association (of ALA; formerly ISAD)
LITA AVS	LITA Audiovisual Section
LITA ISAS	LITA Information Science and Automation Section
LITA VCCS	LITA Video and Cable Communications Section
LITE	Legal Information Through Electronics (of NAL)
LIV	Legislative Indexing Vocabulary (of LC)
LJ	Library Journal (periodical)
LL	Library Literature (periodical)
LLA (1)	Lebanese Library Association (Lebanon)
LLA (2)	Louisiana Library Association
LLBA	Language and Language Behavior Abstracts (publication)

LLC	Lakeland Library Cooperative (Grand Rapids, Mich.)
LLCUNAE	Law Library of Congress United Association of Employees
LLE	Leadership in Library Education (of School of Library Science, Florida State University)
LLI	Laubach Literacy International
LLJ	Law Library Journal
LLS	Local Library System (of OCLC Inc.)
LLU	Lending Library Unit (Dept. of Scientific and Industrial Research, U.K.) (later NLLST and NLL; now BLLD)
lm	Lumen (SI) (luminous flux)
lmp (1)	Lines per Minute (computer term)
LMP (2)	Literary Market Place (publication, R.R. Bowker Co.)
LMPIC	Library Materials Price Index Committee (of RTSD RS)
LMRU (1)	Library Management Research Unit (Loughborough University of Technology, Loughborough, U.K.)
LMRU (2)	Library Management Research Unit (Univ. of Cambridge, U.K.; also known as CMU)
LMS	Library Micrographic Services Inc., U.S.)
LMTA	Library/Media Technical Assistants
LNAC	Librarians for Nuclear Arms Control (U.S.)
LNR	Louisiana Numerical Register (a computer produced catalogue)
LNUGs	Library Network User Groups (of CCBCS)
LOCAS	Local Catalogue Service (of BLAISE)
LOCATE	Library of Congress Automation Techniques Exchange
LOCIS	Library of Congress Information System
LOCNET	Libraries of Orange County Network (Calif.)
LODES	Library On-line Data Entry System (used by UTLAS Inc.)
LOEX	Library Orientation Exchange (network, U.S.)
LOGO	(a computer language, designed specifically for educational purposes)

LOIS (1)   Library Order Information System (of LC)

LOIS (2)   Library Order Information System (of Northwestern University)

LOLA   Library On-line Acquisitions (Washington State University)

LOLITA   Library On-line Information and Text Access (Oregon State University)

LOMS   Library Organization and Management Section (of LAMA)

LONSEC   London and South East Branch of CTFE Section (of LA (1))

LOOP   Library Operated Outreach Program (U.S.)

LOPAC   Liaison of Provincial Associations Committee

LORLS   Lake Ontario Regional Library System

LOS   Loss of Signal (computer term)

LOVE   Let Our Values Emerge (an organization)

LP   Linear Programming (computer term)

LPFs   Library Processing Facilities (of CCBCS)

LPL   Lorain Public Library (Ohio)

LPM   Lines per Minute (computer term)

LPP   Library Professional Publications (U.S.)

LPRC   Library Public Relations Council (U.S.)

LPRT   Library Periodicals Round Table (of ALA)

LPSC (1)   Library Planning Study Committee (of Univ. of Wisconsin)

LPSC (2)   Library Publishers of Southern California

LPSS   Law and Political Science Section (of ACRL)

LQ   Library Quarterly

LRACCC   Learning Resources Association of California Community Colleges

LRC (1)   Library Research Center (of Univ. of Illinois)

LRC (2)   Library Resources Centre

LRI   Library Resources, Inc. (a subsidiary of Encyclopaedia Britannica)

LRRS	Library Reports & Research Service, Inc. (U.S.)
LRRT	Library Research Round Table (of ALA)
LRS	Legislative Reference Service (of LC; now CRS)
LRTS	Library Resources and Technical Services (publication of RTSD)
LSA (1)	Library Science Abstracts (now Library and Information Science Abstracts, of LA (1) and Aslib)
LSA (2)	Library Services Act (U.S.)
LSB	Least Significant Bit or Byte (computer term)
LSBPHF	Library Service to the Blind and Physically Handicapped (also known as ASCLA/LSBPHF)
LSBPHS	Library Services to the Blind and Physically Handicapped Section (now ASCLA/LSBPHF)
LSC (1)	Library Collections Services (U.S.)
LSC (2)	Library Science Classification (also known as CLS (2))
LSCA	Library Services and Construction Act (U.S.; now known as LISDA)
LSCG	Literature Searching and Consulting Group (of Tianjin University, China)
LSCU	Library Statistics of Colleges and Universities (U.S.)
LSD (1)	Least Significant Digit (computer term)
LSD (2)	Library Service to the Disadvantaged (of ALA)
LSDS	Library Service to the Deaf Section (of ASCLA)
LSEP	Library Service Enhancement Program (of CLR)
LSG	Local Studies Group (of Reference, Special and Information Section (of LA (1))
LSI	Large-scale Integrated Circuit or Large-scale Integration
LSIES	Library Service to the Impaired Elderly Section (of ASCLA)
LSLA	Leeds School of Librarianship Association (U.K.)
LSP (1)	Library Skills Program (East Organge, New Jersey Public Library, U.S.)
LSP (2)	Library Software Package (of BSD)
LSP (3)	Linked Systems Project (of LC's NACO Project)

LSPS	Library Service to Prisoners Section (of ASCLA)
LSP/SNI	Linked Systems Project/Systems Network Interconnection
LSQA	Local System Queue Area (computer term)
LSSI	Library Systems and Services, Inc. (U.S.)
LSSIG	Library School Students Interest Group (of CLA)
LSU (1)	Library Space Utilization
LSU (2)	Louisiana State University
LT	Library Trends (periodical)
LTA	Library Technical Assistant
LTP	Library Technology Program (formerly Library Technology Project)
LTR	Library Technology Reports (publication of ALA)
LTRS	Letters Shift Character (computer term)
LUC	London Union Catalogue (absorbed into LASER (2))
LUCIS	London University Central Information Services (U.K.)
LUG	LOCAS Users Group (U.S.)
LUIS	Library User Information Service/System (of Northwestern University, U.S.)
LULOP	London Union List of Periodicals (of LASER (2))
LUTFCSUSTC	Librarians United to Fight Costly, Silly Unnecessary Serial Title Changes (defunct)
LV	Laser Optical System
LVA	Literacy Volunteers of America Inc.
LVAHEC	Lehigh Valley Area Health Education Center (library consortium, Pa.)
LVN	Library Video Network (U.S.)
lx	Lux (SI) (illuminance)
M (1)	Mega (1,000,000 or 1,048,576 (=2^{20})) (refers to computer storage capacity)
m (2)	Metre (Metric) = 1,000 mm
M (3)	Milli

M (4)   Millimeter

MA (1)   Masters Abstracts (of UMI)

mA (2)   Milliamp (10^{-3} amp)

MAB (1)   Mail-a-Book

MAB (2)   MARC Application Books (of LC)

MAB (3)   Massachusetts Association for the Blind

MABI   Maschinelles Austauschformat für Bibliotheken, Version I
               (German exchange format - computers)

MAC (1)   Machine Aided Cognition (of MIT)

MAC (2)   Man and Computer

MAC (3)   Multi-Access/Application Computer

MACARS   Microfilm Aperture Card Automated Retrieval System

Macsyma   Project MAC's Symbol Manipulation (computer language)

MACUL   Michigan Association of Computer Users in Learning

Mad   Michigan Algorithm Decoder (computer language)

MAESTRO   Machine-Assisted Educational System for Teaching by
               Remote Operation

MAGB   Microfilm Association of Great Britain (also known as
               MAOGB)

MAGERT   Map and Geography Round Table (of ALA)

MAHSL   Maryland Association of Health Sciences Librarians

MAI   Machine-aided Indexing

MALA   Malawi Library Association

MALC (1)   Madison Area Library Council (Wis.)

MALC (2)   Midwestern Academic Librarians Conference (U.S.)

MALCAP   Maryland Academic Library Center for Automated Processing
               (Maryland University)

MALIMET   Master List of Medical Indexing Terms (Excerpta Medica
               Foundation, Netherlands)

MALLCO   Mid-Atlantic Law Library Cooperative (a cooperative
               among twelve law libraries of Penn., Del. and N.J.)

MAL MARC	Malaysian MARC
MALS	Master of Arts in Library Science
MALT	Manitoba Association of Library Technicians
MAME	Michigan Association for Media in Education
MAMMAX	Machine Made and Machine Aided Index
MANS	Metro Area Networks
MANTIS	Manchester Technical Information Service (U.K.)
MAOGB	Microfilm Association of Great Britain (also known as MAGB)
MAP	Multi-Media Access Project (started in 1979 for resource sharing of audiovisual materials in 18 Illinois multitype library systems)
MAPICS	Morphological Analysis with Parameters Information Coding System
MAR	Memory Address Register (computer term)
MARA	Machine-readable Accession Reporting (of NLC (2))
MARBI	Machine-readable Form of Bibliographic Information (committee of RASD/RTSD/LITA)
MARC	Machine Readable Cataloging (a generic term referring to bibliographic information that has been encoded and transcribed into machine-readable form to permit its manipulation using the technology of electronic data processing)
MARCAL	Latin-American MARC
MARCF	MARC Fiche
MARCIVE	(MARC-based library system at five academic libraries, San Antonio, Tex.)
MARC RECON	MARC Retrospective Conversion (of selected older LC printed cards)
MARC (S)	Machine-readable Cataloguing for Serials
MARLF	Middle Atlantic Regional Library Federation (U.S.)
MARLIB	(an information service based on the Institute of Marine Engineers Library)
MARLIN	Middle Atlantic Research Libraries Information Network

MARML	Mid-Atlantic Regional Medical Library (U.S.)
MARN	Manitoba Association of Registered Nurses
MARS	Machine-Assisted Reference Section (of RASD)
MARSS	Machine-Assisted Reference Services Section (of RASD)
MARVEL	Managing Resources for University Libraries (Univ. of Georgia Library System)
MARVLS) MARVYLS)	MARC and REMARC Videodisc Library System (of International Thomson/Carrollton Press containing MARC, REMARC and LAWMARC databases)
MASIS	Maruzen Scientific Information Service (an information retrieval service for scientific and technical literature, Japan)
MASS (1)	Marc-based Automated Serials System (Birmingham Libraries Cooperative Mechanisation Project and Loughborough University of Technology, U.K.)
MASS (2)	Materials Acquisition Subsystem (of Univ. of Waterloo, Ont.)
MASTIR	Microfilmed Abstract System for Technical Information Retrieval (Illinois Institute of Technology, U.S.)
MATE	Marc Translate and Edit (Yale University Medical Library, U.S.)
MATH-PAC	Mathematical Program (software developed by General Electric Co.)
MATICO	Machine Applications to Technical Information Centre Operations (Lockheed Missiles and Space Co., U.S.)
MAVI	Medical Audio-Visual Institute (of AAMC)
Mb (1)	Megabit (10^6 bits)
MB (2)	Megabyte (10^6 bytes)
mbar	Milibar (10^{-3} bar (cgs units of pressure))
MBI	Maslach Burnout Inventory
MBIP	Medical Books in Print (R.R. Bowker)
MBLC	Massachusetts Board of Library Commissioners
MBM	Magnetic Bubble Memory (computer term)
MBO	Management by Objectives
MBQ	Modified Biquinary Code (computer term)

MBR	Management by Results
MBS	Multilingual Biblioservice (of NLC (2))
Mc	Megacycle (10^6 cycles)
MCA	Microfilming Corporation of America
MCALS	Minnesota Computer Aided Library System (Minnesota University)
MCB	Music Cataloging Bulletin (periodical)
MCC	Multi-channel Communications Control Unit
MCCIC	Model Cities Community Information Center (Philadelphia, Pa.)
MCCLPHEI	Massachusetts Conference of Chief Librarians in Public Higher Educational Institutions
MCFLS	Milwaukee County Federated Library System
MCIC	Metals and Ceramics Information Center (of Columbus Laboratories, Columbus, Ohio)
MCL (1)	Metro Central Library (Toronto, Ont.)
MCL (2)	Movement for Canadian History (established 1978)
MCLS	Metropolitan Cooperative Library System (Pasadena, Calif.)
MCLU	Minnesota Civil Liberties Union
MCP	Master Control Program (computer term)
MCPS	Mechanical Copyright Protection Society (U.K.)
MCR (1)	Master Control Routine (computer term)
MCR (2)	Ministry of Culture and Recreation (Ont.)
MCRMLP	Midcontinental Regional Medical Library Program (U.S.)
MCRR	Machine Check Recording and Recovery (computer term)
MCRS	Micrographic Catalog Retrieval System (of LC)
MCS (1)	Master Control System (computer term)
MCS (2)	Multiple Character Set (of IBM)
MCST	Magnetic Card Selectric Typewriter
MCU	Ministry of Colleges and Universities (Ont.)

MCVF	Multi-channel Voice Frequency
MDC	Machinability Data Center (Cincinati, Ohio)
MDF	Main Distribution Frame (computer term)
MDMLG	Metropolitan Detroit Medical Library Group
MDO	MARC Development Office (of LC)
MDOS	Micropolis Disk Operating System
MDPL	Miami Dade Public Library
MDS (1)	Master Data Structure
MDS (2)	Microprocessor Development System
MDT	Mean Down Time (computer term)
MEC	Media Exchange Cooperative (of BCTF)
MECC	Minnesota Education Computing Consortium
MECCA	Mechanized Cataloguing
MEDCORE	Medical Resources Consortium (of Central New Jersey)
MEDI	Marine Environmental Data Information (of UNESCO)
MEDICAT	Medical Catalog (of LC)
MEDINC	Medical Information for Consumers, Inc. (Chevy Chase, Md.)
MEDLARS	Medical Literature Analysis and Retrieval System (of NLM)
MEDLEARN	Method of Learning Teaching Techniques for Searching on Library Computer (developed by NLM and George Washington University's Office of Computer-Assisted Education and Services to teach techniques in using MEDLINE)
MEDLI	Medical & Scientific Libraries of Long Island (N.Y.)
MEDLINE	MEDLARS On-line (of NLM)
MEDLIT	Medical Literature (Retrieval) (a DIALOG database)
MEET	McGill Elementary Education Teaching Teams (Quebec)
Megaflop	Million Floating-Point Operations per Second (computer term)
MELA	Middle East Librarians Association
MELCOM	Middle Eastern Libraries Committee

MELSA	Metropolitan Library Services Agency (St. Paul, Minn.)
MELVYL	(University of California's nine-campus online public catalogue)
MEMIS	Network Management Information System
MEMO	Minnesota Educational Media Organization
MERC (1)	Media Equipment Resource Center (N.Y.)
MERC (2)	Middle Atlantic Educational and Research Center (Pa.)
MERIP	Middle East Research and Information Project (Cambridge, Mass.)
MERLIN	Machine Readable Library Information (of BSD)
MERMLS	Mid-Eastern Regional Medical Library Service (Pa.)
MeSH	Medical Subject Headings
METADEX	Metals Abstracts Index (of American Society for Metals, Ohio)
METAPLAN	Methods of Extracting Text Automatically Programming Language
METRINS	Metrication Information and Sources (London Borough of Lewisham, U.K.)
METRO	New York Metropolitan Reference and Research Library Agency
METRO/CAP Catalog	Metro's Cooperative Acquisitions Program Catalog
MF (1)	Medium Frequency
MF (2)	Microfiche/Microfilm
MF (3)	Multi-frequency
MFBD	MARC Format for Bibliographic Data
MFLA	Midwest Federation of Library Associations (U.S.)
MFT	Multi-programming with Fixed Number of Tasks (computer term)
mg	Milligram (Metric)
MGA	Meteorological and Geoastrophysical Abstracts (of AMS (2))
MHECB	Minnesota Higher Education Coordinating Board
MHLS	Mid-Hudson Library System (Poughkeepsie, N.Y.)

MHSLN	Midwest Health Sciences Library Network (U.S.)
MHZ	Megahertz (10^6 cycles/sec)
MIBF	Montreal International Book Fair
MIC (1)	Management Information Corp. (N.J.)
MIC (2)	Mechanized Information Center (Ohio State University)
MIC (3)	Medical Information Center (Stockholm)
MICCLE	Michigan Interorganization Committee on Continuing Library Education
MICR	Magnetic Ink Character Reader Recognition
MICRO	Multiple Indexing and Console Retrieval Options (of SDC (2))
MICUA	Maryland Independent Colleges and University Association
MIDAC	Michigan Digital Automatic Computer
MIDAS (1)	Medical Information Dissemination Using ASSASSIN
MIDAS (2)	Multimode International Data Acquisition Service (a satellite communication system that permits Australian libraries to have direct access to commercial online services such as DIALOG and ORBIT)
MIDLNET	Midwest Region Library Network (U.S.)
MIDORI	Modern Information and Documentation Organizing and Rearrangement, Inc. (Japan)
MIG	Membership Initiative Group (of ALA)
MILC (1)	Manchester Inter-Library Cooperative (Manchester City Library, N.H.)
MILC (2)	Midwest Inter-library Center (of CRL (1))
MILCS	Metropolitan Interlibrary Cooperative System (database of NYPL)
MILO (1)	Maryland Interlibrary Organization
MILO (2)	Miami Valley Library Organization
MIMC	Microform International Marketing Corporation (U.S.)
MIMIC	Microfilm Information Master Image Converter
MIMP	Magazine Industry Market Place (publication, R.R. Bowker)

MIMR	Magnetic Ink Mark Recognition
MIMS	Medical Information Management System (of NASA)
MINE	Montana Information Network and Exchange
MINET	Metropolitan Information Network (of Kansas City libraries)
MINI-CATS	Miniaturization of Federal Catalog System Publications (U.S. Dept. of Defense)
MINICS	Minimal Input Cataloguing System
MINISIS	(a minicomputer-based acquisition-cataloguing-information retrieval system developed by the Canadian International Development Research Centre)
MINITEX	Minnesota Interlibrary Telecommunication Exchange
MIPS	Million Instructions Processed per Second (computer term)
MIRABILIS	(a microsystem for interactive bibliographic searching)
MIRACODE	Microfilm Information Retrieval Access Code (Kodak Co.)
MIRPS	Multiple Information Retrieval by Parallel Selection
MIS	Management Information System
MIS-IRPAT	Patent Information Retrieval System (Japan)
MISLIC	Mid-Staffordshire Libraries in Cooperation (U.K.)
MISON	Meždunarodnaja Informacionnaja Sistema po Obščestvennym Naukam (International Social Sciences Information System, Moscow, U.S.S.R.)
MIT	Massachusetts Institute of Technology (U.S.)
MITE	Mycroft Intelligent Terminal Emulator
MITINET	(pronounced mighty-net; a system designed for microcomputers, used by Wisconsin libraries)
MITS (1)	Michigan Information Transfer Source (of Univ. of Michigan)
MITS (2)	Microfiche Image Transmission System
MKE	Magyar Könyvtárosok Egyesülete (Association of Hungarian Librarians)
ml	Millilitres (Metric)
MLA (1)	Maine Library Association

MLA (2)	Malta Library Association
MLA (3)	Manitoba Library Association
MLA (4)	Marine Librarians Association (U.K.)
MLA (5)	Maryland Library Association
MLA (6)	Massachusetts Library Association
MLA (7)	Medical Library Association
MLA (8)	Michigan Library Association
MLA (9)	Minnesota Library Association
MLA (10)	Mississippi Library Association
MLA (11)	Missouri Library Association
MLA (12)	Modern Languages Association (U.S.)
MLA (13)	Montana Library Association
MLA (14)	Music Library Association
MLAA	Medical Library Assistance Act (U.S.)
MLAB	Medical Library Association Bulletin
MLA/CEA	Medical Library Association Continuing Education Activity
MLAN	Music Library Association Notes (periodical)
MLC (1)	Michigan Library Consortium
MLC (2)	Minimal Level Cataloging (at LC)
MLC (3)	Mississippi Library Commission
MLC-NY	Medical Library Center of New York
MLCS	Multitype Library Cooperation Section (of ASCLA)
MLGSCA	Medical Library Groups of Southern California & Arizona
MLIS	Master of Library and Information Studies (of Univ. of Calif. at Berkeley, School of Library and Information Studies)
MLP (1)	Moon Literature Project (Lunar Science Institute, U.S.)
MLP (2)	Machine Language Program
MLS (1)	Machine Literature Searching

MLS (2)	Master of Library Science
MLS (3)	Metropolitan Libraries Section (of PLA (7))
MLS (4)	Microtext Library Services (U.S.)
MLTA (1)	Manitoba Library Trustees' Association
MLTA (2)	Massachusetts Library Trustees Association
MM (1)	Micromedia Ltd.
mm (2)	Millimetre (Metric)
MMIS	Medicaid Management Information System (Ohio)
MMML	Monastic Manuscript Microfilm Library (St. John's Abbey & University of Minnesota)
MMP	Microform Market Place (publication)
MMR	Motorized Microfilm Reader
MMS	Microfiche Management System
MMSC	Metro Multilanguage Services Committee (Toronto)
MMSCS	Meta Micro Serials Control System (San Antonio, Tex.)
MODEM	Modulate-demodulate or Modulator-demodulator (computer term)
MOF	Multiple Order Form
MOL (1)	Machine Oriented Language
mol (2)	Mole (SI) (amount of substance)
MOLDS	Management On-line Data System (Syracuse University, U.S.)
MOLO	Mideastern Ohio Library Organization
MONOCLE	(Project de)Mise en Ordinateur d'une Notice Catalographique de Livre (Processing format based on MARC II and Frech cataloguing practices)
MOP	Multiple On-line Programming
MOS	Metal-Oxide Semiconductor
MOUG	Music OCLC User's Group
MP	Microprocessor

MPA (1)	Magazine Publishers Association Inc. (U.S.)
MPA (2)	Music Publishers Association (U.K.)
MPAA	Motion Picture Association of America
MPDC	Mechanical Properties Data Centre (Mich.)
MPHEC	Maritime Provinces Higher Education Commission (also known as CESPM)
MPI	Monthly Periodical Index (of National Library Services Co., Princeton, N.J.)
MPL (1)	Minneapolis Public Library
MPL (2)	Moline Public Library (Ill.)
MPLA	Mountain-Plains Library Association (U.S.)
MPLIC	Minneapolis Public Library and Information Center
MPMI	Magazine and Paperback Marketing Institute (formerly BIPAD)
MPS	Multi-programming System
MPSX	Mathematical Programming System Extended (computer language)
MPU	Microprocessor Unit
MQ (1)	Minimum qualifications
MQ (2)	Multiplier-Quotient (computer term)
MQR	Multiplier-Quotient Register (computer term)
MR	Microform Review (publication)
MRAP	Management Review and Analysis Program (a study done by Wilbur Cross Library of the Univ. of Connecticut for ARL)
MRB	Microcircuit Reliability Bibliography (a database governed by RADC (2))
MRC	Medical Research Council (also known as CRM)
MRD	Media Review Digest (Pierian Press)
MRDF	Machine-readable Data Files
MRDS	MARC Records Distribution Service (of LC)

MRF (1)	Machine Readable File
MRF (2)	Microform Reference File (of ASIS)
MRIS (1)	Maritime Research Information Service (of National Academy of Sciences, U.S.)
MRIS (2)	Medical Record Information Service (of Univ. of Vermont)
MRLS	Midwestern Regional Library System
MRR	Main Reading Room (of LC)
MS (1)	Manuscript
ms (2)	Milisecond (10^{-3})
MSB	Most Significant Bit or Byte (computer term)
MSC (1)	Management Systems Corporation (of CTI (2))
MSC (2)	Metropolitan Special Collection
MSC (3)	Multistate Centers (established by LC in 1970. Serves as a resource point for books, equipment and supplies for the regional libraries)
MSCM	Multistate Center for the Midlands (a major materials support center for LC Braille & Talking Book Programme in Cincinati, Ohio)
MSD	Most Significant Digit (computer term)
MSDC	Mass Spectrometry Data Center (of Atomic Energy Authority, U.K.)
MS-DOS	Microsoft Disk Operating System (also known as 86 DOS, Z-DOS and DOS)
MSF	Master Source File (computer term)
MSH	Magazine Supply House (Worcester, Mass.)
MSI (1)	Maxwell Scientific Information Inc. (Pergamon Press, U.K.)
MSI (2)	Medium Scale Integration (computer term)
MSLAVA	Manitoba School Library Audio-Visual Association
MSLS) MSLSc)	Master of Science in Library Science
MSO	Multiple System Operation

MSOS	Membership, Subscription and Order Services (of ALA)
MSPLT	Master Source Program Library Tape
MSR (1)	Mechanical Storage and Retrieval
MSR (2)	Mechanical Storage and Retrieval (Working Committee on) (of FID)
MSS (1)	Manuscripts
MSS (2)	Mass Storage System
MSSS	Mass Spectral Search System
MSTC	Micrographic Systems Technology Corporation (Falls Church, Va.)
MSU (1)	Mankato State University (Minn.)
MSU (2)	Montana State University
MSUDC	Michigan State University Discrete Computer
MSUL	Mississippi State University Library
MSUS/PALS	Minnesota State University System Project for Automated Library Systems
MTAK	Magyar Tudományos Akadémia Könyotára (Library of Hungarian Academy of Sciences, Hungary)
MTBF	Mean Time Before Failure (computer term)
MTDATA	Metallurgical Thermodynamic Data Bank
MTL	Metro Toronto Library
MTLA	Micropublishers' Trade List Annual (publication)
MTLB	Metropolitan Toronto Library Board
MTLT	MARC Tape to Local Tape
MTS (1)	Manitoba Telephone System
MTS (2)	Michigan Terminal System
MTSR	Magnetic Tape Selectric Recorder (of IBM)
MT/ST	Magnetic Tape/Selection T pewriter
MTTI	Muszaki Tudomanyos Tajekoztato Intezetben (Hungarian Institute of Scientific & Technical Information)

MUCIA	Midwest Universities Consortium for International Activities (of Michigan State University)
MUDG	MARC Users Discussion Group
MUDPIE	Museum and University Data, Program and Information Exchange (Smithsonian Institution newsletter, U.S.)
MUG	MARC Users Group (U.K.)
MUGLNC	Microcomputer Users Group for Librarians in North Carolina
MULS	Minnesota Union List of Serials (Univ. of Minnesota)
MULTICS	Multiplexed Information and Computer Service
MUM	Miami University-Middletown
MUMA	Museum of Modern Art (U.S.)
Mumps	Massachusetts General Hospital Utility Multi-programming System (computer language)
MUMS	Multiple Use MARC System (of LC)
MUN	Memorial University of Newfoundland
MUSTARD	Museum and University Storage and Retrieval of Data (Smithsonian Institution, U.S.)
MUX	Multiplexor (computer term)
mv	Millivolt (10^{-3} volt)
MVL	Miami Valley Libraries
MVT	Multi-programming with Variable Number of Tasks
mw	Milliwatt (10^{-3})
MWCOG	Metropolitan Washington (Library) Council of Governments
MWLC	Metropolitan Washington (D.C.) Library Council
MWRLS	Midwestern Regional Library System
MYCIN	(a system developed at the Stanford Heuristic Programming Project)
N	Newton (SI) (force)
NA (1)	Not Assigned
NA (2)) N/A)	Not Available

NAACP	National Association for the Advancement of Colored People (U.S.)
NAALD	Nigerian Association of Agricultural Librarians and Documentalists
NABER	National Association of Business and Educational Radio (U.S.)
NAC	Network Advisory Committee (of LC)
NACAE	National Advisory Council on Adult Education (U.S.)
NACILA	National Council of Indian Library Associations (India; became FILA in 1975)
NACL	National Advisory Commission on Libraries (U.S.; also known as NACOL)
NACO	Name Authorities Cooperative Project (of LC and NAL)
NACOL	National Advisory Commission on Libraries (U.S.; also known as NACL)
NACS (1)	National Association of College Stores (U.S.)
NACS (2)	National Association of Computer Stores (U.S.)
NADL	Newspaper Archive Developments Ltd. (U.S,)
NAEB	National Association of Educational Broadcasters (U.S,)
NAEP	National Assessment of Educational Progress (U.S.)
NAF	Nouvelle Architecture des Fichiers (of UTLAS Inc.; also known as NFA)
NAFS	Name Authority File Service (of LC)
NAG	Networking Advisory Group (of LC)
NAGC	National Association of Government Communicators (U.S.)
NAIP	North American Imprints Program (of LC)
NAIPRC	Netherlands Automatic Information Processing Research Centre
NAL	National Agricultural Library (U.S.; also called National Agriculture Library)
NALA (1)	Laubach Literacy International (U.S.)
NALA (2)	National Affiliation for Literacy Advance (Syracuse, N.Y.)
NALA (3)	Noth Alabama Library Alliance

NALNET	NASA Library Network (D.C.)
NALT	Nevada Association of Library Trustees
NANTIS	Nottingham and Nottinghamshire Technical Information Service (U.K.)
NAPCO	Northwest Association of Private Colleges and Universities (U.S.)
NAPCU	Northwest Association of Private Colleges and Universities (a network, U.S.)
NAPL	National Air Photo Library (Directorate of Topographical Surveys)
NAPLPS	Northern American Presentation Level Protocol Standards
NAPS	National Auxiliary Publications Service (of ASIS)
NAPTIC	National Air Pollution Technical Information System (U.S.)
NARA	North American Radio Archives
NARDIS	Navy Automated Research and Development Information System (U.S.)
NARIC	National Rehabilitation Information Center (of the Catholic University of America's Mullen Library, Washington, D.C.)
NARISCO	North American Rockwell Information Systems Co. (U.S.)
NARS	National Archives and Records Service (U.S.)
NAS (1)	National Academy of Sciences (U.S.)
NAS (2)	Needs Assessment Surveys
NASA	National Aeronautics and Space Administration (U.S.)
NASEMP	National Association of State Educational Media Professionals (U.S.)
NASIC	Northeast Academic Science Information Center (computer-based reference service at MIT)
NASIS	National Association for State Information Systems (U.S.)
NASL	Nevada Association of School Librarians
NASM	National Association for School Magazines (U.K.)
NAS-NRC	National Academy of Sciences - National Research Council (U.S.; also known as NRC (2))
NASSL	National Association of Spanish Speaking Librarians (U.S.)

NASTA	National Association of State Text Book Administrators (U.S.; previously NASTBD)
NASTBD	National Association of State Text Book Administrators (U.S.; now NASTA)
NAT	Name Authority Tape (of LC)
NATIS	National Information Systems (of Unesco)
NATO	North Atlantic Treaty Organization
NATS	National Activity to Test Software (U.S.)
NATTS	National Association of Trade and Technical Schools (U.S.)
NAUCA	National Association of Users of Computer Applications (U.S.)
NAVA	National Audio-visual Association (U.S.; now ICIA)
NAVAC	National Audio-visual Aids Centre (U.K.)
NBA (1)	National Book Agreement (U.K.)
NBA (2)	National Book Awards
NBA (3)	National Braille Association (U.K.)
NBB	Nederlandse Boekverkopersbond (Association of Dutch Booksellers, Netherlands)
NBC (1)	National Bibliographic Control (U.S.)
NBC (2)	National Bibliographical Center (National Central Library, Taiwan)
NBC (3)	National Book Council (U.K.; now NBL (1))
NBC (4)	National Broadcasting Company (U.S.)
NBCN	National Biomedical Communications Network
NBECN	New Brunswick Education Computer Network
NBER	National Bureau of Economic Research (U.S.)
NBKM	Norodna Biblioteka Kiril i Metodij (National Library of Cyril, Bulgaria)
NBL (1)	National Book League (U.K.; formerly NBC (3))
NBL (2)	Norsk Bibliotekarlag (Association of Norwegian Public Librarians)

NBLC	Nederlands Bibliotheek en Lektuur Centrum (Dutch Library and Literature Centre)
NBLTA	New Brunswick Library Trustees' Association
NBM	Non-book Material
NBN (1)	National Bibliography Number
NBN (2)	National Book Number
NBS (1)	National Bureau of Standards (U.K.)
NBS (2)	National Bureau of Standards (U.S.)
NBS-SIS	NBS - Standards Information Services (U.S.)
NBW	National Book Week
NC	National Centre (of ISDS)
NCA	National Communications Association (U.S.)
NCAB	National Cyclopedia of American Biography (U.S.)
NCAC (1)	National Coalition Against Censorship (U.S.)
NCAC (2)	National Conservation Advisory Council (U.S.)
NCACC	Northampton County Area Community Collections (U.K.)
NCALI	National Clearinghouse for Alcohol Information (U.S.)
NCASL	North Carolina Association of School Librarians
NCATE	National Council for Accreditation of Teacher Education (U.S.)
NCAVAE	National Committee for Audiovisual Aids in Education (U.K.)
NCC (1)	National Computer Center/Conference
NCC (2)	National Computing Center (U.S.)
NCC (3)	National Computing Centre (U.K.)
NCCCD	National Center for Computer Crime Data (U.S.)
NCCLS	Nevada Center for Cooperative Library Services
NCEC (1)	National Center for Educational Communication (U.S.)
NCEC (2)	National Citizens Emergency Committee (to serve public libraries, U.S.)

NCEFT	National Commission on Electronic Fund Transfers
NCEMMH	National Center on Educational Media and Materials for the Handicapped (U.S.)
NCES	National Center for Education Statistics (U.S.)
NCET	National Council for Educational Technology (U.K.: now CET)
NCFLC	North Carolina Foreign Language Center
NCHEMS	National Center for Higher Education Management Systems (of WICHE)
NCIC (1)	National Cartographic Information Center (U.S.)
NCIC (2)	National Crime Information Center (U.S.)
NCIP	National Collection Inventory Project (of CRL (1))
NCJRS	National Criminal Justice Reference Service (of U.S. Dept. of Justice, Washington, D.C.)
NCL (1)	National Central Library (U.K.; now BLLD)
NCL (2)	New Copyright Law (U.S.)
NCLA	North Carolina Library Association
NCLIS	National Commission on Libraries and Information Science (U.S.)
NCME	Network for Continuing Medical Education (U.S.)
NCNMLG	Northern California and Nevada Medical Library Groups
NCOCY	National Council of Organizations for Children and Youth
NCOLUG	North Carolina Online Users Group (Univ. of North Carolina; also known as NCOUG)
NCOUG	North Carolina Online Users Group (also known as NCOLUG)
NCPL	Natrona County Public Library (Caspar, Wyo.)
N&CPR	Newspaper and Current Periodical Reading Room (of LC)
NCPT	National Congress of Parents and Teachers
NCPTWA	National Clearinghouse for Periodical Title Word Abbreviations (U.S.)
NCR (1)	National Cash Register Co. (U.S.)

NCR (2)	No Canadian Rights (used by vendors for acquisition of library materials)
NCRD	National Council for Research and Development (Israel)
NCRLC	National Committee on Regional Library Cooperation (U.K.)
NCRLS	North Central Regional Library System
NCRRRC	North County Reference and Research Resources Council (N.Y.)
NCRY	National Commission on Resources for Youth (U.S.)
NCSDAE	National Council of State Directors of Adult Education (U.S.)
NCSL	North Carolina State Library
NCSTRC	North Carolina Science and Technology Research Center (Durham, N.C.)
NCSUR	North Carolina State University at Raleigh
NCTE (1)	National Council of Teachers of Engineering (U.S.)
NCTE (2)	National Council of Teachers of English (U.S.)
NCWTD	Nationaal Centrum voor Wetenschappelijke en Technische Documentatie (National Centre for Scientific & Technical Documentation, Belgium; also known as CNDST)
NDAB	Numerical Data Advisory Board (U.S.)
NDDP	Nationwide Database Design Project (of NDO)
NDEX	National Newspaper Index (an online file of SDC's ORBIT database)
NDL	National Diet Library (Japan)
NDLA	North Dakota Library Association
NDO	Network Development Office (of LC)
NDPS	National Data Processing Service
NDRO	Non-Destructive Read-Out (computer term)
NEA	National Education Association (U.S.)
NEAT	NCR Electronic Autocoding Technique
NEBASE	(Cooperative On-line Cataloguing Network of Nebraska Library Commission)

NEBHE	New England Board of Higher Education
NEBIC	New England Bibliographic Instruction Committee
NECCUM	Northeast Consortium of Colleges and Universities in Massachusetts
NECHI	Northeastern Consortium for Health Information (Mass.)
NEDCC (1)	New England Document Conservation Center
NEDCC (2)	Northeast Document Conservation Center (U.S.)
NEDL	New England Deposit Library
NEDS	National Emission Data System (U.S.)
N.E.E.D.	New Employment Expansion and Development
NEEDS	New England Education Data System
NEH	National Endowment for the Humanities (Learning Libraries Program, U.S.)
NEIAL	Northeast Iowa Academic Libraries Association
NEICA	National Energy Information Center Affiliate (U.S.)
NEIRC	New England Interinstitutional Research Council
NEL	National Engineering Laboratory
NELA	New England Library Association
NELB	New England Library Board
Neliac	**Naval Electronics Laboratory International Algabraic Compiler (computer language)**
NELINET	New England Library Information Network
NELL	North East Lancashire Libraries (U.K.; defunct 1974)
NEMICRO	(a microcomputer users group in New England)
NEMISYS	New Mexico Information Systems
NEMSINET	National Emergency Medical Services **Information** Network (U S.)
NENON	New England Online Users Group
NENUL	Near East National Union List
NEOMAL	Northeastern Ohio Major Academic Libraries

NEOUCOM	North Eastern Ohio Universities College of Medicine
NEPHIS	Nested Phrase Indexing System (an automated permuted subject indexing system)
NERAC	New England Research Application Center (Univ. of Connecticut)
NERCOMP	New England Regional Computing Program
NERIS	National Energy Referral and Information System (U.S.)
NERLS	Northeastern Regional Library System
NERMLS	New England Regional Medical Library Service
NESLA	New England School Library Association
NESS	New England Serials Service
NET	National Educational Television (U.S.)
NETRC	National Educational Television and Radio Center (U.S.)
NEUL	Near East Union List (an online database)
NEWIL	North East Wisconsin Intertype Libraries Inc.
NEWRIT	Northeast Water Resources Information Terminal (U.S.)
NEXIS	(an on-line database of newspapers)
NFA	New File Architecture (of UTLAS Inc.; also known as NAF)
NFAIS	National Federation of Abstracting and Indexing Services (U.S.; previously NFSAIS)
NFB	National Film Board
NFBS	Nordiske Forskningsbibliotekens Samarbejdskomité (Scandinavian Research Libraries Co-operative Committee)
NFER	National Foundation for Educational Research (U.K.)
NFF	Norske Forskningebibliotekarers Forening (Association of Norwegian Research Library, Norway)
NFLCP	National Federation of Local Cable Programmers (U.S.)
NFRN	National Federation of Retail Newsagents, Booksellers and Stationers (U.K.)
NFSAIS	National Federation of Science Abstracting and Indexing Services (now NFAIS)

NGSD	National Geophysical and Solar Terrestrial Data Center (U.S.; also known as NGSTDC)
NGSTDC	National Geophysical and Solar Terrestrial Data Center (U.S.; also known as NGSD)
NHIR	Natural History Information Retrieval (System) (Smithsonian Institution, U.S.)
NHLA	New Hampshire Library Association
NHLC	New Hampshire Library Council
NHPIC	National Health Planning Information Center (U.S.)
NHPRC	National Historical Publications and Records Commission (U.S.)
NIAC	National Issues Advisory Council (of MLA (7))
NIALSA	Northwest Indiana Area Library Services Authority (a consortium)
NIAM	Nederlands Instituut voor Audio Visuele Middlelen (Netherlands Institute for Audiovisual Media)
NIB	National Information Bureau (U.S.)
NIC	Nineteen Hundred Indexing and Cataloguing
NICE	National Information Conference & Exposition (Washington, D.C.)
NICEM	National Information Center for Educational Media (of UCLA)
NICOC	Nursing Information Consortium of Orange County (Calif.)
NICOL	Nineteen Hundred Commercial Language
NICS	Northern Inter-Library Cooperation Scheme (N.S.W.)
NICSEM	National Information Center in Special Education Materials (of UCLA; formerly NIMIS)
NIDER	Nederlands Instituut voor Documentatie en Registratuur (Netherlands Institute of Documentation and Filing)
NIDOC	National Information and Documentation Centre (Egypt)
NIE	National Institutes of Education (U.S.)
NIER	National Institute for Educational Research (Japan)
NIH	National Institute of Health (of Public Health Service, U.S.)

NIIT   National Institute of Instructional Technology (of NIE)

NIL   Not in Library

NILS   Northern Interrelated Library System (R.I.)

NIM   Newspapers in Microform

NIMIS   National Instructional Materials Information System
            (became NICSEM in 1977)

NIMMS   Nineteen Hundred Integrated Modular Management System

NIMR   National Institute for Medical Research (U.K.)

NIMS   Nolan Information Management Services (Torrance, Calif.)

NIN   Name Index Number (of MERLIN)

NINDS   Neurological Science Information Network (U.S.)

NIOSH   National Institute for Occupational Safety and Health
            (U.S.)

NIP   National Information Policy (U.S.)

NIPDOK   Nippon Documentesyon (Japan Documentation Kyokai Society)

NIRC   National Information Retrieval Colloquium (U.S.; also
            known as ANIRC)

NIRI   National Information Research Institute (U.S.)

NISARC   National Information Storage and Retrieval Centers (U.S.)

NISO   National Information Standards Organization (formerly
            ANSC Z39)

NISP   National Information System for Psychology (U.S.)

NISPA   National Information System for Physics and Astronomy
            (U.S.)

NISSAT   National Information System for Science and Technology
            (of INSDOC)

NITC   National Information Transfer Centre (Unesco)

NJBLN   New Jersey Black Librarians Network

NJCC   National Joint Computer Committee

NJFR   National Joint Fiction Reserve

NJLA   New Jersey Library Association

NJLBH	New Jersey Library for the Blind and Handicapped
NKLS	Northwest Kansas Library System
NL	National Library (also known as NLC (2))
NLA (1)	National Librarians Association (U.S.)
NLA (2)	National Library Authority or National Libraries Authority (U.K.)
NLA (3)	National Library of Australia (also known as ANL (2))
NLA (4)	Nebraska Library Association
NLA (5)	Nevada Library Association
NLA (6)	Newfoundland Library Association
NLA (7)	Nigerian Library Association
NLAB	National Library Advisory Board
NLAQ	Nebraska Library Association Quarterly
NLB	National Library for the Blind (U.K.)
NLBR	National Level Bibliographic Record (of LC)
NLC (1)	National Libraries Committee (of BL)
NLC (2)	National Library of Canada (Bibliothèque Nationale du Canada) (also known as NL)
NLC (3)	National Library of China
NLDRV	National Library of the Democratic Republic of Vietnam
NLISA	National Library and Information Service Act (U.S.)
NLL	National Lending Library (U.K.; formerly LLU and NLLST, now BLLD)
NLLST	National Lending Library for Science and Technology (later NLL; now BLLD)
NLM	National Library of Medicine (U.S.)
NLMBR	National Level Minimal Bibliographic Record (of LC)
NLN	National Library of Nigeria
NLP (1)	National Library, Peking (People's Republic of China)
NLP (2)	Nonlinear Programming

NLS (1)	National Library of Scotland
NLS (2)	National Library Service (of LC)
NLS/BPH	National Library Service for the Blind and Physically Handicapped (of LC; previously DBPH)
NLSLS	National Library of Scotland Lending Services
NLTF	National Libraries Task Force (U.S.)
NLW	National Library Week (a year long programme of ALA for library publicity)
NMA (1)	National Microfilm Association (U.S.)
NMA (2)	National Micrographics Association (now AIIM)
NMAC	National Medical Audiovisual Center (of NLM)
NMHC	National Materials Handling Center (U.K.)
NMLA	New Mexico Library Association (U.S.)
NMPA	National Music Publishers Association
NMSL	New Mexico State Library
NNI	National Newspaper Index
NOAA	National Oceanic and Atmospheric Administration (U.S.)
NOD	National Office on Disability (U.S.)
NOBIN	Nederlands Orgaan voor de Bevordering van de Informatieverzorging (Dutch Organism for the Promotion and Development of Information, Netherlands)
NOBLE	North of Boston Library Exchange (a consortium)
NOISE	Notification and Information on Source Entries (of SHARAF)
NOLA	Northeastern Ohio Library Association
NOLAG	Northwestern Ontario Library Action Group
NORASIS	Northern Ohio Chapter of ASIS
NORC (1)	National Opinion Research Center (Univ. of Chicago)
NORC (2)	Naval Ordnance Research Computer (U.S.)
NORIA	Normes et Reglementation Information Automatisée (France)
NOR-LUCS	Northern Software Consultants Library Updating and Compiling System

NORMARC	Norwegian MARC (Royal University, Norway)
NORWELD	Northwest Library District (U.S.)
NOS (1)	Network Operating System
NOS (2)	Non-on-Shelf
NOSP	Nordisk Samkatalog Over Periodika (Scandinavian union list of serials)
NOTIS	Northwestern On-Line Total Integrated System (of Northwestern University Library, Evanston, Ill.)
NOTS	Naval Ordnance Test Station (U.S.)
NPA	Newspaper Publishers Association (U.K.)
NPAC	National Program for Acquisitions and Cataloging (of LC)
NPC	National Periodicals Center (U.S.)
NPDN	Nordic Public Data Network
NPL (1)	National Physical Laboratory
NPL (2)	New Programming Language
NPL (3)	New South Wales Public Library
NPL (4)	Norman Public Library (U.S.)
NPL/CPIS	National Program Library and Central Program Inventory Service for the Social Sciences (Univ. of Wisconsin)
NPPO	National Preservation Program Office (of LC)
NPS	National Periodicals System (U.S.)
NPSS	Non-Public School Section (of AASL)
NRC (1)	National Referral Center (of LC's Science and Technology Division)
NRC (2)	National Research Council (also known as CNRC and NRCC)
NRC (3)	National Research Council (National Academy of Sciences, U.S.; also known as NAS-NRC)
NRCC	National Research Council of Canada (also known as NRC (2) and CNRC)
NRCd	National Reprographic Centre for Documentation (U.K.)
NRCPUBS	National Research Council Publications (database)

NRCST	National Referral Center for Science and Technology (of LC)
NRL (1)	National Reference Library (U.K.; also known as BLSRL, formerly NRLSI)
NRL (2)	National Registry for Librarians (U.S.)
NRLB	Northern Regional Library Bureau (U.K.)
NRLS	Niagara Regional Library System
NRLSI	National Reference Library of Science and Invention (U.K.; also known as BLSRL or SRL; now NRL (1))
NRMM	National Register of Microform Masters (of LC)
NRZ	Non Return to Zero (computer term)
ns	nanosecond (10^{-9}) (also nsec)
NSA	Nuclear Science Abstracts (U.S. Atomic Energy Commission)
NSC	National Shelflist Count (of CRL (5))
NSCLR	Nova Scotia Council on Library Resources
NSCLS	North State Cooperative Library System (Willows, Calif.)
NSCUFA	Nova Scotia Confederation of University Faculty Associations
NSDC	National Serials Data Centre (part of the Bibliographic Services Division of the British Library)
NSDP	National Serials Data Program (U.S.)
nsec	nanoseconds (10^{-9}) (also ns)
NSF	National Science Foundation (U.S.)
NSIC	Nuclear Safety Information Center (U.S.)
NSL (1)	National Science Library (India)
NSL (2)	National Science Library (now CISTI)
NSLA	Nova Scotia Library Association
NSLS	North Suburban Library System (Ill.)
NSMR	National Society for Medical Research (U.S.)
NSN	National Satellite Network (U.K.)

NSNI   Nova Scotia Nautical Institute

NSPAC   National Standards Policy Advisory Committee (of ANSI)

NSRDS   National Standard Reference Data System (of NBS (2))

NSSC   National Society for the Study of Communications
              (now ICA (2))

NSSDC   National Space Science Data Center (Goddard Space
              Flight Center of NASA)

NSSLA   Nova Scotia School Library Association

NST   New Serial Titles (publication, R.R. Bowker)

NSTC   Nineteenth Century Short Title Catalogue (U.K.)

NSWIT   New South Wales Institute of Technology

NT   Narrower Term (in LCSH)

NTA   Newfoundland Teacher's Association

NTAG (1)   Network Technical Advisory Group (of BSDP)

NTAG (2)   Network Technical Architecture Group (Advisory Committee
              to LC)

NTBL   Nuffield Talking Book Library (for the Blind)

NTC   National Translations Center (of SLA (6) and John
              Crerar Library, Chicago, Ill.)

NTH   Norges Tekniske Høgskole (Library of the Norwegian
              Institute of Technology, Norway)

NTIA   National Telecommunications and Information Adminis-
              tration (U.S.)

NTIAC   Nondestructive Testing Information Analysis Center
              (U.S. Army)

NTIS   National Technical Information Service (U.S.; formerly
              CFSTI and OTS)

NTISearch   National Technical Information Search (Dept. of
              Commerce, U.S.)

NTL Institute National Training Laboratories (provides opportunities
              for librarians in management positions, U.S.)

NTSC   National Television System Committee (U.S.)

NUC (1)   National Union Catalog (U.S.)

NUC (2)	National Universities Commission (government agency responsible for funding, overseeing and coordination of development of all Nigerian universities)
NUCLEUS	Numerical Classification and Evaluation System
NUCMC	National Union Catalog of Manuscript Collections
NUCOM	National Union Catalogue of Monographics (of NLS (3))
NUCPP	National Union Catalog Publication Project (of LC)
NUI	Network User Identifier
NUL	Northwestern University Library (U.S.)
NULOS	National Union List of Serials (held in Papua New Guinea libraries)
NUS	National Union of Students (also known as UNE)
NVB	Nederlandse Vereniging van Bibliothecarissen (Netherlands Association of Librarians)
NVBA	Nederlandse Vereniging van Bedrijfsarchivarissen (Netherlands Association of Business Archivists)
NVBF	Nordiska Vetenskapliga Bibliotekarieforbundet (Scandinavian Association of Science Librarians, Sweden)
NVC	National Video Clearinghouse (U.S.)
NWAHEC	Northwest Area Health Education Center (N.C.)
NWICO	New World Information and Communication Order (Unesco)
NWRLS	Northwestern Regional Library System (U.K.)
NYLA	New York Library Association
NYLIC	New York Library Instruction Clearinghouse (SUNY College of Environmental Science and Forestry)
NYP	Not Yet Published
NYPL	New York Public Library
NYSCAT	New York State Catalogue (based at Mid-Hudson Library System, N.Y.)
NYSILL	New York State Interlibrary Loan Network
NYSL	New York State Library
NYTIB	New York Times Information Bank

NYTIS	New York Times Information Service
NYTSL	New York Technical Services Librarians
NYU	New York University
NZLA	New Zealand Library Association
OAC	Ontario Arts Council
OACUL	Ontario Association of College and University Libraries (of OLA (3) (L'Association des Bibliothèques des Collèges et des Universités d'Ontario; now OCULA)
OAEVH	Ontario Association for the Education of the Visually Handicapped
OAH	Organization of American Historians
OALS	OTIS Automated Library Services (Or.)
OALT	Ontario Association of Library Technicians (also known as ABO (1))
OARS	Organization of Asian Research Scholars (U.S.)
OAS	Organization of American States
OASI	Office Automation Society International (U.S.)
OASIS (1)	Oceanic and Atmospheric Scientific Information System
OASIS (2)	Ohio (Chapters) of ASIS
OASIS (3)	On-line Administrative Information System
OASIS (4)	Ontario Ambulance Services Information System
OASL	Ohio Association of School Librarians
OASLMS	Oklahoma Association of School Libraries Media Specialists
OATS	Original Article Tearsheet or Original Article Text Service (of ISI (3))
OBCH	Overseas Booksellers Clearing House (U.K.)
OBIAS	OTIS Basic Index Access System (U.S.)
OBR	Optical Bar Code
OC (1)	Official Catalogue
OC (2)	Organizational Climate

OCAP	Ontario Career Action Programme
OCCI	Optical Coincidence Coordinate Indexing
OCCIO	Ohio Cooperative Conservation Information Office
OCCS	Office of Computer and Communications Systems (of NLM)
OCDDLS	Ontario Committee of Deans and Directors of Library Schools
OCLC	Online Computer Library Center or Online College Library Center (previously Ohio College Library Center; now OCLC Inc.)
OCPL	Onondaga County Public Library (N.Y.)
OCR	Optical Character Recognition/Reader/Reading
OCS	Online Computer Systems, Inc. (U.S.)
OCTRF	Ontario Cancer Treatment and Research Foundation
OCUA	Ontario Council on University Affairs (also known as COAU)
OCUFA	Ontario Confederation of University Faculty Associations (formerly known as Ontario Council of University Faculty Associations)
OCUL	Ontario Council of University Libriries (Le Conseil des Bibliothèques d'Universités de l'Ontario)
OCULA	Ontario College and University Library Association (of OLA (3); previosly known as OACUL)
ODE	Overseas Data Entry (a project of LC)
ODIN (1)	Online Database Information Network (Pa.)
ODIN (2)	On-Line Dokumentations-und-Informationsetze
ODL	Oklahoma Department of Libraries
OE	Office of Education (also known as USOE)
OECA	Ontario Educational Communications Authority
OECD	Organization for Economic Cooperation and Development
OED	Oxford English Dictionary
OEED	Office of Equal Educational Opportunities (of OE)
OEIMC	Oklahoma Environmental Information and Media Center

OELMA	Ohio Education Libraries Media Association
OEM	Original Equipment Manufacturer
OEMI	Office Equipment Manufacturers Institute (previously BEMA; now CBEMA)
OERI	Office for Educational Research and Improvement (U.S.)
OFA	Ontario Film Association
OFL	Ohio Friends of Libraries
OFR (1)	Office for Recruitment (of ALA)
OFR (2)	Office for Research or Office of Research (of ALA)
ÖGDB	Österreichische Gesellschaft für Dokumentation und Bibliographie (Austria)
ÖGDI	Österreichische Gesellschaft für Dokumentation und Information (Austrian Society for Documentation and Information)
OHIONET	Ohio Network
⌒	Ohm (SI) (electric resistance)
ÖIBF	Österreichische Institut für Bibliotheksforschung, Dokumentations - und Informationswesen (Austrian Institute for Library Research, Documentation and Information Science)
OIF	Office of Intellectual Freedom (of ALA)
OISE	Ontario Institute for Studies in Education
OJT	On-the-Job Training
OKDT	Országos Könyvtárügyi és Dokumentációs Tanács (National Board for Librarianship and Documentation, Hungary)
OKULS	Oklahoma Union List of Serials
OLA (1)	Ohio Library Association
OLA (2)	Oklahoma Library Association
OLA (3)	Ontario Library Association
OLA (4)	Oregon Library Association
OLAC	Online Audiovisual Catalogers (of OCLC Inc.)
OLAS	On-Line Acquisitions System

OLC (1)	Office of Library Coordination
OLC (2)	Ontario Library Council
OLE	Office for Library Education (of ALA)
OLF	Ohio Library Foundation
OLLR	Office of Libraries and Learning Resources (of USOE)
OLLT	Office of Libraries and Learning Technologies (U.S.)
OLN	Outreach Library Network (New Hampshire University)
OLOS	Office for Library Outreach Services (of ALA)
OLPR	Office for Library Personnel Resources (of ALA)
OLR	Ontario Library Review (publication)
OL'SAM	Online Database Search Assistance Machine (Franklin Institute, U.S.)
OLSD	Office for Library Service to the Disadvantaged (of ALA)
OLSUS	Online System Use Statistics File (of OCLC Inc.)
OLTA (1)	Ohio Library Trustees Association
OLTA (2)	Ontario Library Trustees' Association (of OLA (3))
OLTEP	On-line Test Executive Program (computer term)
OLTS	On-line Test System (computer term)
OLUC	Online Union Catalog
OMA	Ontario Medical Association
OMB	Office of Management and Budget (of LC)
OMKDK	Országos Müszaki Könyvtár és Dokumentácios Központ (Central Technical Library and Documentation Centre, Hungary)
OMNITAB II	(computer language)
OMPB	Oriental Manuscripts and Printed Books (of BL)
OMPI	Organisation Mondiale de la Propriété Intellectuelle (also known as WIPO)
OMR	Optical Mark Reading
OMS/ARL	Office of Management Studies (of ARL)

OMSS	Online Manuscripts Search Service
ONLICAT	(Online Cataloging System of NYPL)
ONQ	Order of Nurses of Quebec
ONSITE	On-line Site Evaluation
ONTAP	On-line Training and Practice File (of DIALOG)
ONTERIS	Ontario Educational Research Information System (of the Ontario Ministry of Education)
ONULP	Ontario New Universities Library Project (terminated in March 1969)
OO	Outreach Ontario
OOKDK	Országos Orvostudományi Könyvtár és Dokumentációs Központ (National Medical Library and Centre for Documentation, Hungary)
OONL/NSP	(Newspaper Division of the National Library of Canada)
OONL/OPD	(Official Publications Division of the National Library of Canada)
OONL/SHP	Service to the Handicapped persons (of NLC (3))
OP	Out of Print
OPAC	On-line Public Access Catalogue
OPACS	Online Public Access Catalog Systems
OPAL	Ontario Puppetry Association
OPC (1)	Office of the Principal Cataloger (of LC)
OPC (2)	Overseas Press Club of America
OPIRG	Ontario Public Interest Research Group
OPL (1)	Official Publications Library (of BL)
OPL (2)	Ottawa Public Library
OPLA	Ontario Public Library Association (of OLA (3); formerly RPLD)
OPLAC	Ontario Public Libraries Advisory Committee
OPLB	Ontario Public Library Board
OPLC	Ontario Provincial Library Council

OPLIC	Office of Public Libraries & Interlibrary Cooperation (of College of St. Catherine, St. Paul, Minn.)
OPLPR	Ontario Public Libraries Programme Review (started in 1981)
OPM (1)	Office of Personnel Management (U.S.)
OPM (2)	Operations per Miniute (computer term)
OPMA	Overseas Press and Media Association (U.K.)
OPRIS	Ohio Project for Research in Information Service (U.S.)
OPTIM	Order Point Technique for Inventory Management
OR	Operational Research or Operations Research (Management term)
ORACE	Optimal Reception of Announcement by Coded Viewdata
ORACLE (1)	On-Line Retrieval of Acquisitions, Cataloguing and Circulation Details for Library Enquiries (developed by the State Library of Queensland, Australia; modified version known as LIBSAC at Acadia University, Wolfville, N.S.)
Oracle (2)	Optical Reception of Announcements by Coded Line Electronics
ORALL	Ohio Regional Association of Law Libraries
ORAU	Oak Ridge Associated Universities (Tenn.)
ORBIT	On-line Retrieval of Bibliographic Information Time Shared (of SDC (2))
ORCHIS	Oak Ridge Computerized Hierarchical Information System (U.S. Atomic Energy Commission)
ORCUP	Ontario Region of the Canadian University Press
ORD	Office for Research and Development (of ALA)
ORDVAC	Ordnance Variable Automatic Computer
ORION	On-line Retrieval of Information Over a Network
ORLIS	Ohio Regional Library and Information Systems
ORRMIS	Oak Ridge Regional Modeling Information System
ORS	Operations Research Society (U.K.)

ORSA	Operations Research Society of America
ORSTOM	Office de la Recherche Scientifique et Technique d'Outre-Mer (Office of Overseas Scientific and Technical Research, France)
OS (1)	Operating System (computer term)
OS (2)	Out of Stock
OSCAN	Oklahoma Special Collections and Archives Network
OSI	Open Systems Interconnection (adopted by Linked Systems Project)
OSIRIS	On-line Search Information Retrieval Information Storage (U.S. Navy)
OSIS	Office of Science Information Service or Office of Scientific Information Service (of NSF)
OSLA	Ontario School Library Association (of OLA (3))
OS/MFT	Operating System/Multiprogramming a Fixed Number of Tasks
OS/MVT	Operating System/Multiprogramming a Variable Number of Tasks
OSRD	Office of Scientific Research and Development (U.S.)
OSS	Office of Strategic Services (of National Archive's Modern Military Headquarters Branch, U.S.)
OSSHE	Oregon State System of Higher Education
OSTI	Office for Scientific and Technical Information (Dept. of Education and Science, U.K.; now BLRDD)
OSU	Ohio State University
OSUL	Ohio State University Libraries
OTAF	Office of Technology Assessment and Forecasts (Washington, D.C.)
OTI	Office of Technical Information (U.S. Atomic Energy Commission) (now Technical Information Center)
OTIS (1)	Oklahoma Telecommunications Interlibrary System
OTIS (2)	Oklahoma Teletype Interlibrary System
OTIS (3)	Oregon Total Information System

OTIU	Overseas Technical Information Unit (of Dept. of Industry, U.K.)
OTP	Office of Telecommunications Policy (U.S.)
OTS	Office of Technical Services (U.S.; later CFSTI, now NTIS)
OUBCP	Ontario Universities Bibliographic Centre Project
OUCA	Ontario Universities Council on Admissions (also known as CAUO)
OUGL	Odegaard Undergraduate Library
OULCS	Ontario Universities Library Cooperative System
OUP	Oxford University Press
OUPID	Ontario Universities Program for Instructional Development
OURA	Ontario University Registrars' Association (also known as ARUO)
OVAL	Ohio Valley Area Libraries
OVD	Optical Videodisc
OVGTSL	Ohio Valley Group of Technical Services Librarians
Pa (1)	Pascal (SI) (pressure, stress)
PA (2)	Publishers Association (U.K.)
PABX	Private Automatic Branch Exchange
PAC (1)	Packaged Assembly Circuit (computer term)
PAC (2)	Public Access Catalog
PAC (3)	Public Archives of Canada
PAC/II	Public Access Catalog (of CLSI)
PACE	Public Affairs Council for Education
PACFORNET	Pacific Coast Forest Research Information Network (now WESTFORNET)
PACT	Paterson Area Community Television (U.S.)
PACX	Private Automatic Computer Exchange (computer term)

PAD (1)	Packet Assembler/Disassembler (computer term)
PAD (2)	Pontiac-Allen Park-Detroit (a consortium)
PAIGH	Pan-American Institute of Geography and History
PAIN	Philadelphia Acquisitions Information Network
PAIS	Public Affairs Information Service (a major indexing service in social sciences)
PALA (1)	Pennsylvania Library Association
PALA (2)	Polish-American Library Association
PALINET	Pennsylvania Library Network (U.S.)
PALs	Programmable-Logic Arrays (computer term)
PAMAI	Program of Action for Mediation, Arbitration, and Inquiry (of ALA; also known as SCMAI)
PAMI	Prairie Agricultural Machinery Institute
PANCM	Programming Aids to Numerically Controlled Manufacturing
PANSDOC	Pakistan National Scientific and Technical Documentation Centre (now PASTIC)
PAPADI	Perhimpunan Ahli Perpustakaan Arsipdan Dokumentasi (Indonesian Association of Librarians, Archivists and Documentalists)
PAPERCHASE	(on-line system at Beth Israel Hospital, Boston)
PAPRICAN/IRS	Pulp and Paper Research Institute of Canada/Information Retrieval Service
PARENTS	People of America Responding to Educational Needs of Today's Society
PARIF	Program for Automation Retrieval Improvement by Feedback (Euratom)
PAS (1)	Personnel Administration Section (of LAMA)
PAS (2)	Publisher's Alert Service (of USOE)
PASAR	Psychological Abstracts Search and Retrieval
Pascal (1)	(computer language)
PASCAL (2)	Programme Applique a la Selection et a la Compilation Automatique de la Litterature (a database of CNRS)

PASLIB	Pakistan Association of Special Libraries
PASSIM	President's Advisory Staff on Scientific Information Management (U.S.)
PASTIC	Pakistan Scientific and Technical Information Centre (formerly PANSDOC)
PATELL	Psychological Abstracts Tape Editions Lease License (a database generated by American Psychological Association)
PATRICIA	Practical Algorithm to Retrieve Information Coded in Alphanumeric
PATSEARCH	(U.S. Patent and Trademark Office database)
PATSY	Programmer's Automatic Testing System
PATT	Project for the Analysis of Technology Transfer (Univ. of Denver, U.S.)
PB	Peripheral Buffer (computer term)
PBA	Planning and Budget Assembly (of ALA)
PBAA	Periodical and Book Association of America
PBC	Provinciale Bibliotheek Centrale (Central Provincial Library, Netherlands)
PBP	Paperbound Books in Print (publication, R.R. Bowker)
PBS (1)	Personal Bibliographic System (U.S.)
PBS (2)	Public Broadcasting System (U.S.)
PBX	Private Branch Exchange (a computerized telephone circuit switch that can provide both voice and data communication service)
PC (1)	Paper Copy
PC (2)	Personal Computer
PC-AT	Personal Computer-Advanced Technology (of IBM)
PCB	Printed Circuit Board (computer term)
PCCER	Planning Council on Computing in Education and Research (U.S.)
PCHE	Pittsburgh Council on Higher Education
PCI	Programmable Communications Interface (computer term)

PCLA	Polish Canadian Librarians' Association
PCLD	Pierce County Library District (U.S.)
PCLS	**Parish and Community Libraries Section (of CLA (4))**
PCM (1)	Plug Compatible Mainframe (computer term)
PCM (2)	Punched Card Machine
PCMI	Photo-Chromic Micro-Image (computer term)
PC/MIS	Production Control/Management Information System
PCP	Primary Control Program (computer term)
PCR	Program Control Register (computer term)
PCS	Print Contrast System (computer term)
PDC	Publications and Distribution Center (U.S. Air Force Logistics Command)
PDIN	Pusat Dokumentasi Ilmiah Nasional (Indonesian Scientific and Technical Documentation Centre)
PDIs (1)	Picture Description Instructions (Decoder) (computer term)
PDIS (2)	Pusat Dokumentasi Ilmu-Ilmu Sosial (Indonesian Social Sciences Documentation Centre)
PDP	Programmed Data Processor (a computer)
PDS	Problem Descriptor System (a computer language for mathematical programme generation)
PEA	Public Education Association (N.Y.)
PEARL	Periodicals Automation Rand Library (Rand Corp., U.S.)
PEAS	Pacific's Electronic Acquisitions System
PEBUL	Project for the Evaluation of Benefits from University Libraries (an OSTI-supported study, 1969)
PEBUQUILL	Prêts Entre Bibliothèques des Universités de Québec University Inter-library Loans (Quebec)
PEISLA	Prince Edward Island School Library Association
PEL	Professional Education Libraries
PELB-IF	Project Every Library Board-Kit on Intellectual Freedom (of ALTA (2))

PEMD	Program for Export Market Development (U.S.)
PENNTAP	Pennsylvania Technical Assistance Program
PER	Periodex
PERLINE	(periodicals and serials control and management system of Blackwell Library Systems, Inc.)
PERT	Program Evaluation and Review Technique
PESTDOC	Pesticidal Literature Documentation (U.K.)
PET	(a personal computer manufactured by Commodore Business Machines)
PETREL	Professional Education and Training for Research Librarianship (a project of CLR)
PFL	Public Free Library (Guyana)
PGCMLS	Prince George County Memorial Library Service (Md.)
PGI	General Information Program (of Unesco, adopted in 1976 in Nairobi integrating Unesco's former Divisions of Scientific and Technological Documentation and Information and of Documentation, Libraries, and Archives)
PGIS	Project Grant Information System (of USOE)
PHRA	Poverty and Human Resources Abstracts
PI	Programmed Instruction (computer term)
PIA (1)	Peripheral Interface Adaptor (computer term)
PIA (2)	Printing Industry of America
PIB	Publishers Information Bureau (U.S.)
PICA (1)	Project for Integrated Catalogue Automation (a project of Dutch University Libraries)
PICA (2)	Public Interest Computer Association (U.S.)
PID	Peripheral Interface Device (computer term)
PIF	Process Information File (a manual of LC)
PILOT	(a computer language)
PIMNY	Printing Industries of Metropolitan New York
PIN	Personal Identification Number (computer term)
PIO (1)	Parallel Input/Output (computer term)

PIO (2)	Public Information Office (of ALA)
PIP (1)	Peripheral Interchange Program (computer term)
PIP (2)	Pollution Information Project (of NRC (2))
PIPS	Professional Institute of the Public Service
PIRA	Printing Industry Research Association (U.K.)
PIRS (1)	Personal Information Retrieval System
PIRS (2)	Philosophers Information Retrieval Service (U.S.)
PIT (1)	Processing of Indexing Terms
PIT (2)	Programmed Instruction Text (computer term)
PL (1)	Plain-Letter (Romanization System)
PL (2)	Public Library
PL/I	(a computer language (often erroneously thought to stand for Programming Language/1)
PLA (1)	Pakistan Library Association
PLA (2)	Pennsylvania Library Association
PLA (3)	Philippine Library Association
PLA (4)	Polish Librarians Association (Poland)
PLA (5)	Private Libraries Association (U.K.)
PLA (6)	Programmed Logic Array (computer term)
PLA (7)	Public Library Association (of ALA)
PLA AEPS	PLA Alternative Education Programs Section (of PLA (7))
PLA AFLS	PLA Armed Forces Librarians Section (of PLA (7))
PLA CIS	PLA Community Information Section (of PLA (7))
PLAIN	Piedmont Library Acquisitions Information Network
PLA MLS	PLA Metropolitan Libraries Section (of PLA (7))
PLAN (1)	Practical Library Applications Now (U.S.)
PLAN (2)	Public Library Association of Nevada
PLAN (3)	Public Library Automation Network (U.S.)
PLA PLSS	PLA Public Library Systems Section (of PLA (7))

PLASH   (Australian Subject Headings, 1978)

PLA SMLS   PLA Small and Medium-sized Libraries Section (of PLA (7))

PLATO   Programmed Logic for Automatic Teaching Operations
               (of Univ. of Illinois at Urbana-Champaign)

PLAY   Public Library Association of Youngstown (Ohio)

PLC (1)   Progressive Librarians' Council (U.S.)

PLC (2)   Public Library Commission (of provinces)

PLCFC   Public Library of Columbus and Franklin County (Ohio)

PLCHC   Public Library of Cincinnati and Hamilton County (Ohio)

PLIP   Public Library Improvement Program (U.S.)

PL/M   (a computer language)

PLMS   Preservation of Library Materials Section (of RTSD)

PLP   Preservation Level Protocol (for videotex, issued by
               AT&T in 1981)

PLPG   Publishers' Library Promotion Group (a group of trade
               books publishers)

PLQ   Public Library of Queensland (Australia; also known
               as QPL)

PLR   Public Lending Right (U.S.)

PLRG   Public Libraries Research Group (of Brighton Area
               Library, Brighton, Sussex)

PLS   Provincial Library Service (Ont.)

PLSS   Public Library Systems Section (of PLA (7))

PLT   Public Library Trustee

PLUG (1)   Participating Libraries Users' Group (of MRLS Processing
               Centre, Ont.)

PLUG (2)   Public Library Users Group (U.S.)

PLUTO   Parts Listing and Used on Techniques (computer term)

PLYMC   Public Library of Youngstown and Mahoning County (Ohio)

PM (1)   Phase Modulation (computer term)

PM (2)   Popular Music (An Annotated Index of American Popular
               Songs)

PMB	Post Mortem Dump (computer term)
PMC	Princeton Microfilm Corp. (U.S.)
PMCLS	Pioneer Multi-County Library System (U.S.)
PMD	Pharmaco-Medical Documentation (of Biomedical Information Sciences)
PMEST	Personality, Matter, Energy, Space, Time (Colon Classification, S.R. Ranganathan)
PML	Pierpont Morgan Library (N.Y.)
PMLA	Publications of the Modern Language Association
PMS (1)	People's Message System (of Chicago Public Library's North Pulask Branch Library)
PMS (2)	Processor-Memory-Switch (computer term)
PMS (3)	Project Management System
PMS (4)	Public Message Service
PNBC	Pacific Northwest Bibliographic Center (Washington State University)
PNGLA	Papua New Guinea Library Association
PNI	Pharmaceutical News Index (Louisville, Ky.)
PNLA	Pacific Northwest Library Association (U.S.)
PNRHSLS	Pacific Northwest Regional Health Sciences Library Service (Wash.)
PO	Purchase Order
POCS	Patent Office Classification System (U.S.)
POISE	Practices-oriented Information Systems Experiment
POL (1)	Patent Office Library (of BL)
POL (2)	Procedure-Oriented Language or Problem-Oriented Language
POLYDOC	Polytechnical Documentation (Scandinavian computer system)
PONYU	Parents of New York United
POP	Print-on-Paper
POPSI	Postulate-based Permuted Subject Index
POS	Point of Sale (computer term)

POSDCORB	Planning, Organizing, Staffing, Directing, Controlling, Reporting and Budgeting
PP (1)	Paris Principles
PP (2)	Peripheral Processor (computer term)
PPA	Periodical Publishers Association (U.K.)
PPBS	Planning, Programming, Budgeting Systems
PPE	Program Planning and Evaluation
PPG	Process Planning Group (of ALA)
PPI	Popular Periodical Index (Camden, N.J.)
PPITB	Printing and Publishing Industry Training Board (U.K.)
PPL (1)	Polymorphic Programming Language
PPL (2)	Providence Public Library
PPLD	Pikes Peak Library District (Colorado Springs)
PPM	Persatuan Persustakaan Malaysia (Library Association of Malaysia)
PPS	Persatuan Perpustakaan Singapura (also known as LAS (2))
PPU	Payment for Public Use
PR	Public Relations
PRC	Project Review Committee (of BCUC)
PRE	Prefix
PRECIS	Preserved Context Index System
PRIDE	Promote Real Independence for the Disabled and Elderly (U.S.)
PRIM (1)	Program for Information Managers (of AIM (3))
PRIM (2)	Program for Information Managers (of NICE)
PRINCE	Parts Reliability Information Center (of NASA)
PRINFOD	Printed Information Distribution (Air Canada)
PRISM	Personnel Records Information System for Management (U.K.)
PRLC (1)	Pittsburgh Regional Library Center
PRLC (2)	Pittsburgh Regional Library Council

PRO	Public Research Office (U.K.)
PROM	Programmable Read-only Memory (computer term)
PROMPT	Production, Reviewing, Organizing and Monitering of Performance Techniques
PROMT	Predicasts Overviews of Marketing and Technology (a file on DIALOG)
PROSPER	Profit Simulation Planning and Evaluation of Risk
PROXI	Projection by Reflection Optics of Xerographic Images
PRS	Public Relations Section (of LAMA)
ps (1)	Picosecond (10^{-12}) (also psec)
PS (2)	Publishing Services (of ALA)
PSAC (1)	President's Sciences Advisory Committee (U.S.)
PSAC (2)	Public Service Alliance of Canada
PSE (1)	Packet Switching Exchange (computer term)
PSE (2)	Post-Secondary Education
psec	Picoseconds (10^{-12}) (also ps (1))
PSEP	Program for the Study of Ethnic Publications (Kent State University, Ohio)
PSI (1)	Pakistan Standards Institute
PSI (2)	Permuterm Subject Index (of ISI (3))
PSI (3)	Popular Song Index (publication)
PSIEP	Project on Scientific Information Exchange in Psychology (American Psychological Association)
PSL/PSA	Problem Statement Language/Problem Specification Analyzer
PSN	Public Switched Network
PSPL	Palm Springs Public Library (Calif.)
PSRMLS	Pacific Southwest Regional Medical Library Service
PSS	Packet Switching Service (computer term)
PSSC	Public Services Satellite Consortium (U.S.; also known as PSSL)

PSSL	Public Service Satellite Consortium (U.S.; also known as PSSC)
PSSLA	Peel Secondary School Librarians' Association (Ont.)
PSTIAC	Pavement and Soil Trafficability Information Analysis Center (U.S.)
PSTN	Public Switched Telephone Network
PSU	Power Supply Unit (computer term)
PTA	(New) Periodical Title Abbreviations (Gale Research)
PTC	Process Type of Last Change (control field in LHF, of UTLAS Inc.)
PTIC	Patent and Trade Mark Institute of Canada
PTL	Public Television Library (U.S.)
PTLA	Publishers Trade List Annual (R.R. Bowker)
PTP	Point to Point (computer term)
PTS	Predicasts Terminal System (a file on DIALOG)
PTST	Prime Time School Television (U.S.)
PUC	Presse Universitaire Canadienne (also known as CUP (1))
PUDISCO	(New York) Public Library System Directors Organization (also known as PULISDO)
PUFFT	Purdue University Fast Fortran Compiler (computer term)
PUL	Princeton University Library
PULISDO	(New York) Public Library System Directors Organization (also known as PUDISCO)
PW	Publisher's Weekly (R.R. Bowker)
QACLD	Quebec Association for Children with Learning Disabilities
QASL	Quebec Association of School Librarians
QBPL	Queens Borough Public Library (Jamaica, N.Y.)
QCB	Queue Control Block (computer term)
QCIM	Quarterly Cumulative Index Medicus (of NLM)

QED	Quick Text Editor (computer term)
QISAM	Queued Indexed Sequential Access Method (computer term)
QJ	Quarterly Journal (of LC)
QLA	Quebec Library Association (also known as ABQ)
QPBC	Quality Paperback Book Club (a Division of Book of the Month Club)
QPL	Queensland Public Library (also known as PLQ)
Q & Q	Quill and Quire (periodical)
QTAM	Queued Telecommunications Access Method (computer term)
QUBE	(Warner Communications' two way cable television system in Columbus, Ohio)
QUIC/LAW	(Legal information service, Queens University, Ont.)
QUOBIRD	Queens University On-line Bibliographic Information and Dissemination (Belfast, Northern Ireland)
q.v.	quod vide ("which see")
QWERTY	(kayboard layout for alphanumeric characters)
QWL	Quality of Work Life
RA	Research Abstracts (of UMI)
RAC (1)	Regional Advisory Committee (of GBRLS)
RAC (2)	Reliability Analysis Center (N.Y.; also known as RADC (1))
rad (1)	Radian (SI) (plane angle)
RAD (2)	Rapid Access Disc (computer term)
RADC (1)	Reliability Analysis Data Center (also known as RAC (2))
RADC (2)	Rome Air Development Center (U.S.)
RADCOL	RADC Automatic Document Classification On-line (of RADC (2))
RADIALS	Research and Development - Information and Library Science (of LA (1))
RADIICAL	Retrieval and Automatic Dissemination of Information from Index Chemicus and Line Notations
RADIR	Random Access Document Indexing and Retrieval

RAG	Retrieval Advisory Group (of LC)
RAI	Random Access and Inquiry
RAIDS	Rapid Availability of Information and Data for Safety
RAILS	Reference and Inter-Library Loan Service (Ohio)
RAK	Regeln für die alphabetische Katalogisierung (German Cataloguing Code)
RAL	Register of Additional Locations (of LC)
RALF	Rapid Access to Literature via Fragmentation Codes
RAM (1)	Random Access Memory (computer term)
RAM (2)	Remote Access Module (Univ. of Guelph's On-line System)
RAMAC	Random Access Methods of Accounting and Control (of IBM)
RAMIS	Rapid Access Management Information System
RANN	Research Applied to National Needs
RAP	Reference Assistance Project (program for minority students, developed by Library/Learning Center at the Univ. of Wisconsin-Parkside)
RAPID (1)	Random Access Personal Information Dissemination
RAPID (2)	Random Access Photographic Index and Display
RAPID (3)	Research in Automatic Photo-Composition and Information Dissemination
RAPID (4)	Retrieval through Automated Publication and Information Digest (of SDC (2))
RAPID (5)	Rotating Associative Processor for Information Dissemination
RARE	Rochester Area Resources Exchange (a consortium)
RAS	Readers Advisory Service (of Science Associates International, Inc., N.Y.)
RASD	Reference and Adult Services Division (of ALA)
RASD HS	RASD History Section
RASD MARS	RASD Machine-assisted Reference Service Section
RASP	Retrieval and Statistical Processing (U.K.)
RASTAD	Random Access Storage and Display (computer term)

RBB	Reference Books Bulletin (new name of RSBR - changed April 1983)
RBMS	Rare Books and Manuscripts Section (of ACRL)
RBT	Rapid Bibliographic Transfer (of Rutgers University, U.S.)
RBUPC	Research in British Universities, Polytechnics and Colleges (formerly SRBUC)
RC	Register of Copyrights (U.S.)
RCA	Radio Corporation of America
RCAA	Régles de Catalogage Anglo-Américaines (Symposium, Univ. du Québec)
RCCPL	Riverside City/County Public Library (Calif.)
RCD(C)	Royal College of Dentists of Canada (also known as CRCD(C))
RCE	Repertoire Canadien sur l'Éducation (also known as CEI)
RCHA	Regional Conference of Historical Society (U.S.)
RCI	Remote Console Information Corporation (McLean, Va.)
RCLS	Rampaco Catskill Library System (N.Y.)
RCMP	Royal Canadian Mounted Police
RCOP	Research Committee on the Punjab (U.S.)
RCPS(C)	Royal College of Physicians and Surgeons of Canada (also known as CRMC(C))
RD (1)	Research and Development
R & D (2)	Research and Development (of BL)
RDC (1)	Regional Dissemination Center (of NASA)
RDC (2)	Rules for Descriptive Cataloguing (of LC)
RDES	Retrospective Data Entry System
REACH	Research Education and Assistance for Canadians with Herpes (a Toronto-based organization)
READI	Remote Electronic Access to and Delivery of Information
RECBIR	Regional Coordination of Biomedical Information Resources (New York Academy of Medicine)
RECI	Reading Enrichment Company, Inc. (West Peterson, N.J.)

RECON (1)	Remote Console (of NASA and European Space Research Organization)
RECON (2)	Retrospective Conversion (converting records in machine-readable form)
REDIC	Red de Documentacion e Información de Colombia (Network of Documentation and Information for Colombia)
REDINSE	Red de Información Socio-Económica (Network of Socio-Economic Information, Venezuela)
Reduce	(a computer language)
REEC	Register and Examinations Committee (of LA (1))
RE/EIC	Regional Energy/Environment Information Center (U.S.)
REFCATSS	Reference Catalogue Support System (of UTLAS Inc.)
REFLECS	Retrieval From the Literature on Electronics and Computer Science/Service (of IEEE)
REFLES	Reference Librarian Enhancement System
REFORMA	(National Association to Promote Library Services to the Spanish Speaking Community, U.S.)
REFSEARCH	(Reference Materials Searching System at the Univ. of California, Berkeley)
REIC	Radiation Effects Information Center (U.S.)
RELAIS (1)	(On-line Retrieval System for Searching Bibliographic Files; also known as CAN/OLE)
RELAIS (2)	Relance de l'Aide à l'Emploi
REMARC	Retrospective MARC (of LC)
REMCO	Reference Materials Council Committee (of ISO (2))
REMPA	Reference Materials Party (of ISO (2))
REMSTAR	Remote Electronic Microfilm Storage Transmission and Retrieval
REMUS	Retrospective Music Project (of Univ. of Wisconsin at Milwaukee)
RESPONSA	Retrieval and Special Portions from Nuclear Science Abstracts (of AEC (2))
RETROSPEC	Retrospective Search System (of INSPEC Database)
RF	Radio Frequency

RFB	Recordings for the Blind (N.Y.)
RFI	Request for Information
RFP	Request for Proposal
RFQ	Request for Quotation
RG	Readers' Guide to Periodical Literature (H.W. Wilson Co.; also known as RGPL)
RGB	(red, green, blue monitor) (computer term used for VDTs)
RGPL	Readers' Guide to Periodical Literature (H.W. Wilson Co.; also known as RG)
RIA	Research Institute of America
RIAA	Recording Industry Association of America
RIACT	Retrieval of Information about Census Tapes (U.S.)
RIBDA	Reunion Interamericana de Bibliotecarios y Documentalistas Agrícolas
RIBLIN	Réseau Informatique des Bibliothèques/Library Information Network (of NLC)
RICASIP	Research Information Center and Advisory Service on Information Processing (sponsored by NSF and NBS (2))
RICC	Regional Information Coordinating Center (Fla.)
RICE	Regional Information and Communication Exchange (of Rice University, Tex.)
RIdIM	Répertoire International d'Iconographie Musicale
RIE (1)	Research in Education (periodical) (of ERIC; now RIE (2))
RIE (2)	Resources in Education (periodical) (of ERIC; formerly RIE (1))
RILA	Rhode Island Library Association
RILM	Répertoire International de Littérature Musicale
RIMS	Remote Information Management System (of Northwestern University, Ill.)
RIS (1)	Regulatory Information System
RIS (2)	Research Information Services (U.S.)

RIs (3)	Rule Interpretations (of LC)
RISE	Register for International Service in Education
RISM	Répertoire International des Sources Musicales (International Society of Musicology and International Association of Music Libraries)
RIT	Rochester Institute of Technology (N.Y.)
RJE	Remote Job Entry (computer term)
RLA	Rhodesia Library Association (defunct)
RLAC	Research Library Advisory Committee (of OCLC Inc.)
RLB	Regional Library Bureau (U.S.)
RLG	Research Libraries Group (formed by Columbia, Harvard, Yale Universities and NYPL to develop common bibliographic systems)
RLG/CJK	RLG Chinese, Japanese, Korean (System) (a project of RLG and LC)
RLIN	Research Libraries Information Network (formerly BALLOTS)
RLMS	Reproduction of Library Materials Section (of RTSD)
RML (1)	Regional Medical Libraries (of NLM)
RML (2)	(Southeastern-Atlantic) Regional Medical Library Services (Md.)
RMLN	Regional Medical Library Network (of NLM)
RMM	Read Mostly Memory (computer term)
RNC	Resource Network Committee (of National Library Advisory Board)
ROBINS	Roberts Information Services (Va.)
ROCAPPI	Research on Computer Applications in the Printing and Publishing Industries (of Lehigh Press, N.J.)
ROM	Read Only Memory (computer term)
RPG	Report Program Generator (computer term)
RPL	Richmond Public Library (Va.)
RPLD	Regional and Public Libraries Division (of OLA (3))
RPM	Revolutions per Miniute

RPS	Revolutions per Second
RPWG	Reference/Processing Working Group (of LC)
RQ	Research Quarterly (of RASD)
RRI	Ryan Research International (Chico, Calif.)
RRIS	Railroad Research Information Services (Penn.)
RRL	Registered Record Librarian
RRRLC	Rochester Regional Research Library Council (N.Y.)
RRS	RLIN Report System
RS	Resources Section (of RTSD)
RSAA	Romanian Studies Association of America
RSBR	Reference & Subscription Book Reviews (publication)
RSBRC	Reference and Subscription Books Review Committee (of ALA)
RSC	Revised Statutes of Canada
RSD	Reference Services Division (of ALA)
RSIC	Radiation Shielding Information Center (Oak Ridge, Tenn.)
RSIS	Reference, Special and Information Section (of LA (1))
RSL	Requirements Specification Language
RSN	Record Sequence Number (of UTLAS Inc.)
RSR	Reference Services Review (publication)
RSS	Regional Support System (of SOLINET)
RSSDA	Research Social Science Data Archives (of Univ. of Iowa)
RSVP	Retired Senior Volunteer Program (U.S.)
RSWK	Regeln für den Schlagwortkatalog (Rules for the Subject Heading Catalogue developed by Deutsches Bibliotheksin- stitut)
RT (1)	Register Transfer (computer term)
RT (2)	Related Term (in LCSH)
RTECS	Registry of Toxic Effects of Chemical Substances (of BLAISE)

RTL	Register-Transister Logic (computer term)
RTLB (1)	Round Table of Libraries for the Blind (of IFLA, at the 1982 Conference, Montreal)
RTLB (2)	Round Table of Libraries for the Blind (of LC)
RTM	Register Transfer Module (computer term)
RTSD	Resources and Technical Services Division (of ALA)
RTSD/AAP	RTSD Automated Acquisitions Program
RTSD/AS	RTSD Acquisitions Section
RTSD/CCS	RTSD Cataloging and Classification Section
RTSD/PLMS	RTSD Preservation of Library Materials Section
RTSD/RLMS	RTSD Reproduction of Library Materials Section
RTSD/RS	RTSD Resources Section
RTSD/SS	RTSD Serials Section
RTTY	Radio Teletypewriter
RUC	Regional Union Catalog (U.S.)
RUIN	Regional Urban Information Network (Washington, D.C.)
RUSTIC	Regional and Urban Studies Information System (U.S.)
RVM	Répertoire de Vedettes-Matière (a file of Université Laval)
R/W	Read/Write (computer term)
s (1)	Second (SI)
S (2)	Siemens (SI) (electric conductance)
SAA (1)	Society of American Archivists
SAA (2)	Standards Association of Australia
SAALCK	State Assisted Academic Library Council of Kentucky
SAALIC	Swindon Area Association of Libraries for Industry and Commerce (U.K.)
SAB	Sveriges Allmänna Biblioteksförening (Swedish General Library Association)
SABIR (1)	Semi-Automatic Bibliographic Information Retrieval (U.S. Naval Postgraduate School)

SABIR (2)   Système Automatique de Bibliographie d'Information et de Recherche (France)

SABS (1)   South African Bureau of Standards

SABS (2)   Stanford Automated Bibliography System (Stanford University, U.S., and Social Research Council)

SABS (3)   Statistical Analysis of Bibliographic Structure (North Western Polytechnic and HERTIS, U.K.)

SABV   Suid-Afrikaanse Biblioteekvereniging (South African Library Association) (also known as SALA)

SAC (1)   Subject Analysis Committee (of ALA/RTSD/CCS)

SAC (2)   Systems Advisory Committee (of TRLN; also known as Advisory Systems Committee)

SACAP   Selection, Acquisition, Cataloguing and Processing (Bro-Dart Industries, U.S.)

SACHEM   Southeastern Association for Cooperation in Higher Education in Massachusetts

SACS   South Asian Languages Section (of Descriptive Cataloging Division of LC)

SADC   Southwest Asia Documentation Centers (of IRANDOC)

SADPO   Systems Analysis and Data Processing Office (of NYPL; now LIONS)

SADSACT   Self Assigned Descriptors from Self and Cited Titles (National Bureau of Standards, U.S.)

SAE   Society of Automotive Engineers (U.S.)

SAEMS   Saskatchewan Association of Educational Media Specialists

SAERIS   South Australian Education Resources Information System

SAGE   Services to the Aging (programme of Brooklyn Public Library, N.Y.)

SAHLC   Seattle Area Hospital Library Consortium

SAILA (1)   Sault Area International Library Association (resource sharing among Sault Sainte Marie, Mich., and Sault Sainte Marie, Ont.)

SAILA (2)   South African Indian Library Association

SAILIS   South African Institute for Librarianship and Information Science

SAIS	Specific Area Intellegence System (a demographic database)
SALA	South African Library Association (also known as SABV)
SALALM	Seminar on the Acquisition of Latin American Library Materials
SALCKIN	Subject Access to Library Catalogues through Keyword Indexes (programme of Bath University, U.K.)
SALINET	Satellite Library Information Network (a consortium of libraries, a library school, and regional agencies with headquarters at Denver Graduate School of Librarianship, U.S.)
SALLA	Sierra Leone Library Association
SALS	Southern Adirondack Library System
SALT (1)	Saskatchewan Association of Library Technicians
SALT (2)	Society for Applied Learning Technology (U.S.)
SAM	Sequential Access Method (computer term)
SAMANTHA	System for the Automated Management of Text from Hierarchical Arrangement (U.S.)
SAMKAT	(a Danish short-form acronym for shared cataloguing)
SAMMIE (1)	Southwest Area Multi-County Multy-type Interlibrary Exchange (Minn.)
SAMMIE (2)	System for Aiding Man-Machine Interaction Evaluation
SAMP	South Asia Microform Project
SAMS	Small and Medium-size Libraries Sub-Committee (of GBRLS)
SAN	Standard Address Number (identification code assigned by book industry organizations for ordering purposes)
SANB	South African National Bibliography
SANZ	Standards Association of New Zealand
SAOLM	Subject Analysis and Organization of Library Materials Committee (of RTSD/CCS)
SAP (1)	Subject Access Project (which outlines procedures for the selection of terms directly from the content pages and indexes of books being catalogued for use as descriptors)
SAP (2)	Symbolic Assembly Program

SAPIR	System of Automatic Processing and Indexing of Reports Univ. of Calif., U.S.)
SAPRISTI	Système Automatique de Production d'Information Scientifique
SARBICA	Southeast Asian Regional Branch of the International Council on Archives (Malaysia)
SAROAD	Storage and Retrieval of Aerometric Data (also called Storage and Retrieval of Air Quality Data)
SAS	Statistical Analysis System
SATCOM	Scientific and Technical Communication (a Committee formed by NAS (1))
SATIRE	Semi-automatic Technical Information Retrieval (of SDC (2))
SATRA	Science and Technology Research Abstracts (of G.K. Hall, U.S.)
SBARN	South Bay Area Reference Network (Calif.)
SBC (1)	Single Board Computer
SBC (2)	Société Bibliographique du Canada (also known as BSC)
SBCL	San Bernadino County Library (Calif.)
SBD	Standard Bibliographic Description
SBN	Standard Book Number
SBP	Stowarzyszenie Bibliotekarzy Polskich (Polish Library Association, Poland)
SBPR	Sociedad de Bibliotecarios de Puerto Rico (Society of Librarians of Puerto Rico)
SBS (1)	Satellite Business Systems (a consortium of IBM, COMSAT and Aetna Insurance Co., U.S.)
SBC (2)	Svenska Bibliotekariesamfundet (Swedish Association of Research Librarians)
SBSE	Science Book and Serial Exchange (Ann Arbor, Mich.)
SC	Subject Classification (Brown)
SCAD	Société Canadienne pour l'Analyse de Documents (also known as IASC)
SCALS	Standing Conference of African Library School (Senegal)

SCAN (1)	Service Center for Aging Information (U.S.)
SCAN (2)	Southern California Answering Network (administered by California State Libraries)
SCAN (3)	Stock Control and Analysis
SCANDOC	Scandinavian Documentation Centre (Washington, D.C., maintained by Nordforsks Dockumentationscentral)
SCANS	Scheduling and Control by Automated Network
SCATS	Sequentially Controlled Automatic Transmitter Start (computer term)
SCATT	(National) Scientific Communication and Technology Transfer System (Pennsysvania University, U.S.)
SCAUL	Standing Conference of African University Librarians
SCAULEA	Standing Conference of African University Libraries Eastern Area (Nairobi)
SCAULWA	Standing Conference of African University Libraries Western Area (Ghana)
SCBW	Society of Children's Book Writers (U.S.)
SCCLYP	Southern California Council on Literature for Children & Young People
SCDC	State-wide Collection Development Committee (of CCLD (2))
SCE	Superior Council of Education
SCEA	Société Canadienne d'Éducation par l'Art (also known as CSEA)
SCEB	Société Canadienne des Études Bibliques (also known as CSBS)
SCEC	Société Canadienne des Études Classiques
SCECI	Société Canadienne d'Éducation Comparée et Internationale (also known as CIESC)
SCECSAL	Standing Conference for Eastern Central and Southern African Librarians
SCEE	Société Canadienne pour l'Étude de l'Éducation (also known as CSSE)
SCEES	Société Canadienne pour l'Étude de l'Enseignement Supérieur (also known as CSSHE)
SCEL	Standing Committee on Education in Librarianship (U.K.)

SCEPTRE	(a computer language for circuit design)
SCFC	Southern California Film Circuit
SCH	Student Contact Hours (B.C.)
SCHOLAR	Schering-Oriented Literature Analysis and Retrieval System (of MeSH)
SCI (1)	Science Citation Index (of ISI (3))
SCI (2)	Simulation Councils, Inc. (U.S.)
SCICAT	Science Reference Library Catalogue (of BL)
SCIL	Small Computers in Libraries (periodical; Meckler Publishing)
SCILL	Southern California Interlibrary Loan Network
SCIM	Selected Categories in Microfiche (of NTIS)
SCI-MATE	(ISI Personal Data Management Software for several microcomputers; of ISI (3))
SCIP	Stanford Center for Information Processing (U.S.)
SCIPIO	(an index of art sales catalogs)
SCISEARCH	Science Citation Index Search
SCI-TECH	Science-Technology Division (of SLA (6))
SCITEL	Institute for Scientific Information (U.K.)
SCKLS	South Central Kansas Library System (Hutchinson, Kan.)
SCL (1)	Scottish Central Library (merged with National Library of Scotland in 1974 to form National Library of Scotland Lending Services)
SCL (2)	Society of County Librarians (Wiltshire, U.K.)
SCL (3)	South Central Library System (U.S.)
SCLA (1)	South Carolina Library Association
SCLA (2)	Suffolk County Library Association (N.Y.)
SCLL	State and Court Law Libraries (of U.S. and Canada)
SCLS (1)	Southwestern Connecticut Library System
SCLS (2)	Suffolk Cooperative Library System (N.Y.)

SCM (1)	Smith Corona Merchant Co.
SCM (2)	Society for Computer Medicine (U.S.)
SCMAI	Staff Committee on Mediation, Arbitration and Inquiry (of ALA; also known as PAMAI)
SCOLCAP	Scottish Libraries Co-operative Automation Project
SCOLE	Standing Committee on Library Education (of ALA; supersedes LED (1))
SCOLIS	Spokane Cooperative Library Information System (Wash.)
SCOLLUL	Standing Conference of Librarians of Libraries of University of London
SCOLMA	Standing Conference on Library Materials on Africa
SCOMMA	Subcommittee on the Monitering of Microform Advertising (of RTSD)
SConMeL	Standing Conference for Mediterranean Librarians
SCONUL	Standing Conference of National and University Libraries (U.K., established 1950)
SCOP	Single-Copy Ordering Plan (of ABA (1))
SCOPE (1)	Systematic Computerized Processing in Cataloguing (Guelph University)
SCOPE (2)	Systematic Control of Periodicals (Pfizer Inc., U.S.)
SCORPIO	Subject-Content-Oriented Retriever for Processing Information Online (of LC)
SCOTAPLL	Standing Conference on Theological and Philosophical Libraries in London (now ABTPL)
SCPI	Scientists Committee for Public Information (U.S.)
SCRAP	Special Committee to Review Program Assessment Processes (of ALA)
SCRLC	South Central Research Library Council (U.S.)
SCRLS	South Central Regional Library System (U.S.)
SCS	Society for Computer Simulation (U.S.)
SCSN	(American National Standard Computer Software Number)
SCTPG	Southern California Technical Processes Group

SCTRPAP	Special Committee to Review Program Assessment Processes
SCUC	Slavic Cyrillic Union Catalog (of pre 1956 imprints)
SCUL	Simulation of the Columbia University Libraries (U.S.)
SCUR	Southwest Center for Urban Research (Tex.)
SDC (1)	Scientific Documentation Centre (Scotland)
SDC (2)	System Development Corp. (U.S.)
SDD	Selected Dissemination of Documents
SDE (1)	Society of Data Educators (U.S.)
SDE (2)	State Department of Education (Calif.)
SDI	Selective Dissemination of Information
SDILINE	Selective Dissemination of Information On-line (of NLM)
SDIM	Système de Documentation et d'Information Métallurgique (System for Documentation and Information in Metallurgy) (Commission of the European Communities, Italy)
SDLC	Synchronous Datalink Control (a high level data communications protocol (of IBM)
SDM	Selective Dissemination of Microfiche (Clearinghouse for Federal Scientific and Technical Information, U.S.)
SD METRO	San Diego Greater Metropolitan Area Library & Information Agency Council (a network)
SDPL	San Diego Public Library
SDS (1)	Scientific Data Systems
SDS (2)	Serials Data System
SDS (3)	Space Documentation Service (European Space Research Organization)
SDSL	South Dakota State Library
SDTF	State Documents Task Force (of GODORT)
SDTI	Selective Dissemination of Technical Information (Institute of Paper Chemistry, U.S.; and Pulp and Paper Research Institute of Canada)
SEAC	Standards Electronic Automatic Computer
SEALA	South East Asia Library Association

SEALLINC	Southeast Louisiana Library Network Cooperative
SEAMIC	Southeast Asian Medical Information Center (Japan)
SEAM/NAP	Southeast Asia Microfilm Project/North American Pool
SEARCH (1)	System for Electronic Analysis and Retrieval of Criminal Histories (Calif.)
SEARCH (2)	Systematized Excerpts, Abstracts & Reviews of Chemical Headlines (Fort Lee, N.J.)
SEARS	Song Index and Supplement
SEBC	Southeastern Bibliographic Center (N.Y.)
SECLA	Southeastern Connecticut Library Association
SED	South East Division (of Association of Assistant Librarians, LA (1); also known as AALSED)
SEDIX	Selective Dissemination of Indexes
SEEDIS	Socio-Economic-Environmental Demographic Information System
SEES	Slavic and East European Section (of ACRL)
SEFA	Scottish Educational Film Association (Scotland)
SEFT	Society for Education in Film and Television (U.K.)
SEIAC	Science Education Information Analysis Center (of ERIC)
SEIMC	State Special Education Instructional Materials Center (N.Y.)
SEIS	Service d'Échange d'Informations Scientifiques (France)
SELA	Southeastern Library Association (U.S.)
SELCO	Southeastern Libraries Cooperating (a consortium of public libraries, U.S.)
SELDOM	Selective Dissemination of MARC (a service of the Univ. of Sask.)
SELINET	South East Library Information Network (U.S.)
SEMCO	Southeastern Massachusetts Health Sciences Libraries Consortium
SEMIS	State Extension Management Information System (U.S.)
SEMLOL	Southeastern Michigan League of Libraries

SEMSQ	Société des Editeurs de Manuels Scolaires du Québec
SENDOC	Small Enterprises National Documentation Centre (India)
SENTOKYO	Senmon Toshokan Kyôgikai (Special Libraries Association, Japan)
SENYLRC	South Eastern New York Library Resources Council (U.S.)
SEOM	(Values of the) Standard Error of Measurement
SEPSA	Society of Educational Programmers and Systems Analysts (now part of SDE (1))
SERB	South East Regional (Library) Bureau (also known as SERLB; now LASER (2))
SERIN	Serials Acquisition and Holdings Information (Govt. of Ontario)
SERLB	South East Regional Library Bureau (part of SERLS; also known as SERB, now LASER (2))
SERLINE	Serials On-line (of NLM)
SERLS	South East Regional Library System (now London and South Eastern Library Region, U.K.)
SERMLP	South Eastern Regional Medical Library Program (U.S.)
SESAM	Système Electronique de Selection Automatique de Microfilms (Bruxelles, Belgium)
SEWHSL	Southeastern Wisconsin Health Sciences Libraries
SFF	Svenska Folkbibliotekarie Förbundet (Union of Swedish Librarians)
SFL	Society of Federal Linguists (U.S.)
SFPL	San Francisco Public Library
SFRA	Science Fiction Research Association (U.S.)
SFU	Simon Fraser University (B.C.)
SFWA	Science Fiction Writers of America
SFYA	Selected Films for Young Adults
SGA	Schweizerische Gessellschaft für Automatic (Association Suisse pour l'Automatique; Swiss Association for Automation; also known as ASSPA)
SGJP	Satellite Graphic Job Processor (computer term)

SGLA   Saskatchewan Government Libraries Association

SGSR   Society for General Systems Research (U.S.)

SHAL   Subject Heading Authority List (computer program -
                Rand Corp., U.S.)

SHAPE   Special Handicapped Adults Program (of New Jersey
                State Library)

SHARAF   Shared Authority File (maintained by a group of UTLAS
                clients)

SHARE   Sisters Have Resources Everywhere (a feminist library
                group, Chicago, Ill.)

SHARES (1)   Shared Acquisitions and Retention System (of New York
                Metropolitan Reference & Research Library Agency)

SHARES (2)   (Shared Resource System - performs retrospective
                conversion tasks for OCLC member libraries)

SHARP (1)   Ships Analysis and Retrieval Project (of U.S. Navy)

SHARP (2)   Special Handicapped Adults Recreation Program (New
                Jersey State Library program)

SHE   Subject Headings for Engineering (Engineering Index, U.S.)

SHF   Super High Frequency

SHIRTDIF   Storage, Handling and Retrieval of Technical Data in
                Image Formation

SHORE   Sussex Help Organization for Resources Exchange (Del.)

SHSU   Sam Houston State University (Tex.)

SHSW   State Historical Society of Wisconsin

SHUL   Sullivant Hall Undergraduate Library (of OSU)

SI   Système Internationale d'Unités (International System
                of Units)

SIA   Service in Informatics and Analysis

SIAL   Southeast Iowa Academic Libraries

SIALSA   Southeastern Indiana Area Library Services Authority

SIAM   Society for Industrial and Applied Mathematics

SIAR   Swedish Institute for Administrative Research

SIBIL	Système Intégre pour les Bibliothèques Universitaires de Lausanne (an automated system of acquisition, cataloguing and circulation, Switzerland)
SIBMAS	Société Internationale des Bibliothèques - Musées des Arts du Spectacle (International Society of Libraries and Museums of the Theatre Arts, France)
SIC (1)	Songs in Collection (de Charms & Breed)
SIC (2)	Standard Industrial Classification (of DIALOG)
SIC (3)	Survival Information Center (U.S.)
SICI	Shastri Indo-Canadian Institute (also known as IICS)
SICOLDIC	Sistema Colombiano de Información Cientifica Y Technica
SID (1)	Society for Information Display (U.S.)
SID (2)	System of Information Documentation
SIDAR	Selective Information Dissemination and Retrieval
SIE	Science Information Exchange (Smithsonian Institution, U.S.; now SSIE)
SIECOP	Scientific Information and Educational Council of Physicians (U.S.)
SIECUS	Sex Information and Education Council of the U.S.
SIG	Special Interest Group
SIG ACT	SIG on Automata and Computability Theory (of ACM)
SIG AH	SIG on Arts and Humanities (of ASIS)
SIG ALP	SIG on Automated Language Processing (of ASIS)
SIG ARCH	SIG on Computer Architecture (of ACM)
SIG ART	SIG on Artificial Intellegence (of ACM)
SIG/BC	SIG on Biological and Chemical Information Systems (of ASIS)
SIG BDP	SIG on Business Data Processing (of ACM)
SIG BIO	SIG on Biomedical Computing (of ACM)
SIG/BSS	SIG on Behavioral and Social Sciences (of ASIS)
SIG CAI	SIG on Computer-Assisted Instruction (of ACM)

SIG CAPH	SIG on Computers and the Physically Handicapped (of ACM)
SIG CAS	SIG on Computers and Society (of ACM)
SIG/CBE	SIG on Costs, Budgeting and Economics (of ASIS)
SIG/CIS	SIG on Community Information Services (of ASIS)
SIG COMM	SIG on Data Communications (of ACM)
SIG COSIM	SIG on Computer Systems Installation Management (of ACM)
SIG CPR	SIG on Computer Personnel Research (of ACM)
SIG/CR	SIG on Classification Research (of ASIS)
SIG/CRS	SIG on Computerized Retrieval Services (of ASIS)
SIG CSE	SIG on Computer Science Education (of ACM)
SIG CUE	SIG on Computer Uses in Education (of ACM)
SIG DA	SIG on Design Automation (of ACM)
SIG/ED	SIG on Education for Information Science (of ASIS)
SIG/ES	SIG on Education of Information Science (of ASIS)
SIG/FIS	SIG on Foundations of Information Science (of ASIS)
SIG GRAPH	SIG on Computer Graphics (of ACM)
SIG/IAC	SIG on Information Analysis Centers (of ASIS)
SIG/IP	SIG on Information Publishing (of ASIS)
SIG IR	SIG on Information Retrieval (of ACM)
SIG/ISE	SIG on Information Services to Education (of ASIS)
SIG/LA	SIG on Library Automation and Networks (of ASIS; also known as SIG/LAN)
SIG/LAN	SIG on Library Automation and Networks (of ASIS; also known as SIG/LA)
SIG LASH	SIG on Language Analysis and Studies in Humanities (of ACM)
SIG/LAW	SIG on Law and Information Technology (of ASIS)
SIGLE	System for Information on Gray Literature in Europe
SIGMA	(a make of computers, such as used by UTLAS Inc.)
SIG MAP	SIG on Mathematical Programming (of ACM)

SIG METRICS	SIG on Measurement Evaluation (of ACM)
SIG/MGT	SIG on Management Information Activities (of ASIS)
SIG MICRO	SIG on Microprogramming (of ACM)
SIG MINI	SIG on Minicomputers (of ACM)
SIG MOD	SIG on Management of Data (of ACM)
SIG/MR	SIG on Medical Records (of ASIS)
SIG/NDB	SIG on Numerical Data Bases (of ASIS)
SIG/NPM	SIG on Non-Print Material (of ASIS)
SIG NUM	SIG on Numerical Mathematics (of ACM)
SIG OPS	SIG on Operating Systems (of ACM)
SIG PLAN	SIG on Programming Languages (of ACM)
SIG/PPI	SIG on Public Private Interface (of ASIS)
SIG/RT	SIG on Reprographic Technology (of ASIS)
SIGs	Special Interest Groups (of ASIS)
SIG/SDI	SIG on Selective Dissemination of Information (of ASIS)
SIG SIM	SIG on Simulation (of ACM)
SIG SOC	SIG on Social and Behavioral Science Computing (of ACM)
SIG/TIS	SIG on Technology, Information and Society (of ASIS)
SIG UCC	SIG on University Computing Centers (of ACM)
SIG/UOI	SIG on User On-line Interaction (of ASIS)
SII	Standards Institute of Israel
SIIRS	Smithsonian Institution Information Retrieval System (U.S.)
SILAS	Singapore-based Integrated Library Automation System
SILC	System for Interlibrary Communication (of ARL)
SIM (1)	Self-Instructional Module
SIM (2)	Standards Institute of Malaysia
SIMS	Socioeconomic Information Management System (Univ. of Wisconsin, U.S.)

SIMSCRIPT II.5 (a computer language)

Simula 67   Simulation Language 67 (a computer language)

SIN   Subject Indicator Number (of PRECIS)

SINE   Society for Indian and Northern Education

SINET   Louisiana State University System Interlibrary Network

SINTO   Sheffield Interchange Organization (U.K.)

SIO   Serial Input/Output (computer term)

SIPI   Scientists' Institute for Public Information (U.S.)

SIPRI   Stockholm International Peace Research Institute

SIR (1)   Selective Information Retrieval

SIR (2)   Statistical Information Retrieval

SIRC   Sport Information Resource Centre (Ottawa) (publishes sport and recreation index)

SIRCULS   San Bernadino, Inyo, Riverside Counties United Library Services (Calif.)

SIRE   (An experimental retrieval system at Syracuse University)

SIRLS   (An information retrieval system for the sociology of leisure and sport, of the Univ. of Waterloo, Ont.)

SirS   Social Issues Resources Series, Inc. (Boca Raton, Fla.)

SIS (1)   School of Information Studies (of Syracuse University, N.Y.)

SIS (2)   Science Information Service (U.S.)

SIS (3)   Special Interest Section (of AALL)

SIS (4)   Specialized Information Services (of NLM)

SIS (5)   Standard Information Services (of NBS (2))

SISAC   Serials Industry Systems Advisory Committee (of BISAC)

SISIR   Singapore Institute of Standards and Industrial Research

SIST   Standard for Information Science and Technology

SITC   Standard International Trade Classification

SITES   Smithsonian Institution Travelling Exhibition Service (U.S.)

SITM	Subject Index Term (sybsystem of CRS Bill Digest System of LC)
SIU	Southern Illinois University
SIUC	Southern Illinois University, Carbondale
SJCC	Spring Joint Computer Conference (U.S.)
SJF	Shortest Job First (computer term)
SJSU	San Jose (Calif) State University
SKCSR	Statni Knihovna Ceskosloveneke Socialisticke Republiky (Czechoslovakia) (State Library of the Czechoslovak Socialist Republic)
SKWOC	Structured Keyword Out of Context
SL (1)	Shelf-list
SL (2)	Subject List
SLA (1)	Saskatchewan Library Association
SLA (2)	School Library Association
SLA (3)	Scottish Library Association
SLA (4)	Southeastern Library Association (U.S.)
SLA (5)	Southwestern Library Association (also known as SWLA)
SLA (6)	Special Libraries Association (U.S.)
SLA (7)	Sudan Library Association
SLAAM	Student Librarian Assistants Association of Michigan
SLACES	Syndicat de la Libraire Ancienne et du Commerce de l'Estampe en Suisse (Switzerland; also known as VEBUK)
SLAIS	School of Library, Archival and Information Studies (renamed School of UBC (2))
SLAM	Simulation Language for Alternative Modeling (computer language)
SLANG	Systems Language
SLAP	System Level Access Project (Calif.)
SLAPNG	School Library Association of Papua, New Guinea
SLAS	State Library Agency Section (of ASLA)

SLC (1)	Schools of Librarianship Committee (U.K.; later ABLS (1); now ABLISS)
SLC (2)	Senate Library Committee (of Univ. of Pittsburgh)
SLCLS	Salt Lake County Library System
SLESR	Société des Libraires et Éditeurs de la Suisse Romande (Booksellers and Publishers Association of French-speaking, Switzerland)
SLF	Systems Library File (computer term)
SLIC	Selective Listing in Combination
SLICE (1)	Southwestern Library Interstate Cooperative Endeavor (U.S.)
SLICE (2)	Surrey (University) Library Interactive Circulation Experiment (U.K.)
SLIN	Standard Library Identification Number
SLIS (1)	School of Library and Information Science (of Univ. of Western Ontario)
SLIS (2)	Shared Laboratory Information System (U.S.)
SLJ	School Library Journal (R.R. Bowker)
SLLA (1)	Sierra Leone Library Association
SLLA (2)	Sri Lanka Library Association
SLMP	School Library Manpower Project
SLMQ	School Library Media Quarterly
SLO	State Library of Ohio
SLP (1)	Session Level Protocol (of AT&T)
SLP (2)	Small Libraries Publications (of LAD)
SLS (1)	School of Library Science or School of Library Service
SLS (2)	Seminary Libraries Section (of CLA (4))
SLS (3)	Suburban Library System (Ill.)
SLSENY	School Librarians of Southeastern New York
SLSI	Super-Large Scale Integration (computer term)
SLT (1)	Solid Logic Technology (used in 2nd generation computers)

SLT (2)	The Sourcebook of Library Technology (annual cumulation of LTR)
SLTA	Saskatchewan Library Trustees Association
SLV	State Library of Victoria (Australia)
SMAC	Special Materials and Cataloging (Group of LC)
SMART (1)	Salton's Magical Automatic Retrieval of Texts (of Cornell University, N.Y.)
SMART (2)	System for Mechanical Analysis and Retrieval of Texts
SMARTS	Sexism : Minority Awareness - Review Thinking Sessions (LAMA/PAS Racism and Sexism Awareness Training Committee's programmes at ALA Conferences)
SMCCL	Society of Municipal and County Chief Librarians (U.K.)
SMCL	Southeastern Massachusetts Cooperating Libraries
SMCSLA	Special Libraries Association, Section de Montréal Chapter
SMD	Specific Materials Designation (used in descriptive cataloguing - AACR II)
SMERC	San Mateo Educational Research Center (Calif.)
SMF	System Management Facilities
SMI	Simulated Machine Indexing
SMIAC	Sail Mechanics Information Analysis Center (U.S.)
SMILE	Southcentral Minnesota Interlibrary Exchange
SMIRS	School Management Information Retrieval System (of ERIC)
SMIS	Society for Management Information Systems (U.S.)
SML	Symbolic Machine Language (computer language)
SMLS	Small and Medium-Sized Libraries Section (of PLA (7))
SMM	Start of Manual Message (computer term)
SMPTE	Society of Motion Picture and Television Engineers (U.S.)
SMQ	School Media Quarterly
SMSA	Standard Metropolitan Statistical Area (U.S.)
SMUG	SOLINET Microcomputer Users' Group
SNA	System Network Architecture

SNI	Standard Network Interconnection
SNICT	National Systems of Scientific and Technological Information (Brazil)
Snobol 4	String-Oriented Symbolic Language (computer language)
SO	Standing Order
SOA	State of the Art
SOAP	Symbolic Optimizer and Assembly Program (computer term)
SOAS	School of Oriental and African Studies (U.K.)
SOASIS	Southern Ohio Chapter of ASIS
SoCCS	Study of Cataloguing Computer Software (project funded by the British Library and the Microelectronics Education programme)
SOCRATES	System for Organising Current Reports to Aid Technologists and Scientists (Defence Scientific Information Service)
SOFTCON	Software Conversion (and Exposition) (U.S.)
SOKRATUS	Státni Knihovna ČSSR, Klementinum (of State Library, Czechoslovakia)
SOLACE	School of Librarianship Automated Cataloguing Experiment (New South Wales University, Australia)
SOLAPIC	Solar Applications Information Center
SOLAR	Storage and On-line Automatic Retrieval (Washington State University)
SOLID	Self-Organizing Large Information Dissemination
SOLINET	Southeastern Library Network (U.S.)
SOLO	Southeastern Ohio Library Organization
SOLOS	(A Student-Oriented Information Retrieval System Using MARC Records)
SOM	Small Office Microform
SOMD	Specialized Office for Materials Distribution (of Indiana University)
SOQUIP	Société Québeçoise d'Initiatives Pétrolières
SORT	Staff Organization Round Table (of ALA)

SOS (1)	Search of Software (computerized search service)
SOS (2)	Share Operating System (computer term)
S.O.S. (3)	Sharing Our Specialties (conference theme of CLA's 37th Annual Conference)
SOS (4)	Super Operating System (of Apple III computer)
SOSC	Southern Oregon State College
SOTA	State of the Art
SP	Structured Programming
SPA	Systems and Procedures Association (U.S.)
SPACE	Symbolic Programming Anyone Can Enjoy
SPAN	Systems Planning and Analysis
SPARC (1)	Standards Planning and Requirements Committee (of ANSI)
SPARC (2)	Strategic Planning and Research Coordination Group (of BL)
Speakeasy	(computer language)
SPEC	Systems and Procedures Exchange Center (of ARL)
SPECOL	Special Customer Oriented Language
SPEEDI	System for the Publication and Efficient, Effective Dissemination of Information (a system proposed for chemical literature)
SPIEL	Spokane Inland Empire Libraries (consortium, Wash.)
SPIEs	Specialized Professional Information Expeditors
SPIL	Society for the Promotion and Improvement of Libraries (Pakistan)
SPIN	Searchable Physics Information Notices (of American Institute of Physics)
SPINDEX	Selective Permuting Index (U.S. National Archives)
SPINES	Science Policy Information System (also called Science and Technology Policies Information Exchange System, Unesco)
SPIRES (1)	Stanford Personnel Information Retrieval System (of U.S. Military)
SPIRES (2)	Stanford Physics Information Retrieval System (of Stanford University, U.S.)

SPIRES (3)	Stanford Public Information Retrieval System (of Stanford University, U.S.)
SPIRIT	Sensible Policy for Information Resources and Information Technology (U.S.)
SPIRS	Special Purpose Information Retrieval System (Business Computer Systems Ltd.)
SPIT	Selective Printing of Items from Tape
SPL (1)	Scranton Public Library (Pa.)
SPL (2)	Simple Programming Language
SPL (3)	Sound Pressure Level
SPLC	Student Press Law Center (sponsored by ALA and other organizations)
SPLQ	Scandinavian Public Library Quarterly
SPM	Separately Published Monograph
SPN	Switched Public Network
SPOOL	Simultaneous Peripheral Operations On-Line
SPP	Society of Private Printers (U.K.)
SPPL	Saint Paul Public Library (Minn.)
SPRBP	Small Press Record of Books in Print (publication)
SPRD	Science Policy Research Division (of LC's Congressional Service)
SPSS	Statistical Package for the Social Sciences
SQT	Square Root
Sr	Steradian (SI) (solid angle)
SRA	Science Research Associates (of IBM)
SRBUC	Scientific Research in British Universities and Colleges (now RBUPC)
SRC	Science Research Council (U.K.)
SRCDL	Survey Research Center Data Library (at UCLA; previously IDL & RS)
SREB	Southern Regional Education Board

SRG	Sound Recordings Group (of LA (1); now Audiovisual Group; also known as LASRG)
SRI (1)	Stanford Research Institute (Calif.)
SRI (2)	Statistical Reference Index (a service of SRI-CIS, Washington, D.C.)
SRIM	Selected Research in Microfiche (of NTIS)
SRIS	Safety Research Information Service (of National Safety Council, U.S.)
SRL	Science Reference Library (also known as BLSRL; formerly NRL (1), NRLSI)
SRRT	Social Responsibilities Round Table (of ALA)
SRRTAC	SRRT Action Council (of ALA)
SRS (1)	Selective Record Service (of BLAISE)
SRS (2)	System Reference Service (of NSLS)
SRSA	Scientific Research Society of America
SRTF	Shortest Remaining Time First (computer term)
SS (1)	Serials Section (of RTSD)
SS (2)	Statistics Section (of LAMA)
SS (3)	Supervisors Section (of AASL (1))
SSC	Synagogue, School, and Center Division (of AJL)
SSCI	Social Sciences Citation Index (of ISI (3))
SSDC	Space Science Data Centre (also known as NSSDC)
SSDL	Society for the Study of Dictionaries and Lexicography (now DSNA)
SSEC	Selective Sequence Electronic Calculator
SSHELCO	State System of Higher Education Libraries Council (Pa.)
SSHRCC	Social Sciences and Humanities Research Council of Canada
SSI	Small-Scale Integration (computer term)
SSIE	Smithsonian Science Information Exchange (previously SIE)
SSIPP	Social Science Instructional Programming Project (U.S.)

SSIS	Social Science Information System (of York University)
SSN	Standard Serial Number
SSO	Subject Systems Office (of BSD)
SSP (1)	Scientific Subroutine Package (computer term)
SSP (2)	Society for Scholarly Publishing (U.S.)
SSRC	Social Sciences Research Council (U.K.)
SSRCC	Social Sciences Research Council of Canada (also known as CCRSS)
SSRR	Social Sciences Reading Room (of LC)
STA	Status Control Field (of UTLAS Inc.)
STAIRS	Storage and Information Retrieval System (of IBM)
STAIS	Student Advisory Information Service (Univ. of Dayton, Ohio)
STAR (1)	Scientific and Technical Aerospace Reports (U.S.)
STAR (2)	Sharing through Alliances (Roundtable of NYLA)
STARC	Study Team on Automatic Record Creation (of BL)
STARS	Solano-Travis Access and Resource Sharing (a project at Travis Air Force, Calif, and Solano County Library using CLSI circulation system)
START	Summary Tape Assistance Research and Training Community
STATMUX	Statistical Multiplexor (computer term)
STC (1)	Short Title Catalogue (publication, U.K.)
STC (2)	Society for Technical Communication (U.S.)
STDM	Synchronous Time-Division Multiplexing (computer term)
STI	Scientific and Technical Information (Dissemination)
STID	Scientific and Technical Information Division (of NASA)
STISEC	Scientific and Technological Information Services Enquiry Committee (of NLA (3))
STM	(International Group of) Scientific, Technical, and Medical Publishers
STR	Synchronous Transmitter Receiver (computer term)

STRN	Standard Technical Report Number
STRUDL	Structural Design Language
STS	Science and Technology Section (of ACRL)
STX	Start of Text Character (computer term)
SUB	Substitute Character (computer term)
SUC (1)	Saskatchewan Universities Commission (also known as CUS)
SUC (2)	Slavic Union Catalog (of LC; previously SCUC)
SUCO	Service Universitaire Canadien Outre-mer (also known as CUSO)
Su-Docs	Superintendent of Documents (of USGPO)
SUERF	Société Universitaire Européenne de Recherches Financières
SUL (1)	Small University Libraries Section (of CACUL)
SUL (2)	Stanford University Libraries (U.S.)
SULIRS	Syracuse University Libraries Information Retrieval System
SUNY	State University of New York
SUNYAB	State University of New York at Buffalo
SUNY-BCN	SUNY Biomedical Communications Network
SUNYLA	State University of New York Librarians Association
SUNY-OCLC	State University of New York - OCLC Library Network
SUPARS	Syracuse University Psychological Abstracts Retrieval System
SUZDKS	Stáni Ústav pro Zdravotnickou Dokumentačm a Knihovnickou Sluzbu (State Institute for Medical Documentation and National Medical Library, Czechoslovakia)
SVAL	Sangamon Valley Academic Library (a consortium, Ill.)
SVD	Schweizerische Vereinigung für Dokumentation (also known as ASD (2))
SVP	S'il Vous Plait (network of Information Clearing House, Inc.)
SVPL	Sierra Vista (Ariz.) Public Library

SVSF	Sveriges Vetenskapliga Specialbiblioteks Förening (Association of Swedish Special Research Libraries)
SWA	Schweizerisches Wirtschaftsarchiv (Swiss Economic Archives; Switzerland)
SWAC	Standard Western Automatic Computer
SWALCAP	South-West Academic Libraries Cooperative Automation Project (Bristol, Exeter and Wales (Cardiff) Universities, U.K.; formerly SWULSCP)
SWALO	Southern Wisconsin Academic Librarians Organization
SWCC	Southwest Computer Conference (U.S.)
SWELP	South Western Educational Library Project (Mich.)
SWIFT	Society for Worldwide Interbank Financial Telecommunications
SWIRS	Solid Waste Information Retrieval System (of Environmental Protection Agency, U.S.)
SWLA	Southwestern Library Association (also known as SLA (5))
SWLC	Southwestern Connecticut Library Council
SWORCC	Southwestern Ohio Regional Computer Center
SWORL	Southwestern Ohio Rural Libraries
SWRA	Selected Water Resources Abstracts (of Water Resources Scientific Information Center, U.S.)
SWRL	Southwest Regional Laboratory (for Educational Research and Development) (Los Alamitos, Calif.)
SWRLS	Southwestern Regional Library System (Ont.)
SWRSIC	Southern Water Resources Scientific Information Center (N.C.)
SWULSCP	South-West University Libraries Systems Cooperation Project (now SWALCAP)
SWVLAC	Southern West Virginia Library Automation Corporation
SYEP	Summer Youth Employment Program (U.S.)
SYN	Synchronous Idle (computer term)
SYNTOL	Syntagmatic Organization Language (computer language)
SYSOP	System Operators (computer term)

T (1)	Tesla (SI) (magnetic flux density)
t (2)	Tonne (Metric) = 1,000 kg
TAAG	Toronto Area Archivists' Group
TABA	The American Book Awards (of AAP (2))
TABAMLN	Tampa Bay Medical Library Network (Fla.)
TABSIM	Tabulating Simulator (computer term)
TACOL	Tasmanian Advisory Committee on Libraries (Australia)
TAFE	(Committee on) Technical and Further Education (Australia)
TAICH	Technical Assistance Information Clearinghouse (U.S.)
TALIC	Tyneside Association of Libraries for Industry and Commerce (U.K.)
TALINET	Telecommunications or Telefax Library Information Network (of Univ. of Denver, Colo.)
TALON	Texas, Arkansas, Louisiana, Oklahoma and New Mexico (South Central Regional Medical Library Program)
TANDOC	Tanzania National Documentation Centre
TAP	Training, Appraisal and Promotion (a program of LC)
TAPPI	Technical Association of the Pulp and Paper Industry (U.S.)
TASL	Texas Association of School Librarians
TAXIR	Taxonomic Information Retrieval
TB (1)	Talking Book
Tb (2)	Terabit (10^{12} bits)
TB (3)	Terabyte (10^{12} bytes)
TBRI	Technical Book Review Index
TBT	Talking Book Topics
TCA	Telecommunications Association (U.S.)
TCABMI	Twentieth-Century Author Biographies Master Index (publication)
TCAM	Telecommunications Access Method (of IBM)

TCBC	Twin Cities Biomedical Consortium (Minn.)
TCCL	Tulsa City County Library (U.S.)
TCCLS	Tulsa City County Library System (U.S.)
TCLC	Tri-State College Library Cooperative (Pa.)
TCPL	Toledo-Lucas County Public Library (Ohio)
TCTS	TransCanada Telephone System (now Telecom Canada)
TCU	Transmission Control Unit (computer term)
TCU Library	Texas Christian University Library
TDD	Telecommunications Device for the Deaf (of LC)
TDM	Time-Division Multiplexing (computer term)
TDN	Toronto Disarmament Network
TDTL	Tunnel Diode Transister Logic (computer term)
TEAM-A	Theological Education Association of Mid-America
TEBROC	Teheran Book Processing Centre (Iran)
TEC	Tertiary Education Commission (Australia)
TEIGA	Treasury, Economics and Inter-Governmental Affairs (Ministry of Ontario)
TELECAT	Telecommunications Catalogue (of UNICAT/TELECAT)
TELEX	Automatic Teletypwriter Exchange Service (of Western Union, U.S.)
TEL-MED	(A unique tape library developed by the San Bernadino (calif.) Medical Society; a tape library on approx. 300 frequently requested subjects)
TERC	Technical Education Research Center (Cambridge, Mass.)
TermNet	(International Network for Terminological Agencies)
TESLA	Technical Standards for Library Automation (of LITA)
TEST	Thesaurus of Engineering and Scientific Terms (Engineers Joint Council, U.S.)
TEX	(Automatic Teleprinter Exchange Service (of Western Union, U.S.))
TFW	Task Force on Women (of ALA)

THOMIS	Total Hospital Operating and Medical Information System (U.S.)
THOR	Tape Handling Option Routines (computer term)
3M	Minnesota Mining and Manufacturing Company (U.S.)
3Rs	Reference and Research Library Resources (a consortium; New York State Library)
TI	Texas Instruments
TIB	Technische Informationsbibliothek (Technischen Universitat, W. Germany)
TIC	Telecommunications Information Center (Washington, D.C.)
TICCIT	Time-Shared Interactive Computer-controlled Information Television
TIE (1)	Texas Information Exchange (of Rice University, Tex.)
TIE (2)	Total Interlibrary Exchange (a consortium, Calif.)
TIES (1)	Total Information for Educational Systems (Minn.)
TIES (2)	Total Integrated Engineering System
TIMP	Terminal Interface Message Processor (also known as TIP (3))
TIMT	Toronto Institute of Medical Technology
TINA	Technology Innovation Alert (U.S.)
TINFO	Tieteellisen Informoinnin Neuvosto (Council for Scientific and Research Libraries, Finland)
TIP (1)	The Information Place
TIP (2)	Technical Information Program/Project (of MIT)
TIP (3)	Terminal Interface Message Processor (also known as TIMP)
TIP (4)	Topics in Personnel (kit: covers areas of labour relations, initial organizing contract procedures, etc., U.S.)
TIP (5)	Toxicology Information Program (of NLM)
TIPTOP	Tape Input/Tape Output (computer term)
TIRC	Toxicology Information Response Center (Oak Ridge, Tenn.)

TIRMMS	Technical Information Reports for Music - Media Specialists (of MLA (14))
TIS	Technical Information Service (of NRC (2))
TISA	Technical Information Support Activities Project (formerly ATLIS, TISAP; ceased 1974)
TISAP	Technical Information Support Activities Project (formerly ATLIS (2); later TISA, ceased 1974)
TISCO	Technical Information Systems Committee (of two U.S. firms)
TITUS	**Textile** Information Treatment Users' Service (of Institut Textile de France)
TJID	Terminal Job Identification (computer term)
TKD	Türk Kütüphaneciler Dernegi (Turkish Librarians Association, Turkey)
TKV-VBT	Tieteellisten Kirjastojen Virkailijat-Vetenskapliga Bibliotekens Tjänstemannaförening r.y. (Association of Research and University Librarians, Finland)
TLA (1)	Tennessee Library Association
TLA (2)	Texas Library Association
TLA (3)	Thai Library Association (Thailand)
TLA (4)	Theatre Library Association (U.S.)
TLA (5)	Toy Library Association (Chicago, Ill.)
TLC (1)	(Cumulative Title Index to the Classical Collections of LC)
TLC (2)	Tri-County Library Council (Wis.)
TLCPL	Toledo-Lucas County Public Library (Ohio)
TLIRT	Tennessee Library Instruction Roundtable
TLS (1)	Tekniska Litteratursällskapet (Swedish Society for Technical Documentation)
TLS (2)	Total Library System (developed by Claremont, includes acquisitions, circulation, and online catalog support functions, U.S.)
TLX	Telex
TMP (1)	Terminal-Management Processor (computer term)
TMP (2)	Terminal Monitor Program (computer term)

TNAN	Trial Network Access Node
TOBIAS	Terminal Oriented Bibliographic Information Analysis Program (of Institute for Research in Social Sciences, N.C.)
TODS	Transaction on Database Systems
TOHYOP	Hanguk Tosogwan Hyophoe (also known as KLA (3))
TOL	TRIS-on-Line (a database of Transportation Research Board, Washington, D.C.)
TOLIS	Total Online Information System (of DRA)
TOMAS	(Carlyle Systems, Inc.'s online catalogue)
TON	Top of the News
TOP	Temporarily Out of Print
TOPLAS	Transactions on Programming Languages and Systems
TORTOS	Terminal Oriented Real Time Operating System
TOS (1)	Tape Operating System (computer term)
TOS (2)	Temporarily Out of Stock
TOSCA	Total On-line Searching and Cataloging Activities (of LC)
TOTAL	(Cincom Systems, Inc.'s database)
TOXLINE	Toxicology Information On-line (a database of Toxicology Information Program, U.S.)
TPB	Swedish Library of Talking Books
TPL (1)	Toronto Public Library
TPL (2)	Tucson Public Library (U.S.)
TPRC	Thermophysical Properties Research Center (Center for Information and Numerical Data Analysis and Synthesis, U.S.)
TPSIS	Transportation Planning Support Information System (California. Dept. of Transportation. Library)
TRADOC	United States Army Training & Doctrine Command (Library and Information Network, Va.)
TRANSDOC	Transportation Documentation (France)
TRC	Teaching Resources Center (U.S.)

TRI-AISA	Area 3 Library Services Authority (Cooperative Library Services, Ind.)
TRIAL	Technique for Retrieving Information from Abstracts of Literature
TRIC	Therapeutic Recreation Information Center (Univ. of Colorado)
TRIP	Technical Reports Indexing Project (Research Report Project of Purdue University, U.S.)
TRIPS	TALON Reporting and Information Processing System (of NLM)
TRISNET	Transportation Research Information Systems Network
TRIUL	Tri-University Libraries of British Columbia (of UBC, Simon Fraser and Univ. of Victoria)
TRLN	Triangle Research Libraries Network (master database of Duke University, NCSUR and UN(CH))
TROLL	Time-Shared Realtime Online Lab (Mass.)
TSAMSRLDG	Technical Services Administrators of Medium-sized Research Libraries Discussion Group (of ALA)
TSC	Time Sharing Control Task (computer term)
TSCG	Technical Services Coordinating Group (of CLA)
TSDLRL	Technical Services Directors of Large Research Libraries (of RTSD)
TSG	Technical Support Group (of UTLAS Inc.)
TSI	Transworld System Inc. (a collection agency for libraries, U.S.)
TSL	Tasmania State Library
TSO	Time Sharing Option (computer term)
TSS	Time-Shared System or Time Sharing System (computer term)
TT	Teletype
TTCP	The Technical Cooperative Program (U.S., U.K., Canada and Australia - research)
TTHM	Turk Teknik Haberlesme Merkezi (Turkish Technical Information Centre)
TURDOK	Turk Billimsel ve Teknik Dokumentasyon Merkesi (Turkish National Scientific and Technical Documentation Centre)

TUSC	Technology Use Studies Center (now KIAC)
TUTOR	Teaching Users to Operate RECON (European Space Research Organisation Space Documentation Service)
TWX	Teletypewriter Exchange Service
TWXILL	TWX Interlibrary Loan Network
TX	Telex
TYMNET	Time-Sharing Communications Network
UAAC	Universities Art Association of Canada (also known as AAUC)
UAF	University of Alaska at Fairbanks
UAP	Universal Availability of Publications (programme of IFLA)
UAPUO	Union des Associations des Professeurs des Universités de l'Ontario
UART	Universal Asynchronous Receiver/Transmitter (computer term)
UBC (1)	Universal Bibliographic Control (of IFLA)
UBC (2)	University of British Columbia
UCAE	Universities Council for Adult Education (U.K.)
UCAL	University of California Library Automation Program
UCASS	University Computer-Assisted Search Service (U.S.)
UCB	University of California at Berkeley
UCB-ILR	UCB - Institute of Library Research
UCC (1)	Unified Classification Code (of INSPEC, U.K.)
UCC (2)	Universal Copyright Convention
UCLA	University of California at Los Angeles
UCLC	Utah College Library Council
UC/LSD	University of California Library Systems Development Program
UCMCL	University of Cincinnati Medical Center Library
UCMP	Union Catalog of Medical Periodicals (of Medical Library Center of New York)

UCNI	Unclassified Controlled Nuclear Information (U.S.)
UCPA	University and College Placement Association (also known as APUC (1))
UCPG	University and College Publishers' Group
UCPL	Union City (N.J.) Public Library
UCRS	University, College and Research Section (of LA (1))
UCS (1)	Universal Character Set (of IBM)
UCS (2)	Universal Classification System
UCSB	University of California, Santa Barbara
UCSC (1)	University City Science Center (Pa.)
UCSC (2)	University of California/Santa Cruz
UCSD	University of California, San Diego
UCUCS	University of California Union Catalog Supplement
UDAS	Unified Direct Access System (computer term)
UDC (1)	Universal Decimal Classification (of FID; also known as CDU, ETO)
UDC (2)	University of the District of Columbia (U.S.)
UDT	Universal Document Transport (computer term)
UDUAL	Unión de Universidades de América Latina (Mexico)
UEC	Universal Entry Control System (Penn State's catalog access system)
UFL	University Federation of Librarians (U.S.)
UGAL	University of Georgia Libraries
UGL	Undergraduate Librarians (Discussion Group of ALA)
UHF	Ultra High Frequency
UHS	Universalist Historical Society's Library (Society found in 1834, Library of Study of Universalism)
UIA (1)	International Union of Architects (Paris, France)
UIA (2)	Union of International Associations (U.S.)
UIA (3)	Universitaire Instelling Antwerpen (The Library of) (Belgium)

UICA	Union of Independent Colleges of Art (Mo.)
UICA/LREP	UICA Learning Resources Exchange Program
UKASE	University of Kansas Automated Serials System
UKCIS	United Kingdom Chemical Information Service (Chemical Society - Consortium on Chemical Information; formerly CSRU)
UKMARC	British MARC Project
UKSAV	Ústredná Kniznica Slovenskej Akademie Vied (Central Library of the Slovak Academy of Sciences, Czechoslovakia)
ULA (1)	Uganda Library Association
ULA (2)	Universal Libinfosci Association (fictitious)
ULA (3)	Utah Library Association
ULAA	Ukranian Library Association of America
ULAC	Ukranian Librarians Association of Canada
ULAP	University-wide Library Automation Program (of Univ. of Calif.)
ULAV	Union List of Audiovisuals
ULC	Urban Libraries Council (U.S.)
ULCN	Union List of Canadian Newspapers
ULC-NCEC	Urban Libraries Council - National Citizens Emergency Committee (to Save Our Public Libraries)
ULIS	Union List of Item Selections (of USGPO)
ULISYS	Universal Library Systems
ULL	University of Liverpool Library (U.K.)
ULMS	University Library Management Studies (of ARL)
ULOSSOM	Union List of Selective Serials of Michigan
ULS (1)	Union List of Serials (H.W. Wilson)
ULS (2)	University Libraries Section (of ACRL)
ULSSCL	Union List of Scientific Serials in Canadian Libraries
ULSSSHCL	Union List of Serials in the Social Sciences and Humanities Held by Canadian Libraries

ULTC	Urban Library Trustees Council (U.S.)
UM	University of Missouri
UMA	University of Mid-America (a consortium of 11 colleges and universities in the Midwest, U.S.)
UMC	Upstate Medical Center (Syracuse, N.Y.)
UMF	Ultra Microfiche
UMI	University Microfilms International
UMIACH	University Microfilms International Article Clearing House
UMIST	University of Manchester Institute of Science and Technology (U.K.)
UMKC	University of Missouri, Kansas City
UMREL	Upper Midwest Regional Educational Laboratory (Minn.)
U.N.	United Nations
UNADS	Univac Automated Documentation System (U.S.)
UNAM	Universidad Nacional Autonóma de México
UNB	University of New Brunswick
UNBIS	United Nations Bibliographic Information System
UNCC	University of North Carolina at Charlotte
UNC(CH)	University of North Carolina at Chapel Hill
UNCL	Utah Network of Cooperating Libraries
UNCRD	United Nations Centre for Regional Development
UNDI	United Nations Documents Index
UNDIS	United Nations Documentation Information Service/System
UNE	Union Nationale des Étudiants (also known as NUS)
UNECA	United Nations Economic Commission for Africa
Unesco	United Nations Educational Scientific and Cultural Organization
UNIBID	UNISIST International Centre for Bibliographic Descriptions (U.K.)

UNICAT/TELECAT	Union Catalogue/Telecommunication Catalogage (name of the Ontario Universities' UTLAS-based Library Cooperative Systems' Union Cataloguing Project - began July 1977 as the Monograph Documentation Project of OULCS; now defunct)
UNICEF	United Nations Children's Fund
UNICIS	University of Calgary Information Systems
UNIMARC	Universal MARC (formerly the MARC International Format) (U.S. and France)
UNIS	United Nations Information Service
UNISIST	United Nations Information System in Science and Techno-logy or Universal System for Information in Science and Technology
UNISTAR	User Network for Information Storage, Transfer, Acquisi-tion and Retrieval
UNITEL	University Information Technology Corporation (of Harvard and MIT)
UNIVAC	Universal Automatic Computer (a first generation computer)
UNIVERSITEL	(an Ontario-based agricultural information system under development by the Univ. of Guelph)
UNM	University of New Mexico
UNO	University of Nebraska at Omaha
UNRISD	United Nations Research Institute for Social Development
UPC	Universal Product Code
UPI	United Press International
UPM	University of Petroleum and Minerals (Dhahran, Saudi Arabia)
UPRLC Inc	Upper Peninsula Region of Library Cooperation, Inc. (an automated multitype library system, Mich.)
UQAM	Université du Québec à Montréal
URBANDOC	Urban Documentation Project (City University, N.Y.)
URI	University of Rhode Island
URIS	Universal Resources Information Symposium (Calif.)
URISA	Urban and Regional Information Systems Association (U.S.)

USACSSEC   United States Army Computer Systems Support and
            Evaluation Command

USASCII   USA Standard Code for Information Interchange

USASI   United States of America Standards Institute (formerly
            ASA (1); now ANSI)

USBE (1)   United States Book Exchange (formerly ABC (2); now
            USBE (2))

USBE (2)   Universal Serials and Book Exchange (formerly USBE (1)
            and ABC (2)

USC   University of Southern California

USE   Univac Scientific Exchange

USGPO   United States Government Printing Office

USGRDR   United States Government Research and Development
            Reports (U.S. Government reports announcements)

USHDI   U.S. Historical Documents Institute

USIA   United States Information Agency (now ICA (1) or USICA)

USIC   Union Sportive Interuniversitaire Canadienne (also known
            as CIAU)

USICA   U.S. International Communications Agency (now ICA (1))

USICF   Union Sportive Interuniversitaire Canadienne Feminine
            (also known as CWIAU)

USIS   United States Information Service (also known as USIA)

USLA   Uganda School Library Association

USMARC   United States Machine-Readable Cataloging

USNARS   United States National Archives (Census) Schedules

USNCFID   United States National Committee for Fédération Interna-
            tionale de la Documentation

USNC/   United States National Committee for the UNESCO General
Unesco - PGI Information Program

USN & WR   U.S. News and World Report (publication)

USOE   United States Office of Education (also known as OE)

USP   United States Patent

USPS   United States Postal Service

USPSD	United States Political Science Documents (Pa.)
UT	User Terminal
UTC	University of Tennessee (at Chattanooga)
UT-Dallas	University of Texas at Dallas
UTLAS Inc.	University of Toronto Library Automation System (now known by its acronym)
UUA	Univac Users Association
UVP	Universal Availability of Publications (of IFLA)
UVPROM	Ultraviolet-Erasable Programmable Read Only Memory (computer term)
UW	University of Wyoming
UWI	University of West Indies
UWM	University of Wisconsin-Milwaukee
UWPC	United World Press Cooperative (U.S.)
V (1)	Volt (SI) (electromotive force)
V (2)	Volume
VABB	Vereniging van Archivarissen en Bibliothecarissen van Belgie (Belgian Association of Archivists and Librarians; also known as AABB)
VALINET	Veterans Administration Library Network (U.S.)
VAMIS	Virginia Medical Information System (Medical College of Virginia, U.S.)
VAN (1)	Value-added Network
VAN (2)	Vereniging van Archivarissen in Nederland (Dutch Association of Archivists, Netherlands)
VASD	Veterans Administration Supply Depot (U.S.)
VASLA	Virginia Chapter, Special Libraries Association (U.S.)
VAT	Value Added Tax
VAX	Virtual Address Extention (computer term)
VBB	Verein der Bibliothekare an öffentlichen Bibliotheken (Association of Librarians in Public Libraries, W. Germany)

VBT	De Vetenskapliga Bibliotekens Tjänstemannaförening (Association of University and Research Libraries, Sweden)
VC	Virtual Circuit (computer term)
VCC	Vancouver Community College
VCCS	Video and Cable Communications Section (of LITA)
VCL	Vigo County Library (Ind.)
VCPL	Vigo County Public Library (Terre Haute, Ind.)
VdA	Verein Deutscher Archivare (Association of German Archivists, W. Germany)
VDB	Verein Deutscher Bibliothekare e.V. (Association of Chief Librarians, W. Germany)
VDD	Verein Deutscher Dokumentare (Association of German Documentalists, W. Germany)
VdDB	Verein der Diplom-Bibliothekare an Wissenschaftlichen Bibliotheken (Association of Certified Librarians of Research Libraries, W. Germany)
VDL	Vienna Definition Language (computer language)
VDOL	Vermont Department of Libraries
VDT	Video Display Terminal
VDU	Video or Visual Display Unit
VDV	Verein Deutscher Volksbibliothekare (Association of German Public Librarians, W. Germany)
VEBUK	Vereinigung der Buchantiquare und Kupferstichhändler in der Schweiz (Switzerland; also known as SLACES)
VEMA (1)	Vermont Educational Media Association
VEMA (2)	Virginia Educational Media Association
VENISS	Visual Education National Information Service for Schools (U.K.)
VESIAC	VELA Seismic Information Analysis Center (Michigan University)
VETDOC	Veterinary Literature Documentation (U.K.)
VF	Voice Frequency

VGBIL	Vshesoyuznoi Gosudarstvennoi Biblioteki Innostrannoi Literaturi (All-Union State Library of Foreign Literature, U.S.S.R.)
VGCLIS	Virginia Governor's Conference on Libraries and Information Science
VHD	Video High Density
VHF	Very High Frequency
VHS	Video Home System (Matsushito - a Japanese firm)
VIA	Versatile Interface Adapter (computer term)
VIDEOTEX	Visual Data Entry On-line Text
VID-R	Visual Information Display and Retrieval (U.S.)
VILINET	Virgin Islands Library & Information Network
VIM	(Name of CDC 600 and Cyber services users organization (Roman 6(VI) and Roman 1000 (M))
VINITI	Vsesojuzny Institut Naučnotehničeskoi Informacii (All-Union Institute of Scientific and Technical Information, U.S.S.R.)
VIPs	Videodisc Innovation Projects (began 1976 at the Utah State Dept. of Instructional Media)
VIROC	Visible System of Information Retrieval by Optical Coordination
VISC	(VIS Consultant's Vis-a-vis Software Package installed on the Suburban Audio-Visual Services Computer, U.S.)
VISCO	Visual Controller (computer term)
VISPAC	Videotex Information Service Providers Association of Canada
VLA (1)	Vermont Library Association
VLA (2)	Virginia Library Association
VLF (1)	Very Low Frequency
VLF (2)	Volumes per Linear Foot
VLSI	Very Large-Scale Integration (computer term)
VM	Virtual Memory (computer term)

VM/PC	Virtual Machine/Personal Computer (of IBM/PC)
VNIIKI	Vesesojuznii Naučno-Issle-Covatel'skii Institut Techniceskoi Informaccii, Klassifikaccii i Kodirovaniia (All-Union Scientific Research Institute for Technical Information, Classification and Codification, U.S.S.R.)
VNLW	Virginia National Library Week
VOA	Voice of America (radio network)
VÖB	Vereinigung Österreichischer Bibliothekare (Association of Austrian Librarians, Austria)
VOC	(vocabulary used in WLN authority records)
VOLS	Voluntary Overseas Libraries Service
VPD	Vapor Phase Deacidification
VPI	Virginia Politechnical Institute and State University
VPL	Vancouver Public Library
VRB	Vereiniging van Religieus-Wetenschappelijke Bibliothe-carissen (Association of Theological Librarians, Belgium)
VRC (1)	Vertical Redundancy Check (computer term)
VRC (2)	Visible Record Computer
VSAM	Virtual Storage Access Method (computer term)
VSB	Vereinigung Schweizerischer Bibliothekare (also known as ABS (1) and ABS (2))
VSIC	Visual Science Information Center (of UCLA)
VSMF	Visual Search Microfilm Files
VSN	Vendor Sequence Number (of UTLAS Inc.)
VSPX	Vehicle Scheduling Program Extended (computer term)
VT	Vertical Tab (computer term)
VTAM	Virtual Telecommunications Access Method (computer term)
VTB	Vereniging voor het Theologisch Bibliothecariaat (Netherlands)
VTLS	Virginia Technical Library System
VTOC	Volume Table of Content
VTR (1)	Videotape Recorder

VTR (2)	Vidicord Television Reproducer
VTS	Viewscan Text System (a learning device for visually-impaired)
VUBIS	(Interactive on-line library system, based on minicomputer)
VULBS	Virginia Union List of Biomedical Serials
VVBADP	Vlaamse Vereniging van Bibliotheek-Archief en Documentatie-Personeel, Vereniging Zonder Winstoogmarken (Flemish Association of Librarians, Archivists and Documentalists; formerly VVBAP, Belgium)
VVBAP	Vlaamse Vereniging van Bibliotheek-en Archief Personeel (Flemish Library Association; now VVBADP)
VWD	Vereinigte Wirtschaftsdienste (stock exchange data, in Eschborn)
W	Watt (SI) (power, radiant flux)
WAA	World Aluminum Abstracts (American Society for Metals, Ohio)
WAB	Wissenschaftliche Allgemein-bibliotheken (Public Research Libraries, E. Germany)
WABLC	Wilmington Area Biomedical Library Consortium (Del.)
WAC	Wyoming Academic Consortium
WACL	Worcester Area Cooperating Libraries (Mass.)
WAITRO	World Association of Industrial and Technological Research Organizations
WALA	West African Library Association (1953-1962)
WALIC	Wiltshire Association of Libraries of Industry and Commerce (U.K.)
WALL	Western Association of Law Libraries
WALT	West Automatic Law Terminal (developed by WESTLAW)
WALU	Waukesha Academic Library Union (Univ. of Wisconsin)
WAML	Western Association of Map Libraries (U.S.)
WANDPETLS	Wandsworth Public, Educational and Technical Library Services (U.K.)
WASL	Wyoming Association of School Libraries

WATDOC	Water Resources Document Reference Centre (a database produced by Environment Canada)
WATFOR	(University of) Waterloo FORTRAN
WATS	Wide Area Telephone Service
Wb	Weber (SI) (magnetic flux)
WBS	Welsh Bibliographical Society (Wales)
WCGA	World Computer Graphics Association
WCLRC	West Campus Learning Resources Center (of OSU)
WDC	World Data Centre (International Council of Scientific Unions)
WDLS	Wisconsin Division of Library Services
WDPC	Western Data Processing Center (U.S.)
WDRC	World Data Referral Centre (of Unesco ICSU/WFEO)
WEBNET	Western Pennsylvania Buhl Network
WEBS	Westchester Educational Brokering Service (a joint marketing of the Westchester Library System and the Cornell University School of Industrial and Labor relations, U.S.)
WEECN	Women's Educational Equity Communications Network (Calif.)
WEMA	Wisconsin Educational Media Association
WESRAC	Western Research Application Center (of NASA - Univ. of Southern California based)
WESS	Western European Specialists Section (of ACRL)
WESTEX	Western Continuing Education Information Exchange and Network
WESTFORNET	Western Forest Information Network (U.S.; previously PACFORNET)
WESTLAW	(an on-line computer-assisted legal search service of West Publishing, Minn.)
WFEO	World Federation of Engineering Organizations
WFNS	Writers' Federation of Nova Scotia
WGA	Weekly Government Abstracts (of NTIS)
WHCA	White House Conference on the Aging

WHCLIS	White House Conference on Library and Information Services (also known as WHCLOS)
WHCLIST	White House Conference on Library and Information Services Taskforce
WHCLOS	White House Conference on Library and Information Services (also known as WHCLIS) .
WHIM	Western Humor & Irony Membership (holds annual conferences, U.S.)
WHNPA	White House News Photographers Association
WHO	World Health Organization
WHRC	Women's History Research Center (Berkeley, Calif.)
WHSTC	Western Hemisphere Short-Title Catalog (U.S.)
WICHE	Western Interstate Commission for Higher Education
WILCO	Western Interstate Library Coordinating Organization
WILL	Workshop in Library Leadership
WILS	Wisconsin Interlibrary (Loan) Service
WILSONLINE	(H.W. Wilson Co.'s database)
WILS/WLC	Wisconsin Interlibrary Loan Service/Wisconsin Library Consortium
WIMA	Wyoming Instructional Media Association
WINMIC	Windsor Metric Information Centre
WIP	Women in Information Processing (U.S.)
WIPCUS	Washtenaw IBM Personal Computer User Society
WIPIS	Who Is Publishing In Science (Institute for Scientific Information, U.S.)
WIPO	World Intellectual Property Organization (also known as OMPI)
WIRL	West Indies Reference Library (Jamaica)
WISCAT	Wisconsin (State Library) Cataloging System (online catalog)
WISE (1)	World Information Synthesis and Encyclopedia
WISE (2)	World Information Systems Exchange

WLA (1)	Washington Library Association (Washington, D.C.)
WLA (2)	Welsh Library Association (of LA (1))
WLA (3)	Westchester Library Association (N.Y.)
WLA (4)	Wisconsin Library Association
WLA (5)	Wyoming Library Association
WLB	Wilson Library Bulletin (publication)
WLC (1)	Wisconsin Library Consortium
WLC (2)	World Literacy of Canada
WLDCARD	(an RLIN catalog card production system)
WLN	Washington Library Network (U.S.)
WLW	Women Library Workers (U.S.)
WMP	World Microfilm Publications Ltd.
WMRPLS	Western Massachusetts Regional Public Library System
WMU	Western Michigan University Libraries
WN	(Wellington) National Library of New Zealand
WNBA	Women's National Book Association
WNLA	West Newfoundland Library Association (defunct)
WNPLA	Washington Non-Professional Library Association (now CLEWS)
WNYHSL	Western New York Health Sciences Librarians
WOLF	Wayne Oakland Library Federation
WORLDS	Western Ohio Regional Library Development System
WORM	Write Once, Read Many (computer term)
WP	Word Processing
WPA (1)	Work Progress Administration (U.S.)
WPA (2)	Work Projects Administration (city libraries cooperation with the state level projects, U.S.)
WPI	World Patents Index (Derwent Publications, U.K.)
WPL	Westville Public Library (Ill.)

WPLA	West Pakistan Library Association (defunct)
WPLHCL	Working Party on Library Holdings of Commonwealth Literature
WPOM	Word Processing Output Microfilm (computer term)
WRA	Welfare and Recreation Association (of LC)
WRISC	Western Regional Information Service Center (Calif.)
WRLS	Welsh Regional Library System (U.K.)
WRMS	W.Ross Macdonald School (Brantford) (Provincial Resource Centre for the Visually Handicapped)
WRSIC	Water Resources Scientific Information Center (U.S.)
WRU	Case Western Reserve University (now CWRU)
WSCC	Westmount Senior Citizens' Centre (Quebec)
WTE	World Tape for Education (U.K.)
WUC	Writers Union of Canada
WUSC	World University Service of Canada
WUSML	Washington University School of Medicine Library
WVLA	West Virginia Library Association
WVLAC	West Virginia Library Association Commission
WVLC	West Virginia Library Commission
WWNSS	World Wide Network of Standard Seismograph Stations
XDM	(a silverless updatable electrophotographic dry microfilm developed by Xerox)
XDS	Xerox Data Systems
XIP	Xerox Individualized Publishing
XMIT	Transmit (computer term)
XMTR	Transmitter
XOR	Exclusive-or (computer term)
YA	Young Adult
YAKUTOKYO	Nippon Yakugaku Toshokan Kyogikai (Japan Pharmaceutical Library Association)

YAP	Young Adult Project (of two library systems in California)
YASC	Young Adult Services Committee (of WOLF)
YASD	Young Adult Services Division (of ALA)
YCCIP	Youth Community Conservation and Improvement Project
YETP	Youth Employment and Training Program
YEWTIC	Yorkshire (East and West Ridings) Technical Information Centre (U.K.)
YRLS	Yorkshire Regional Library System (U.K.)
ZAED	Zentralstelle für Atomkernenergie Dokumentation (Atomic Energy Documentation Center, W. Germany; also known as AED (1))
ZBB	Zero Based Budgeting
ZLA	Zambia Library Association
ZNB	Zimbawe National Bibliography
ZSKBIP	Zväz Slovennských Knihovníkov, Bibliografov a Informačných Pracovníkov (Association of Slovak Librarians, Bibliographers and Documentalists, Czechoslovakia)

****